Psychological Care
in Physical Illness

KEITH A. NICHOLS

Ⓟ

THE CHARLES PRESS, PUBLISHERS
Philadelphia

©1984 1989 Keith A. Nichols

Croom Helm Ltd, Provident House, Burrell Row,
Beckenham, Kent BR3 1AT

Croom Helm Australia Pty Ltd, First Floor, 139 King Street,
Sydney, NSW 2001, Australia

The Charles Press, Publishers
Post Office Box 15715
Philadelphia, Pennsylvania
19103

13.95

Library of Congress Catalog Card Number: 84-71617

ISBN 0-914783-04-1 Hbk
ISBN 0-914783-06-8 Pbk

CONTENTS

ACKNOWLEDGEMENTS

Lorna Sealy has worked enormously hard preparing and refining the manuscript for me and she has also contributed a valued chapter. Polly Woodhams (Sister-in-charge of the Exeter Kidney Unit) evaluated the material from the nursing standpoint and has contributed much through her discussion and suggestion. My thanks to them both.

The case studies presented in this book, while based on first-hand experience, are fictional composites and do not refer to the exact history of specific individuals.

INTRODUCTION

Myrtle Dellbridge struck me as a somewhat unusual name. To be honest though, she was not an unusual woman, living a fairly ordinary life in an ordinary North Devon town. She achieved little that was exceptional in her 40 or so years a valiant struggle against the hardships associated with total kidney failure which overtook her in mid-life. I met her a month or so after her transplanted kidney had also failed. Her experience was, I suppose, much the same as many other people whom I have since met but at the time, in 1977, it felt to me as if she had been dealt with rather savagely by the determinants of fate.

Myrtle had mastered the complex technique of haemodialysis and had adjusted with patience and courage to the deprivations and discomforts involved. She was noted for her cheeriness towards other people and clearly had made enormous efforts to put aside her personal grief and make the best of things. Like many people surviving by dialysis, she longed for a transplant and, to everyone's delight, a matching kidney did materialise and was successfully grafted. It worked well and Myrtle experienced some months which were akin to resurrection. Before that she had been weak, low on energy, dreadfully constrained by the routines of dialysis and assaulted by the nagging minor physical discomforts and illnesses brought about by uraemia. Following the transplant, though, she was her old self − a busy, energised extrovert. Tragically, her time in this comparative paradise was limited to seven months at which point an influenza infection led to the failure of the transplanted kidney and she was plunged once more into the grey world of survival by dialysis. Coping with the overwhelming disappointment and sense of loss required of Myrtle personal resources which she could not give. The effort of adjustment and acceptance had been found once but this second blow broke her emotionally.

I used to visit her once or twice a week. She had been 'referred'. Without any sense of drama I can say that Myrtle unwittingly engendered a profound effect on me and fuelled my already growing interest in the psychological needs of people who are seriously ill or injured. What intruded upon me most powerfully was experiencing how isolated she was with the weight of her sadness. She was in decline, her spirit broken, conscious of the realisation that she no longer wanted to carry on and attempting to deal with her fears of death together with the intense grief of a mother saying goodbye to her child and husband. The staff in the Kidney Unit at that time were kindly and concerned but, it seemed to me, a hundred miles away in terms of understanding her experiences. She was truly alone, surrounded by caring people who were unable to offer the kind of care she needed — that is, companionship and understanding. They wanted to 'cure' her with anti-depressants, persuade, cajole, in some way shake her into struggling on again. It was a difficult experience for me as a psychologist. One could quite easily understand why the staff were like this. They had very strong needs too — they also needed protection and care. At the same time, I found it hard not to be angry and condemning, caught up as I was in Myrtle's distress.

This same conflict of loyalties and this same anger has nagged away for years now. Time and again I meet with people in general hospitals who are in great need of psychological care because they are undergoing great psychological trauma as a consequence of a serious illness or accident. Yet that need, I believe, is usually neither seen nor met — general hospitals do not offer this kind of care on a widespread and formal basis. I will go further and say that the typical general hospital, although supposedly a caring institution, paradoxically manages to be a centre of psychological neglect which actually generates psychological damage in a proportion of its clients. These are rather attacking claims to make and clearly there is need of substantiation. Accordingly, the earlier part of this book presents some of the large volume of material and experiences which back up such claims. I have also included a chapter written by the relative of a man who died whilst in kidney failure as an extended personal example of an era in medical care which, I hope to persuade you, must come to an end (Epilogue by Lorna Sealy).

I assume that most readers will either be training or employed as nurses, doctors or members of the paramedical professions and I write to deliberately burden you with a dilemma. It is this. You must decide whether the position I take is yet another fashionable complaint which will get itself talked out and abandoned, or are we dealing with an issue which matters very much and requires from all of us working in the hospitals an openness to development and a willingness to implement new practices? My mind is made up, so what matters now is how you react. I will put before you the idea of caring as opposed to technical medicine, where caring medicine is a composite of educational, psychological and medical procedures, and where preventative psychological care is absorbed into the practices of the various professions involved as part of the everyday routines. The bulk of the book is given over to describing this approach under such headings as 'emotional care' and 'informational care'. I hope that you will grasp the dilemma and clarify your own position in the debate. If you agree that the insensitive, technical medicine so prevalent today is a needless addition to the difficulties which seriously ill people and their families already face, then the burden of implementing change also falls on you. You must take your share of the responsibility to shift the emphasis.

Deciding how to present the practices of psychological care was problematic. The training phase in psychological work can be frustrating because there are dozens of books which talk in generalities and give various theories on systems of therapy, but few tell you what to actually do. My experiences when teaching nurses and speech therapists during the last few years suggest that they have a particularly strong need for basic, down-to-earth instruction. This has tipped the balance and the book sets out to meet that need directly. What you will find is straightforward instruction aimed at the individual nurse on the ward, or paramedic in the clinic. This is presented by making the temporary assumption of an ideal setting, that is, adequate time, facilities and the attribution of importance to the work by medical and other staff. The intention is to show what happens between an individual nurse and her client when psychological care is being conducted. This is the starting point and if it fires the interest of senior staff in managerial positions, it will be their task to think out the requirements of organising such care on a wider basis. It will also be for them to assess the benefits.

A somewhat hard-headed medical administrator recently said to me, 'What arguments are there in terms of cost effectiveness or increased turnover of patients if you introduce this sort of thing?' Well, there *are* arguments and evidence which demonstrate actual physical and financial benefits but I did not need them in order to force him to concede. My reply was, 'Imagine your wife needs some distressing surgery. There are two units available; one is technically good but being traditional puts little effort into keeping patients informed or caring for them at an emotional level. The other has staff who, as well as medical competence, have also been trained in the basic skills of psychological care. They will care for her emotionally in a professional way and offer counselling in any difficulties arising. Which unit will you choose and why?' He replied, 'Point taken.' I hope you will feel that way too

1 WHEN THERE IS NO PSYCHOLOGICAL CARE

A Case History

I want you to meet someone with me and see him through a psychologist's eyes. In medical terms he is just an 'average patient' but for us he will provide a good example of the ways in which doctors and nurses may unwittingly neglect the psychological needs of the people they care for and, on occasions, actually damage them psychologically. This damaging effect is not usually intentional or malicious but it is a product of the ways in which the medical and nursing professions have developed. In particular, it is a consequence of a way of perceiving people and relating to them which is known as the 'medical style of relating'.

We join Alan on a day three years ago when he is due in at the physiotherapy department of his district orthopaedic hospital for a mid-morning appointment. He has not arrived and now, at the beginning of the afternoon, he is in his bedroom at home sleeping in a restless haze produced by a generous salad of various painkillers and sedatives. He has not gone to physio. because he knows that he will break down emotionally when he is there, just as he has done all week with his fiancée and other people who have looked in to see him. He is ashamed and embarrassed by his sudden loss of emotional control which began shortly after his last visit to the hospital two weeks before. At 23, it is the last thing he expects. He despises himself for it and his instinct is to hide away.

How did Alan get like this? The story started with a road accident some years before which caused extensive damage to his left femur. He was cared for by the staff at the orthopaedic hospital and eventually, after a lengthy time in plaster, was out and about. As the months passed, though, he ran into increasing difficulties with stiffness and pain in the hip joint which progressively worsened. The medical team tried their best but there was no way round the hard fact that the head of the femur was breaking up and Alan was being slowly crippled. He was aware of this happening and began to show his fright and frustration at the hospital. He worried that his job as a trainee car salesman was in jeopardy and believed that his fiancée and other friends were losing patience with his interminable problems and pain, which now had a

4

history of nearly three years.

Alan's consultant knew also that he could not go on as he was and that a decision on surgical procedure had to be made. He requested that Alan attend a joint clinic with other orthopaedic specialists for a final review of the options. For reasons that he now cannot clearly remember, Alan deliberately missed this appointment. 'I was genuinely terrified; three or more of them all standing over you and talking as if you were not there and I knew they were going to make me have a big operation.' The joint clinic decided that the best course was to fuse his femur to the hip joint, that is an arthrodesis of the hip. Accordingly a letter was sent giving the news and arrangements. Alan did keep his next appointment and after a brief discussion of the planned operation a trial period in plaster was organised for a few days' duration as a way of simulating the effect of the operation. He then agreed to go ahead. He was encouraged by what he remembered from his meetings with the consultant and had built up some optimistic expectations. Above all, he believed, the pain would go after the operation and after three years of it, he was desperate for this. He then could expect to spend some months in hospital and maybe six months in plaster, after which the job could be resumed. He would have a stiff hip but it would be possible to learn how to deal with that and then his mobility would be tolerably good. With these thoughts in mind, full of hope and confidence, he entered hospital in June 1978, three years after his accident.

Comment (1)

Now we should freeze the story for a moment and look at the ingredients of the situation. In what state is Alan embarking on this course? As a person, he is typical of a young man from southern England, average in education but quick-witted, not really sure where his future lies, insecure about many things but taking great comfort from two elements in life, namely his job which he feels is the beginning of a ladder and his membership in a close circle of friends similar to himself. He spends much time with them as they move around as a group, often on motor cycles, visiting other towns or dances and pubs. Alan's sense of worth is high in this group but it is based on a psychological make-up which renders him very vulnerable at this moment. He feels secure and accepted as long as he is the same and in no way (to use his language) freaky. Also, to remain a close member of the group it is important for him to be able to join the group in its changing pattern of activities, to be capable of pursuing the latest impulse with them.

It would be unfair to say that Alan has been given false expectations of the arthrodesis operation. No-one has set out to fool him. *However, it is the case that Alan's ideas about how he will be after the operation are, at this point, very unrealistic and badly worked out. He has had no help with this side of the business and without its being noticed, a gross discrepancy has developed between his expectations and the realities of undergoing surgery like this. He is being allowed to undergo the operation with knowledge only of the best possible outcome and has not been prepared for other possibilities.* These include: the risks of continued pain, of the bones not fusing and a second operation being required, of a year or more in plaster. Added to this he has in no way been prepared for the powerful, emotional consequences of being disabled. Nor has provision been made in advance to help him with this.

Why is he so unprepared for these possibilities? The consultant claimed to have warned him of them at some point and clearly felt his duty had been discharged. But anxious people who are searching for relief to pain are not accurate listeners and often recall just the positive and hopeful side of a doctor's communications. Unless their view of events to come is frequently checked and corrected they may idealise the situation, eventually creating unrealistic beliefs. Added to this, many doctors do not feel comfortable with anxious, dependent patients. In encounters with people such as Alan they will attempt to avoid raising anxieties further by playing down the possibilities of difficulties and failure. The business of preparing people for the whole range of outcomes to an operation like the arthrodesis of a hip, which will include information on possible complications or even failure, is often left undone. Simple, idealised versions are presented with the rationalisation that patients are better off without additional worries. It may be a well-meant gesture but you can see that it has introduced a second area of vulnerability for Alan. He is not aware of how things might go wrong and what he will have to deal with as he confronts his disability. He is being left to cope with the outcome of his operation on his own. If there are problems he will feel betrayed, frightened, angry and shaken by the power of his emotional reactions.

The History Continued

No doubt you can anticipate the next stage in this narrative. The operation was undertaken in normal circumstances. Technically it appeared to be a success and Alan joined a ward full of orthopaedic cases to begin his months in plaster. He was attended by kindly but busy nurses with brief, regular visits by one or other of the medical team and occasional contacts by a social worker and a physiotherapist. His fiancée, mother and friends visited frequently. As weeks passed, however, the nurses began to notice some worrying changes. Alan was more irritable now and inclined to be withdrawn and depressed. There were several strange incidents in which he became violently angry and broke his plaster, others in which he was clearly drunk and abusive. The staff became wary and uneasy. He was not expected to be a perfect patient, but surely this behaviour was unreasonable. They sensed an anger, an instability and an *accusation* which was unnerving.

These fears were dealt with by categorising him as a 'difficult' case, a disturbed personality. The doctors and nurses were, of course, concerned but also became angry and exasperated in return. Some tried to approach him to discover what was wrong but were unable to get far and often felt rejected by Alan's angry manner. Things slowly worsened. He complained of pain from the wound, openly speaking of being depressed. The medical social worker felt that he might be clinically depressed so the possibility of calling in outside help was raised. After some discussion, it was agreed to call in a clinical psychologist who worked in the locality. Note, by the way, that this was the first moment in this case history when help from someone specialising in psychological care was seen as necessary. Before such help was sought, it was necessary for Alan to deteriorate to a level which attracted attention to his difficulties and led the staff to label him as disturbed. The implication was that psychological care was to be called for if he became a psychological casualty, but not in order to prevent it happening.

It would be pleasing for me if I could introduce the psychologist as the saviour in the story. This was not to be the case, however. The psychologist was involved too late to make a major contribution — the damage was already done. Anyway, he made errors in judgement which reduced his effectiveness later on. Nevertheless, the two of them got off to a good start. The psychologist called to see Alan several times in the space of two weeks. He offered a counselling style of interaction, that is, with the emphasis on helping Alan express what was in his thoughts and what feelings were associated with these. There was little by way of advice or the interpretations of deep psychotherapy at this point but because Alan felt that he was being listened to without demands or judgement, he was able to relax and explore exactly what was disturbing him.

Somehow he had expected the pain to go away, magically. It had not done so, however, and a despairing feeling that something had gone wrong and that he would never be free of pain was growing by the day. There was also an angry, resentful feeling that sometimes got out of control and made him want to smash things or hurt himself. He was not sure who this was really directed towards. Sometimes it was towards himself, sometimes to the surgeon and staff. It was at its worst during restless nights on the ward, when he visualised himself in the future on the beach, say, with his friends, at a disco perhaps, or involved in sexual encounters. He saw himself as a clumsy cripple with a wasted leg. The leg was, in fact, made shorter than he had expected and that, together with the problem of not being able to move it would, he believed, interfere with so many activities. His group would want to move off and do things but he would be slow and awkward. In his fantasy he was a nuisance and an oddity, thus breaking one of his most important personal rules. The sad image of so many favourite experiences in which he would no longer feel comfortable, or which would be physically impossible, increasingly intruded on him. These sadnesses alternated with the angry periods and often left him in quiet tears.

Two things were happening. Firstly, because of his own values, he was bitterly turning against himself in self-blame and self-rejection. He had, of course, started grieving — rightly so. For a bit of him had died, taking with it, it seemed, access to his group and favoured activities. It was not a weakness nor a neurotic instability on his part but a normal, quite predictable psychological process. A process, though, which no-one had forewarned him about and no-one had watched for in order to help him with it. He was alone with this most powerful of emotional upheavals, not knowing what was happening and surrounded by nurses and doctors who, though they meant well, lacked understanding of the process and were resentful with Alan for his behaviour. To them he was being inconsiderate and unreasonable, making their jobs difficult.

As Alan's experiences were unfolded in these conversations with the psychologist, it became clear that the last few weeks in hospital had forced a complex problem onto him. How was he to endure the interminable weeks of boring ward routine when he was immobilised in plaster, in physical and psychological pain and feeling alienated from the staff and from himself? His instinct was to turn to self-medication to blot things out. It began with alcohol taken together with hoarded painkillers and sleeping tablets. Later, friends brought in other drugs and a solution began to emerge. He could survive by taking lengthy periods of escape during which he no longer felt pain or cared about the future. It seemed ideal to him. From our vantage point now we might feel sympathy yet it was clearly a disadvantageous solution since he was not confronting his problems. He was not beginning the work of adaption and adjustment, he was simply setting everything aside. When he was not able to withdraw in this way his thoughts became more depressed and the emotion more painful. It was during these times that he was difficult with the nurses. Inevitably the urge to exploit every means of escape grew. It was a damaging learning experience, damaging in that he was rehearsing a pattern of defence by drug-induced withdrawal which was later to become unshakably strong.

Comment (2)

If we may take a second pause here it is instructive to ask how someone in a supposedly caring institution surrounded by caring people can become so isolated with personal problems and be forced to find his own solutions? Why was he not helped from the beginning?

In replying to the question I want to stress again that the motive here is not to make accusations or attribute blame. Nobody wished Alan other than well and all the staff involved were concerned to see him recover. However, the case demonstrates one of the key points to be developed in this book, namely, no matter how well intentioned doctors and nurses might be, when they practise with the view that medicine is primarily to do with physical treatment and where they maintain the distant, impersonal, medical style of relating which depersonalises people into 'patients', then the psychological needs of seriously ill people will neither be properly recognised and valued nor be properly met.

In contrast, where the focus of attention is *care, as distinct from just physical treatment*, then there will be an equal concern for the educational, psychological and social aspects of illness, in which case the psychological needs will automatically be recognised and provision made to meet these whenever possible. It is overly simplistic but we might say that the contrast is between two very different approaches — treating bodies versus caring for people. In short, the answer to the question 'how did it happen?' is that Alan's psychological needs were neglected because they were not seen. The focus of attention was elsewhere and the feeling of the staff was, on the whole, that emotional disturbance in physical illness is an unfortunate complication —

something of a nuisance which crops up with the occasional unlucky or weaker patient.

You may think that this is an unreasonable and old-fashioned view. You may want to say 'yes, but it is not like that so much these days'. But as we will see later, the evidence is that this impersonal, treatment-oriented style, remains prevalent in hospitals and there are powerful sociological and psychological forces which keep it so.

The History Concluded

The contact with the psychologist appeared to have a stabilising effect. Reports from the ward staff indicated less 'disturbed' behaviour. At the same time, the news from Alan was not good. The leg continued to be most painful, particularly when any weight was placed on it and, worse, he reported that small movements from the hip could be made within the plaster. These claims, though, were generally dismissed by staff as resulting from imagination and being too tense about things.

After four months in total on the ward, Alan began pressing his doctors for their agreement to a transfer into his own home. The feeling was that he could cope with the estimated two more months in plaster better at home than in hospital. The doctors acquiesced. It was at this point that the psychologist misjudged things. His belief was that the move home was a positive event which would result in Alan feeling less isolated and so facilitate the psychological adjustments which had to be achieved. It was a mistake. As things turned out, the arthrodesis did not fuse and six months were to pass with Alan still in plaster, still in pain, relatively immobilised and with the added problem of being out of contact with his consultant other than brief appraisals by one of the team in a busy outpatients' clinic every six to eight weeks. It became more obvious by the week that there was definite movement at the hip, which technically should by then have fused solid. The arthrodesis had failed.

Many changes took place in Alan's psychological state during this time. Most importantly, there was a growing sense that he had been cheated and abandoned. The difficulties were after all quite unexpected since he had not been forewarned. He became convinced the operation had failed yet he was unable to obtain face-to-face confirmation on his outpatient visits. Four times he had to carry away the simple message of 'Give it another six weeks and we will have another look'. If then he could have shared the consultant's thoughts and sensed the genuine doubt as to whether fusion would ultimately occur he might have seen this period of waiting in a more positive light. But communication was not good and he experienced a frustrating evasiveness. One registrar told him to prepare for the worst but on the whole he was kept minimally informed. (Ideally the psychologist would have liaised and kept him informed but he was a stranger from another department and effective channels of communication and, more importantly, trust, were not established. The medical team saw the psychological care as a parallel but relatively unconnected activity and maintained much the same uncertainty with the psychologist.)

In other words, Alan was stripped of the vital supportive link provided by regular effective communication with the medical and nursing staff responsible for his treatment. He could not know what they were thinking or whether they were aware of his plight because they had retreated from reach. At the time when he most needed their encouragement, their information, their advice and their support, it was cut off almost in total.

The transition from inpatient to outpatient has many risks and is a complex event for those who are seriously disabled and in pain. In this case it was handled in a routine medical manner, without wishing harm yet proving to be a critically damaging event. The staff just did not see the need for their continued contact as a major resource to oppose the drift into despondency and feelings of abandonment.

For a while Alan made some efforts to get out and about on crutches but it was difficult, unrewarding and painful. Increasing amounts of time were spent just lying on his bed at home, resorting inevitably to whatever means of withdrawal and pain relief that came to hand. Seemingly his intolerance to pain grew, as did his resentment and anger towards the hospital staff. His despair mounted daily. He was now discovering, on his own, what one of the alternative outcomes to the surgery could be.

In the sessions with the psychologist, which continued at an interval of every two or three weeks, Alan's distress was evident. He had begun to abandon his links with the future. In particular, he let contact with his employers lapse although they had been holding his job open for him. He turned against many of his friends and stretched his fiancée's loyalty to its limits. Then, unexpectedly for him, he suddenly lost all emotional control. Without warning he would be gripped by periods of intense sadness in which he could not hold back tears and was unable to talk. There were one or two embarrassing incidents for him. In his eyes, to add to the weight of problems, he was now 'going mental'. It was truly frightening. The psychologist tried to increase his support by suggesting more sessions but Alan withdrew saying that he could not face the journey in, or cope with seeing people at the day hospital where they met when he could never be sure of his emotional state.

As an alternative move the psychologist tried to attract the surgeon's interest in Alan's plight. The surgeon, however, felt that although he was concerned by the situation, the arthrodesis must be given more time just in case it finally fused. He saw his brief as limited to orthopaedic problems and not concerned with psychological troubles. There was no recognition that the established manner of doing things in that particular hospital was one of the main sources of Alan's psychological difficulties.

Sadly, although inevitably perhaps, Alan turned increasingly to drugs as a solution. Initially it was relatively safe, orally taken painkillers and sedatives. However, in his locality there was a robust trade in drugs amongst young people and some had learned how to inject their drugs intravenously. Alan's earlier experiences when still in the hospital were that drug-induced escape seemed the best means at his disposal to deal with the physical pain and the oppressive despair that he felt. He was responsive, therefore, to the suggestion of trying an intravenously administered painkiller which had a morphine-like effect. The immediacy of the pain relief and the escape to another world that had nothing to do with plaster and being crippled produced a profound effect in him. Before long the use of drugs became an everyday event and the insidious changes in outlook and personality which this generated began to show.

There is little more to be learned in charting Alan's steady slide into drug dependency and the ensuing problems. For the sake of completion you will probably like to know that about a year after the first operation, a second attempt was made at the arthrodesis. If anything, it was more traumatic for him than the first experience. However, the bones did finally fuse.

So, to a conclusion. This case has been used to demonstrate that the style of communicating with and relating to people in hospitals that has become prevalent in the last few decades is, in *psychological terms*, the opposite of good care. Alan was actually damaged by the approach adopted in the management of his case by the doctors and nurses involved. Yet they did not wish this, or even realise the effect they were having. Fortunately not many cases are as dramatic a demonstration as this one has been. Nevertheless, it is clearly important to discover what exactly the psychological needs of seriously ill people are, to what extent these are neglected, and with what effect. In short, was this an isolated case and thus, in general, there is not too much to worry about, or is the neglect of psychological care a common feature of our hospitals?

2　ILLNESS, DISTRESS AND NEGLECT

No woman can imagine what it is like to awake from an anaesthetic to discover that one of her breasts is gone, to find only bandages where a breast has been. It is such a traumatic experience that scars remain — forever on her body, sometimes for as long in her mind.[1]

Much of this book is set out as a practical guide to those wanting to develop their skills in psychological care. This chapter stands apart in that it draws together some academic and theoretical material which provides a reasoned basis for urging the development of psychological care in medicine, particularly in general hospitals. Without a sound basis of knowledge and argument we would lack direction and conviction. Knowing what we are trying to move away from, and what we are trying to develop in its place is half the battle, so I make no apology in giving space to a little academic work. You may choose to move ahead to the practical side first and look through this chapter later, which is reasonable enough, but I do think familiarity with the material below is important and that it should be worked through at some point.

The last chapter ended with some important questions. We have now to formulate these questions in full and make sure that there are some satisfactory answers. Each section below poses a question, develops it and then looks to some of the research and literature in this field for a reply.

Does Illness Cause Psychological Distress or Disturbance?

It is easy enough to find individual case studies of people in considerable psychological difficulty as a result of illness or injury and it is similarly easy to find instances of individual doctors or nurses who fail to see the need for a psychological side to their work and thus add to the distress of their clients. However, an impassioned argument based on case studies alone lacks real power, and it would fail to convince people who take a broad, critical perspective. Therefore, we must ask, what evidence exists indicating a high prevalence of psychological distress amongst the population of seriously ill and injured people?

14

For our trouble, we run into a problem straight away. It is in the shape of a common psychological defence called denial. Some people gain respite from their distress by blocking out awareness of threat and loss and *repressing* thoughts that excite emotional response. Thus inaccuracies are introduced. Often people are in considerable distress but deny this to themselves and to researchers. The data collected will, therefore, be an underestimate of the true levels of distress. If I may give a couple of examples you will see the problem.

In a study involving 87 men who had sustained severe myocardial infarcts and had been admitted to a coronary care unit, Hackett and Cassem (1976) noted that 70 per cent of these people showed clear signs of an initial denial of anxiety and fear. In interview, they were unable to acknowledge a fear of death and the situation they were in. Subsequently some two-thirds were able to look back and see that they had been very frightened but had resorted to various devices to block out recognition of this. In a more complicated study, Levine and Zigler (1975) used a technique for assessing denial which involved measuring the difference between people's assessment of how they actually see themselves (real self-image) and how they would like to be (ideal self-image). Comparisons were made with a control group of healthy people and three groups of seriously ill people. One group was of stroke victims, one of people with lung cancer and the remainder with coronary heart disease. The relevant finding to us is that these seriously ill people did not show significantly greater discrepancies between their real and ideal self-image than the control group, that is, they denied the implication of the damage they had sustained.

Initial denial is widely reported as a feature of serious illness in clinical descriptive writings from many sectors of medicine. It is a normal, protective response which may collapse after a short while and so lead to a more accurate perception and then perhaps depression or anxiety. We will return to this later but for our purposes now we must note that measures of psychological distress in general hospital populations may well *underestimate actual levels of psychological disturbance* because of the distorting effect of initial denial. I have experienced a powerful, first hand demonstration of this effect in a survey of the psycho-social problems associated with survival by haemodialysis (Nichols, 1984). Several subjects reported very few problems and no emotional difficulties whilst reports from the staff indicated a persistent crop of difficulties and clear signs of emotional distress. Another pattern of defence is that of passive acceptance, a state of emotionally neutral helplessness, which will also affect people's replies to inquiries about their situation.

Bearing all this in mind we must consider the following. The prevalence of psychological disturbance in the British population runs at approximately the 9 per cent level (Goldberg, 1980). However, studies of the population of general hospital patients reveal much higher levels. For example:

1. Moffic and Paykel (1975) screened 150 medical inpatients by means of the Beck depth of depression inventory. The overall prevalence of clinical depression was 28.7 per cent. When considering the sub-category of seriously ill people alone, the proportion rose to 61 per cent (although we must not lose sight of the fact that certain drug therapies induce depression).

2. Johnston (1980) charted the levels of anxiety in four separate groups undergoing surgical procedures of orthopaedic or gynaecological natures using the State Anxiety Inventory. The data revealed that high levels of anxiety occurred before admission to hospital and, with some people, the anxiety level went up *after* the operation. Generally, anxiety levels remained above normal levels until discharge from the hospital.

3. Maguire *et al.* (1974) screened by questionnaire and then interviewed 230 consecutive admissions to two medical wards. The sample included people with degenerative diseases (heart failure, emphysema, osteo-arthritis, etc.), major infections, cancers and so on. Of these, 23 per cent fell within the category 'psychiatrically ill', i.e. they met the criteria for inclusion in formal psychiatric categories. This figure would not, therefore, include the many who were in distress but not psychiatrically disturbed. Later, Hawton (1981) followed up this sample and on finding that after 18 months 90 of them had died, noticed that a higher proportion of those with psychiatric disorders died (38 per cent) compared with those free of disorders (20 per cent). About half of those identified as psychiatrically disordered had remained so during the 18 months.

4. It has for some while been realised that the population of women who ultimately need a hysterectomy include many who are 'fragile' psychologically. This is reflected in the very high incidence of psychological difficulties observed amongst these people. Gath *et al.* (1982) used a very full diagnostic interview schedule called the Present State Inventory to assess 147 women four weeks before surgery and at six and eighteen months after a hysterectomy. Of these, 58 per cent revealed psychological disturbance before surgery, with 38 per cent remaining psychologically disturbed at six months and 29 per cent at

eighteen months after their operation. (By 'psychologically disturbed', it is meant a range of anxiety-based and depressive-type disturbances sufficient in intensity to impair life to some degree and cause considerable anguish.)

5. Similarly, it is clear that breast cancer and mastectomy precipitate high levels of distress in many women which can persist for some considerable time. There is a large literature in this area which, frankly, removes any doubt on the issue. Morris (1979) produced an excellent review of many studies which all demonstrate high levels of psychological distress in significant proportions in the samples studied. For example, Maguire *et al.* (1978) interviewed and compared 75 women who were subjected to a mastectomy with 50 who were diagnosed with breast lumps which proved to be benign. Thirty-one per cent of the women undergoing surgery were depressed and/or anxious to a level that merited treatment prior to the operation and 25 per cent were similarly afflicted one year later. In contrast, the level in the control group was 12 per cent. Morris herself has several important studies which reveal that 22 per cent of 69 breast cancer victims were moderately to severely depressed *two years* after mastectomy, compared with 8 per cent in a control group with benign tumours. Thirty-two per cent of the cancer victims reported changes for the worse in sexual relations during the two-year period.

6. Other instances of disfigurements or loss of body parts reveal similar reactions. Murray Parkes (1976) interviewed 47 people shortly after the amputation of an arm or leg and again one year later. He summarised his findings noting that 'one-third to a half showed moderate emotional disturbance 13 months after the amputation'. Wirsching *et al.* (1975) described high levels of distress in people undergoing a colostomy. Prior to surgery, 39 per cent of the women patients were undermined by feelings of hopelessness, 50 per cent by spells of depression and 35 per cent by anxieties about survival. After surgery, depression was evident in 50 per cent, and 10 per cent had suicidal thoughts.

7. Mayou *et al.* (1978) produced two studies of 100 people in trouble with coronary heart disease. Interviews were conducted while they were in hospital, after two months at home and finally after one year dating from the infarction. Spouses were assessed too. During the phase in hospital, 78 per cent of patients and 53 per cent of spouses revealed mild or moderate distress. At two months, 53 per cent of the patients described moderate to severe distress (including tension, depression, phobic problems, etc.) and 55 per cent of the spouses were

Table 2.1: Percentage of Dialysands Agreeing with Dialysis Problem
Checklist Statements

General Psycho-social Difficulties	% Agreeing
Angry that I can't do the things that I used to	50
Worrying a good deal about the future	50
I'm too moody	43
Craving for liquid	43
Feeling depressed much of the time	38
Feeling irritable much of the time	38
Feeling ruled by the dialysis machine	31
Constantly in fear of injections	31
No interest in life	31
The kidney problems have made me physically unattractive	25
Frightened of any more operations	25
Feeling anxious much of the time	25
Desperate for a transplant	25
Missing being able to travel very much	25
Sometimes wanting to take my life	19
Relationships	
Feeling no good as a parent	60
Feeling that there is too much strain on my partner	57
I feel I'm spoiling my partner's life	50
I'm difficult to live with	43
Sexual relationships are difficult/have stopped	43
Feeling no good as a husband/wife	36
Feeling that I spoil my family's life	31

similarly placed. One year later, Mayou described the psychological
distress as considerable with tension, anxiety, depression and fatigue
occurring with some frequency in the people who had suffered the
coronary; 32 per cent showed moderate distress and 32 per cent
marked distress.

8. As may be expected, kidney failure followed by a life surviving
on haemodialysis or peritoneal dialysis brings great hardship. Amongst
this population the incidence of psychological difficulties and basic
human anguish is known to be high. Kaplan De Nour (1981) in a wide
series of studies found that 53 per cent of her sample of dialysands
experienced moderate to severe depression and 30 per cent considerable anxiety. My own survey at the Exeter Kidney Unit (Nichols, 1984)
returned similar figures, for both dialysands and partners. In this
survey, the people involved used a problem checklist to indicate their
difficulties and were then interviewed by a research assistant for an
expanded account. Tables 2.1 and 2.2 give you some examples of the
stresses and inter-personal strains encountered in this form of treatment

Table 2.2: Percentage of Dialysands' Partners Agreeing with Dialysis
Problem Checklist Statements

Dialysis	% Agreeing
Worried that I won't be able to deal with an emergency	46
Feeling anxious about being in charge of the machine	31
Frightened I'll cause harm or even death during dialysis	31
Feeling anxious about putting needles in	23
Helping with dialysis is a strain — my own health is deteriorating	23
The staff don't realise how difficult life is	23
Feeling anxious whilst dialysis is in progress	23
General Psycho-social Difficulties	
Feeling depressed at how he/she has changed	61
Feeling exhausted	54
Finding his/her depression hard to bear	31
Upset by the way our sexual life has suffered/stopped	31
I badly need a holiday	31
Feeling trapped because he/she depends on me so much now	23
Resenting the way he/she won't do things for him/herself	23
Worried about his/her attitude to other people now	23
Worried about the effects the situation is having on the children	23
Finding his/her tempers hard to bear	23
The future looks bleak	23
I badly need to get away for a day or two but never can	23

during the first year. The figures give the percentage of people who agreed that the problem stated was one which affected them at the time of the interview. Table 2.1 applies to those receiving dialysis treatment and Table 2.2 applies to their partners.

9. The *Lancet* (1979) ran a short but powerful article quoting various studies which estimate the level of psychological distress associated with general hospital patients as ranging between 30 per cent and 60 per cent. The conclusion was 'we now have ample evidence of the high prevalence of undetected and untreated psychiatric disorders' (amongst general hospital patients). To this we must add that with some types of illness there is also a high prevalence of distress amongst the close relatives. Table 2.3 summarises some of the evidence.

I think now that the message is clear. There are dozens of such studies but little will be learnt from adding more. Even if, as suggested, denial causes underestimation, there is still clear evidence of psychological distress or frank disorder amongst seriously ill people which typically runs at 30 per cent or more at the time of hospitalisation and during the first year after the event. We need, therefore, to be clear about what is responsible for this. Illness and injury usually bring two things with them: the experience of threat and the experience of loss.

Table 2.3: Psychological Distress in Hospital Populations

Author	Subjects	Measures	Observations
Moffic and Paykel (1975)	150 Medical	Beck Depression Inventory	28.7% clinically depressed (61% in severe illness)
Johnston (1980)	60 Surgical	State Trait Anxiety Inventory	$\bar{x}$ anxiety above norm before and after surgery
Maguire et al. (1974)	230 Medical	Interview, ratings	23% 'psychiatrically ill'
Gath et al. (1982)	147 Hyster-ectomy	Present State In-ventory	58% disturbed before surgery, 38% 6 months after 29% 12 months after
Maguire (1978)	75 Mastectomy	Interview, ratings, GHQ	31% depressed before 25% depressed after 12 months Control — 12% depressed
Morris (1977)	69 Mastectomy	Interview, ratings	22% depressed after 2 years Control — 8% depressed
Wirsching et al. (1975)	44 Colostomy	Interview	50% depressed
Mayou et al. (1978)	100 Coronary Heart disease	Interview, ratings	78% patients) 'mild-moderate 53% partners) distress'
Kaplan De Nour (1981)	100 Renal failure	Interview, ratings	53% depressed 30% anxious
Nichols (1984)	34 Renal failure	Interview, ratings	51% depressed after first year 35% anxious after first year

The threat may be complex, not just to do with the immediate problems of pain and immobilisation, but also to do with losing control of
events affecting one's own life. Having no control and not knowing
how things will go in the future undermines personal security. How will
a husband respond sexually after his wife's mastectomy? How will a
job be kept with three times a week dialysis training? How can a car be
driven with one arm? How can a family be supported after a stroke has
brought early retirement? It is the not knowing and not having control
over the threat that triggers anxiety.

As for the losses brought about by illness, these will, of course,
relate to the type of illness and the life context in which they are sustained. It may be a body part or function that has literally gone. The
uterus, for example, which takes with it the chance of children, or the
body shape and appearance after burns or amputation. Speech and

vision are obvious losses and, in the case of people in kidney failure, there is a less obvious loss of physical energy. The effect, however, is usually much wider than just physical changes. Serious illness so often leads to the loss of key roles in a person's life − occupational, social, sexual and within the family. The reaction to loss is grief. It is a powerful process that can quite change a person and can mean a year or more of deeply disturbed experience.

The most important thing to pass on to you is that as we list these things rather academically and dispassionately, we lose contact with the feelings of the event. It is all too easy to become detached and dismiss profound distress as 'attention seeking or neurotic behaviour'. *It is vital to understand that the emotional reactions which grip people in these personal crises can have a crushing power. For some, the anguish of the emotional reaction is harder to bear than the illness itself.* Project yourself for a moment into a fantasy centred around you. Imagine finding out that after a bout of influenza you have unexpectedly gone into total kidney failure. Imagine the implication for your career, your relationships, your future as a free person. If you can sense the fright then you are in touch with the reality of the situation. If not, then you have work to do before you can be effective in psychological care.

Does the Psychological Distress Associated with Physical Illness Matter?

If I had extended the quotation from the *Lancet* given above by one more line you would have read, 'We now have ample evidence of the high prevalence of undetected and untreated psychiatric disorders. Does it matter? *Probably it does.*' I will be more decisive on this point. It very definitely does matter in terms of physical recovery, the rate and the extent of rehabilitation and the protection of people from psychic pain and anguish which makes a heavy burden on top of their physical discomforts. I'll examine the issue from several viewpoints:

1. *The effect of psychological distress on physical health and the utilisation of medical services* − the author in the *Lancet* makes the point that psychological distress has a negative effect on recovery from illness. What evidence is there for this? A large scale investigation provided convincing evidence of this point some years ago. Querido (1959) studied 1630 patients admitted over a period of years to the municipal hospital in Amsterdam. Assessments were made of a physical, social and psychological nature, the latter being used to categorise the

people as either distressed or non-distressed (distressed signified 'social or psychic tensions too heavy to bear'). The relevant data for our purposes was collected six months after discharge. The people were assessed as 'in a satisfactory or unsatisfactory medical condition', the latter category comprising a return of former symptoms or continued suffering of former complaints. Of the people who were assessed as psychologically distressed, 70.4 per cent were in an unsatisfactory condition medically six months later, whereas of those classified as non-distressed, only 29.6 per cent were in an unsatisfactory medical condition after the same time lapse.

Taking a different perspective, of the total 1630 cases, 1128 had been given a favourable medical prognosis, yet only 660 of these had lived up to this expectation. The majority of those who failed to improve were psychologically distressed. In fact, Querido counsels caution in leaping to dramatic conclusions. Nevertheless, he allows himself this statement: 'It is plain that such a mental attitude on the part of the patient reduces the efficiency of the hospital staff by almost a half.'

This study is gaining support from a diverse and rapidly growing field of research. We will take just a quick sample. Kallio *et al.* (1979) studied 375 people after they had suffered an acute myocardial infarction. They were divided into two groups. One group met with professional staff on a weekly basis for health education, supportive discussion, guided exercise and general advice (i.e. stress and distress reducing contacts). The control group had no such supportive programme and these people were simply referred back to their GP. After three years the mortality rate for each group stood as follows:

Supportive intervention group	18.6 per cent
Control group	29.4 per cent

Making the very reasonable assumption that the group support programme reduced psychological distress, the obvious conclusion is that less distress contributes to improved health and survival rates after heart failure. Greer *et al.* (1979) had women undergoing mastectomy as their concern. In particular, they wished to assess whether the initial reactions and consequent attitudes which the women displayed towards their breast cancer bore any relationship to their progress after surgery. There was a clear, statistically significant finding that many more of the women who were characterised by a fighting spirit or even denial in relation to their cancer survived without further tumours, in comparison with those who were distressed and felt hope-lessness, or those who reacted with initial distress and then became stoically accepting. 'Of the women who subsequently died, 88 per cent initially reacted with stoic acceptance or helplessness/hopelessness, whereas only 46 per cent of the women who remained alive and well had demonstrated these reactions.'

Lastly, we'll take a glimpse of the expanding field concerning pre-surgical psychological states and the physical response to surgery. Evidence has accrued for some while now that recovery from surgery is influenced by the general psychological state in which an individual undertakes surgery. Here we are not just talking of emotional state but also levels of knowledge and prepared strategies for coping. Thus Ridgeway and Mathews (1982) in their study of various strategies for assisting people undergoing surgery, demonstrated that if the general psychological condition of women undergoing hysterectomy was modi-fied by educational counselling or coaching in coping strategies, then in comparison to patients left on their own without such stress-reducing contact, there was less pre-operative anxiety and worrying and (import-antly) less need of analgesia as indicated by nursing records, and less post-operative pain. These differences held up after discharge when it was shown that the groups without the supportive intervention experi-enced more pain and more symptoms. Similarly, Ray and Fitzgibbon (1981) found that pre-operative stress was positively correlated with post-operative stress and pain in cholecystectomy patients.

2. Another important facet in the relationship between psycho-logical state and recovery from illness is the *failure to comply with necessary treatment regimes, dietary restrictions and behavioural requirements for the best chances of recovery*. Again, a reminder about the introductory case in Chapter 1. The subject, if you remember, became angry in his distress. He broke his plaster on a couple of occasions and probably reduced the chances of his arthrodesis healing since he almost certainly stressed the recently pinned joint. With this and so many other cases, it is quite evident that because of low morale and depressed or angry feelings towards the situation, people behave in a way which is antagonistic to healing or disruptive to medical treat-ment. Dialysis patients are high in the league of compliance problems. They have tremendously difficult restrictions on fluid intake to comply with, sometimes as little as 500 mls per day. They must also regulate with great care the type and quantity of food they take. In fact, failure to comply with these restrictions is often an early sign of emotional disturbance. A good proportion of the cases referred to me

for psychological therapy at the Exeter Kidney Unit were initially seen on the basis of their having difficulty in keeping to their fluid limits. Later, it became clear that this was just a sign of more profound difficulties of adjustment and grief.

The point here is that when people do not understand, are out of communication with their doctors and nurses (even though in their presence), are low in morale or are emotionally disturbed, they often hazard their recovery and make new medical problems by abandoning the behaviour which gives them the best chance of recovery. Extending the example given, a dialysis patient who is restricted to drinking 500 mls of fluid a day but who drinks 1500 mls will accumulate 3000 mls of excess fluid in his body between dialysis sessions. Much of the fluid adds to the volume of the blood system and literally stretches the heart and vascular system physically. Eventually the muscular tissues of the heart change in response to this and permanent damage is done. Some die of heart failure as a consequence of non-compliance with fluid limits.

Kaplan De Nour (1981) noted that in her sample of 100 dialysands, about 75 per cent were not able fully to comply with fluid and dietary regimes. This was associated with the observation that at least 50 per cent had episodes of depression. Ley (1982b) in a very concise, useful review on matters related to compliance and communication, reports studies indicating that typical levels of non-compliance for diets and other forms of medical advice is about 50 per cent of the population of patients. Ley cites Barofsky (1980) who established levels of non-compliance associated with specific drug treatments, e.g. antibiotics, 52 per cent; anti-tuberculosis, 43 per cent; anti-hypertensive, 61 per cent. In fact, some people give up their medical treatments because they directly cause psychological difficulties or unacceptable discomfort. The cost can be high for the individual and for the hospitals. Ley lists reliable surveys in which 20 per cent of hospital admissions could be attributed to non-compliance with medical advice.

3. A further aspect for you to consider is the *effect on doctor/nurse utilisation in relation to psychological distress*. Balint (1964) argues that where neither the doctor nor the patient recognise that the latter is in psychological trouble, then the two parties may spend much time (increased above the normal) in the business of physical investigation and treatment. People will engage a doctor's attention on matters of *physical* health as a means of securing supportive contact when, in fact, there may be no physical pathology present. Tessler *et al.* (1976) measured both psychological distress and the number of visits to a

general practitioner made between this assessment and the passing of one year. There was a positive relationship between the presence of psychological distress and the consultation with a doctor on matters concerning apparent physical symptoms. Rather more alarmingly perhaps, Rawlings (1972) investigated the records of 235 people who were judged to be presenting psychological disorders. They turned out to be operation-prone, having logged 453 operations of which 50 per cent revealed no disease process. Similarly, many cardiologists have spent much time conducting physical investigations of complaints and heart pains which are of a psychogenic nature.

The pain clinics and orthopaedic hospitals give excellent examples of this effect too. The post-operative experience of pain and the long-term pain from injuries to the spine — lower back pain — are known to be amplified by anxiety and depression. Presenting the physical complaint of pain may be an indirect way of presenting a state of psychological distress. Alternatively, the presence of anxiety or depression is known to increase the impact of pain and diminish adaptive behaviour (Bond, 1980; Sternbach, 1974). The exasperation that is a familiar experience with orthopaedic surgeons seems to originate from the fact that they encounter a good number of cases where they suspect complaints of pain are psychologically based, yet they cannot extend their ideas of care beyond that of physical treatment, so a state of impasse is created.

A position has been reached where we can point to three conclusions in answer to the question, 'does it matter?' It does matter, because:

1. recovery from illness and mortality rates can be influenced by psychological distress
2. compliance with treatment regimes and medical advice can be diminished by psychological distress
3. the level of utilisation of medical and nursing services tends to increase where physical illness is associated with psychological stress. This places a burdensome and expensive demand on those services and creates additional work which is often irrelevant to the central problem.

Psychological Stress and Genuine Care

Now we need to think for a moment of the underlying moral philosophy of medicine and nursing. Without getting too involved, we have to ask what is the real point of it all? Two extreme alternatives should be named. The first I will label 'technical medicine' and the other 'caring medicine' to illustrate the point. The differences are probably obvious to you already. The aims of technical medicine are to deal with faulty body parts and functions and restore these physical systems to normal functioning or at least halt deterioration. Technical medicine does not include in its span of attention the personal needs of the individual beyond the minimum necessary to facilitate treatment regimes. To a large extent, the 'person in the body' is an inconvenience and an irrelevance since the requirements for optimum technical medicine often clash with the requirements of the person. To this end, people and their needs are banished by turning them into something less distracting called 'patients'. A patient is not directly equivalent to a person and can be treated in ways which are less inconvenient for technical medicine.

Caring medicine at the other end of the scale involves educational, psychological, social and medical approaches. Here the aim is to minimise the trauma of illness by giving instruction and information, providing supportive intervention to help with psychological reactions and social difficulties when they arise and, of course, standard medical procedures. The difference is that these procedures are not pursued without attention to the other needs, since that produces an outcome which is often psychologically, socially and morally unacceptable. Because, in the pursuit of medical excellence, technical medicine often proves to be the opposite of caring, it leads to the inevitable neglect of psychological needs and the likelihood of people being *made distressed* in addition to the effects of the illness.

Conversely, caring medicine is an ideal with the aim of minimising the damaging impact of illness and actively buffering the individual from additional stresses created by hospitalisation and medical procedures. I recognise that it is an ideal and that arguments about manpower and resources must be heeded. Nevertheless, it seems quite indefensible to me that the medical and nursing professions would opt for technical medicine and remain uncaring in their basic approach. It is morally bizarre to create a set of problems and great distress as a consequence of a narrow attack on another set of problems which, as we will see in the next section, is a very prevalent situation. People who are seriously ill or injured are vulnerable and powerless. Technical medicine, with its associated insensitivity, sometimes amounts to a psychological attack upon them, whereas caring medicine represents a recognition of their vulnerability and a balanced endeavour to meet all their needs.

The question we began with asked, 'does the psychological distress matter?' Here we find a different type of answer to those above. That is, it matters if there is a concern to be humane and to reduce distress in every possible way — and this surely is the only way.

Do the Medical and Nursing Professions Recognise and Respond to Psychological Distress?

Without doubt, there are some very psychologically-minded doctors and nurses who are sensitive, natural counsellors. Some work hard at caring for their clients at all levels. I know several personally and I pay tribute to them. However, in our inquiry, we have to press on to ask whether this is typical. In general, do these two professions actually monitor the psychological state of their clients and does either make appropriate psychological interventions or at least engage other professions to do so on their behalf? Sadly, the answer has to be that, at the time of writing, the majority of people in practice as hospital doctors or nurses appear to have had little training in the detection and management of the type of problem that concerns us. Also, they make little use of the professions who do specialise in psychological care — psychologists and psychiatrists, for example. There are the medical social workers, of course, but most do not claim to be trained as psychological therapists and while few in number they have commitments to many other tasks.

On the positive side, there have been some encouraging recent developments in the nursing professions. Many schools of nursing and the nursing journals now seek to sensitise nurses to the psycho-social side of medicine via the introduction of the nursing process and communication skills generally. Even so, while I would not want to be other than encouraging over this, it is necessary to point out that it falls a long way short of psychological care. If the nurses implementing the nursing process had also received training in basic counselling skills, had the readily available back up of specialists in psychological care such as clinical psychologists and were, as a routine part of their duties, responsible for overseeing psychological care and referring cases on that they felt were too demanding for them, then things would be much more satisfactory. But this is not the case. With the occasional small scale exception, there are no psychological services in the general hospitals, primarily because the hospital management teams fail to realise the need for them. What is available is a referral system to the psychiatric service. This is a service which is separate from the general hospital system and functions curatively. That is, people obtain assistance from this service only when they have deteriorated below certain thresholds and then only when the general sector doctors (physicians, surgeons, etc.) notice the need and decide to refer. Basically, this means that referral for assistance with psychological problems in general hospitals is relatively infrequent (in relation to the high prevalence) and can only be 'earned' by substantial disorder.

Groundless accusations? In the study by Moffic and Paykel (1975) which we encountered earlier, although the overall prevalence of clinical depression on the wards was 43 out of 150 (28.7 per cent), only six of these were mentioned as depressed in their notes, four were receiving anti-depressants and only two had been referred to the psychiatric service. In the survey by Maguire *et al.* (1974), 23 per cent of inpatients were revealed to be suffering 'psychiatric illness' but only 12 per cent were referred for help with 'no evidence in the notes that their problems had been detected by medical staff, treated or dealt with in any other way'. In a later study, Maguire *et al.* (1980) trained a nurse to act as a counsellor to women undergoing mastectomy. She detected and referred 38 women needing psychological help in a group of 77. Tape-recorded interviews were assessed by trained psychological therapists to establish the total number of those in psychological difficulty and it transpired that the nurse had detected 89 per cent. In a control group run by the usual surgical and nursing team, however, only nine (22 per cent) of 41 cases were detected and referred. *That is, most of those needing to be referred for help went unnoticed.*

In my own study of people involved with dialysis, nearly 50 per cent of the subjects agreed that 'the staff do not realise how difficult life on dialysis is'. There was a clear need on the part of staff to see the treatment as worthwhile and their clients as suffering less than was apparent to unbiased observers, which again meant a diminished ability to notice patients' psychological difficulties and arrange help for them. Similarly, Kaplan De Nour and Czaczkes (1974) investigated the accuracy of consultant nephrologists in assessing the state of the people dialysing under their care. Again there was clear evidence of an inability to notice the difficulties and distress of their patients.

Thus the trend of the literature in this area is quite clear. Doctors do seem quite poor at recognising the psychological needs of their clients and in the majority of instances, these needs will go unnoticed or at least unattended to. As Lief and Fox (1963) wrote:

a pathological process of overdetachment begins which may eventually lead them as mature physicians to perceive and treat their patients mechanistically. The process of overdetachment may not stop at the failure to see the patient as a person but go on to the unconscious fantasy that the best patient is the one who is completely submissive and passive.

If then doctors are poor at noticing the psychological needs of their clients, if the nurses are as yet neither trained nor empowered to take the initiative and deal with the problems, if allied professions such as social workers also lack training and are overcommitted with other tasks, and if the hospitals have not made provision for psychological care by the setting up of departments of clinical psychology to develop this side of the hospital care, who looks after the proven, psychological needs of the general hospital patient? The answer is obvious. In most cases nobody does. *The general hospitals are quite clearly places of psychological neglect.*

Does the Behaviour of the Medical and Nursing Professions Create Additional Stress for People in Hospital?

This is difficult territory because it may seem that I am waging a campaign of hostile accusation against doctors and nurses and I might lose your sympathy. This is my last wish. At the same time, though, there is no point in evading the issue and so, in a fair-minded and objective way, we have to pursue the inquiry to its end. I will, however, preface this section with an important point. While I plan to demonstrate that in certain ways doctors and nurses often do impose additional stress, I do not see this as a personal issue, a form of deliberate negligence or punitive behaviour consciously carried out by an individual nurse or doctor. It is more to do with how people are trained into their job and certain psychological factors (detailed in the next section) which have caused the professions to develop certain ways of behaving. As Byrne and Long (1976) surmised in their study of communication by doctors, 'Doctors like any other professional group are both a product and prisoner of the training system that produced them.' I also recognise, as I mentioned above, that at the present time improvements are on the increase within the nursing profession. A small but growing proportion of nurses are extremely active in the pursuit of psychological care. However, whilst the signs are hopeful, there is plenty of evidence that, so far, all is not yet well from the psychologist's viewpoint.

Ivan Illich (1976) wrote, 'The pain, dysfunction, disability and anguish resulting from technical medical intervention . . . *make the impact of medicine one of the most rapidly spreading epidemics of our time*' (my italics).

Illich is a bitter, uncompromising assessor of modern medical practice and occupies an extreme position as a critic, much more so than myself. Nevertheless, I have to say that I know what he means. In the last five years in my role as a psychologist working in the general hospital sector, I have met many people who have been greatly stressed by their encounter with 'medical behaviour' and some who have been undoubtedly damaged by it. So how does it happen? I will examine the problems created by the medical profession under the two headings of communication and emotional aspects. The position of the nurses will be discussed later under a separate heading.

Communication

A much discussed issue in medical sociology and social psychology is the so-called 'medical style of relating'. The basic idea is that in their training and because of the setting in which they first work, young doctors are slowly shaped into a particular way of relating which is responsible for much damage. The profession is, of course, composed of many people with differing personalities and backgrounds, so in reality there will be quite a wide range of expression of the medical style of relating. Our aim here, though, is to establish what is most typical. For a good review of knowledge and research in this area I cannot improve on that given by Hauser (1981). I will also draw on the work of Ley (1982a and b) who deals specifically with the communication of medical information and construct a general summary from the work of these authors together with one or two other contributors.

A key feature of the medical style of relating is the approach to collecting and giving back information and the level of attention given to the general needs of patients. The overwhelming evidence of dozens of studies is that most doctors hold back information or at least make little effort to transmit information in a way which makes it usable. Hence because many of the people who are involved in a significant way with doctors receive too little information, they are often dissatisfied and usually ill-informed. In terms of receiving information, 68 per cent of some 700 patients questioned by Cartwright[2] found their doctors unhelpful. Korsch[3] revealed that 50 per cent of 800 mothers attending a children's clinic were left wondering what had caused their child's illness, and many of the doctors failed to give clear diagnostic and prognostic statements and had also tended to disregard the mother's account of her worries concerning her child's illness and ignore her tension. In Ley's survey involving twelve studies of communication by doctors, the percentage of people found to be dissatisfied with the communication varied from a minimum of 21 per cent from a sample of general practice patients to 57 per cent of medical inpatients and 65 per cent of coronary patients. Webb[4] demonstrated that in *none* of 50 consultations which were studied in depth did patients receive adequate information about treatment.

By the way, it is relevant here to challenge the myth that many patients do not wish to know much about their illness or their treatment. This belief has led to remarkable levels of non-communication. For example, Lipowski (1975)[5] describes a survey which revealed 90 per cent of 219 doctors as believing it was best not to tell people they had cancer (although as Ley comments there is a trend for the proportion of doctors holding this view to decline). In contrast, Wilson-Barnett (1980) cites two studies in which 87 per cent and 93 per cent of cancer patients preferred to be informed. Ley cites similar figures from other research and also points out that there was no evidence found of increased anxiety or depression when patients were given full information about their case, even to the extent of being given their case notes or helping compile them (Stevens *et al.*[6] and Fishbach *et al.*[7]). Ley concludes, 'It would appear from survey evidence that the majority of patients wish to know as much as possible about their illness, its causes, its treatments and its outcome.' There will always be individual exceptions of course and also those who for one reason or another cannot make use of, or understand, the information. The majority it seems, though, do wish to know and are dissatisfied and disturbed by not knowing.

Part of the explanation of withheld information is the controlling style of interaction commonly found in doctors. Byrne and Lang (1976) conducted an intensive study of general practitioners in which they analysed and classified the transactions taking place in 2500 consultations. The most common style observed was described as the 'doctor centred' style, which applied to about 75 per cent of the physicians. In this style, the conversation was controlled by the doctors who tended to adopt an inflexible questioning pattern concerning physical symptoms with the sole purpose of gathering key information to make medical decisions. This blocked any opportunity for the patients to direct conversation to other concerns and meant that the physician was unresponsive to their feelings and needs. Hauser finds

three terms in the literature which are used to describe this predominant style of interaction in doctors, namely doctor-dominated, doctor-
centred and bureaucratic task-oriented. The opposite style of relating
is termed person-oriented. You can see that in the doctor-centred
style effective communication is unlikely. There is little opportunity
for an equal exchange of information — mainly the doctor receives
information and the patient gives it. The need on the part of the
patient to receive information back is not met, nor is the doctor in a
position to react to the needs of the patient since little contact can be
made with them in this kind of conversation.

For those of you who have a taste for straight sociological analysis,
Strong (1979) presented a study of children's clinics which supports
this general claim. His message is a similar one based on the verbatim
analysis of doctor-patient transactions made over three and a half years
in nine Scottish clinics and several American children's clinics. (In
reality the children were the patients but they were basically ignored
and the communication was with the parents.) The prevailing pattern
of interaction was a ritualistic, bureaucratic format. The parents gave
and the doctors took absolute control over the situation and conversation. They would initiate and terminate conversations, control the
content, manipulate conversations by interruptions involving medical
procedures or physical activity of some sort, e.g. talking with other
staff, referring to notes or moving away. The parents remained passive-
dependant and used none of these devices. Much of this could be seen
as motivated by the pursuit of technical efficiency and the limited
availability of time for each case. The overall effect, though, was that
while the doctors obtained the basic medical information, the actual
communication with and care of the people involved was badly
impoverished.

Another study which is also very relevant to our purposes is that
of Millman[8]. She describes three very frequently occurring inter-
personal manoeuvres by doctors that were identified in a two-year
observational study in hospitals. They appeared to be primarily defensive moves as a buffer against being seen to be guilty of error, viz:

Withholding Medical Information. The effect of such a strategy is to
limit the power and autonomy of the patient, since with less knowledge of their condition, patients are in a weak position and are unable
to recognise mistakes in diagnosis or treatment. This particular strategy
is commented upon in depth by Waitzin and Stoeckle (1972) who claim
that, 'A physician's ability to preserve his own power over the patient

. . . depends largely on his ability to control the patient's uncertainty.' They go on to add, 'The postulated association between uncertainty and power may help explain physicians' reluctance to reveal information to the dying patients. A physician's disclosure of fatal illness is equivalent to a declaration of his own powerlessness.'

Refusal to Evaluate or Comment on the Competence and Performance of Other Doctors. There is an almost universal creed amongst hospital doctors which again deprives patients and other professionals of information and so defends the medical power position. It is readily observed when there has been a crisis of some sort which involves medical error.

Discrediting the Patient. Where mistakes occur the communications about the event carry the message that in some way the patient is actually responsible. I have met this on many occasions with kidney patients. For example, '*You* did not react to that drug at all well, did you?' when a prescription error was made and, 'The reason you have heart pains is because you have been overdrinking.' This latter example occurred to a young man two days after a transplant attempt. In fact, an error had been made instructing nurses to encourage a consumption of 2000 mls a day although the output from the recently transplanted kidney was only 1000 mls and falling off. The intake of fluid should have matched the output. Another common form of the defence is frequently encountered by orthopaedic patients who complain of back pain which does not yield to ready diagnosis. They are likely to receive the communication, 'We can find nothing wrong with you, it is probably psychological', the implication being that the experience of pain is not real and they do not merit attention.

A last type of defensive strategy which is worth noticing is described by Duff and Hollingshead[9] and concerns the extent to which 'personal doctoring' is blocked. In the extreme form of the defence called 'committee sponsorship', the patient is never able to deal with the same doctor for any length of time. The experience is of an ever-changing sequence of medical staff making visits, varying from senior house officers to the consultant. In addition, we might add that although the consultant is usually the decision-maker, he has one predominant characteristic. He is absent for most of the time. The use of absence and the system of making doctors interchangeable leaves the patient in a very weak position, blocking the chance of relationships forming and communication developing. This is not so in what Duff and

Hollingshead called 'committed sponsorship' in which an individual doctor would take an interest in a case beyond that of the disease itself.

Emotional Aspects

Moving on now to the issue of personal feeling in doctor-patient relationships, the role of a doctor can involve some harrowing experiences and devastating conflicts. Thus, right from the beginning, trainee doctors are 'shaped' into ways of dealing with the problem. I talked with a doctor recently on this theme and she was recalling some of her training experiences. The emphasis had been to stand back and never get involved for, the tutors stressed, if you began to feel something for a patient, you lost objectivity and became motivated to do things which lead away from good medical practice (for example, over-prescribing painkillers with a risk of drug dependency developing).

One of the strategies for developing this remoteness in medical students was public ridicule. Medical students were severely embarrassed by consultants in front of their colleagues (and sometimes patients) if they revealed sensitivity and concern for the personal experiences of the patient. Hauser found that the literature dealing with the interpersonal training or socialisation of doctors confirmed this to be widespread practice. Lief and Fox[10] wrote of the development of 'detached concern'. It is the beginning of a change towards diminished feelings which eventually results in doctors seeing the people they care for in an incomplete, mechanistic way, symbolised by the label 'patient' as distinct from 'person'. Once started, the process may develop a momentum of its own and can result in 'overdetachment', a gross form of inter-personal insensitivity which can appear to observers to be akin to cruelty. Thus, most doctors relate in a way which is devoid of emotional contact or empathy with their patients. These are best seen then as pseudo-relationships.

There is a strong argument, incidentally, that there are important benefits in the maintenance of 'detached concern', both for the individual doctor and for the good standards of medicine. The benefits are in terms of insulating the doctor from excessive and traumatising contact with other people's distress. I am basically sympathetic with this argument and will give my reply to it in the last two sections of this chapter. However, I can never give support for the more extreme form of overdetachment which can cause extensive psychological damage.

Overall then, the evidence is that doctors do add to the difficulties of their patients by the maintenance of pseudo-relationships and defensive strategies of behaviour. At a time of high dependency and fright, when information is usually all-important, patients and their relatives find themselves dealing with a profession whose members have often been schooled into an impersonal, detached manner of functioning which emphasises minimal levels of communication and inaccessibility.

Communication and Styles of Relating in Nurses

Regrettably (depending on your viewpoint), nurses seem to have received a less intensive investigation than their medical colleagues. As Miller (1979) observed, 'Evidence about nurses' attitudes towards their patients is not readily available.' Nursing is, of course, a very different profession with a large majority of its members being young women most of whom, it seems, were attracted to nursing because of a natural tendency towards caring and nurture. Assessing the characteristic relationship style that nurses adopt is not easy at the moment, though, since the profession does appear to be in a state of transition.

While nursing has developed alongside medicine, its character and history are dissimilar. Healers have always existed but nurses are a comparatively recent development, stemming in this country from the model delineated by Nightingale in the nineteenth century, with its heavy emphasis on discipline, hierarchical bureaucracy and regimentation, reminiscent of the Victorian values of the society in which it was conceived. As we will see, this atmosphere still lingers although two models of nursing now vie for position — the traditional, rather impersonal task-oriented approach and the more recently conceived nursing process which aims for a more person-oriented style (Hawker, 1983a). As I have commented before, there is no reliable information on which to assess the level of implementation of the nursing process, nor the spirit in which it has been implemented. Hawker (1983b) observed that although the nursing process has been a significant movement for a decade particularly in the USA, it is only in the last few years that schools of nursing have attributed it real significance in their syllabus. Further, the implementation of the nursing process on the wards is still relatively weak. Other innovations, such as computer-guided nursing and the extended role of the nurse tend to corrupt attempts at the nursing process and reduce them back to the familiar, task-oriented approach. Certainly in many seminar contacts with nurses during the last few years, it has become a familiar experience for me to hear recently trained nurses complaining that the nursing process oriented training they have received at nursing school is rather stamped on by more traditionally-minded ward sisters and consultants.

Hawker (1983b) also notes some important features of the context in which nurses work. While there is a clear hierarchical structure of authority based on the ward sister, in other terms the situation is not so clear because, although the true superiors are nursing administrators, the nurses take orders from the medical profession. That is, the doctors are in a power-preserving stance towards the nurses, as well as patients.

However, despite these various confusions, let's see what is known about the way the profession conducts its business. An investigation by Menzies (1970) makes a good start for us. Her brief was to make a study of nurse behaviour and nurse relationships in a large London teaching hospital. There were 150 trained nurses and 550 student nurses. In her report which was based solely on clinical observation, Menzies identified several features which had become predictable aspects of nursing organisation and behaviour. Combining various of these together, the following characteristics emerge:

The Splitting of Nurse-patient Relationships. Personal nursing was blocked by the practice of giving nurses a few tasks to perform on a large number of patients, rather than working with just a few patients and coping with the whole range of tasks.

Ritualistic Task Performance – the Task-oriented Approach. The attention of the nurses was directed to the performance of tasks rather than to the patients as individuals. The work tended to be undertaken in a ritualistic manner, that is, without variation or individual interpretation in relation to patients' needs. This again had a blocking effect on nurse-patient relationships.

Denial of Feeling. The young nurses were tutored to hold back their feelings and not to get close or involved with the patients. They would receive rebukes from seniors of the 'pull yourself together' type if there were instances of emotionality.

The Depersonalisation of Nurse and Patient. The basic attitude taught to the students was that nurses were interchangeable with one another – it should not matter to nurse or patient which nurse dealt with which patient. They were all required to approach their job in a standard, regimented way, the uniform symbolising their neutrality as individuals. The student nurses particularly were moved from ward to ward with notable frequency. The patients were similarly depersonalised by the nurses, perhaps referred to as 'the cancer in bed twelve'.

This tendency to depersonalise was also noted in research by Stock-well (1972) and Towell (1975). Now we need to bear in mind that Menzies's work was published in 1970 and change may have occurred. However, I have looked hard and talked to many nurses and the position appears to be that in a large, active hospital, much of this still applies. Hawker (1983a) directed her attention to the relationship between nurses and relatives. She mentions various studies which indicate strategies of avoiding contact with relatives including not noticing their efforts to attract attention, being very busily engaged on seemingly important tasks such that the visiting relative feels inhibited at interrupting her, and being inaccessible by engaging in tasks away from the ward when the relatives are visiting.

A recurring theme then is that of nurses being efficiently and busily engaged in tasks with a manner that discourages communication and relationships by imposing a barrier of activity.

Evidence also exists that nurses are, like their medical colleagues, preoccupied with the threat of making a mistake with the consequent exposure to discipline by senior nurses and medical staff and guilt towards the patient involved. Hawker (1983a) cites Stein (1969, re-published 1978) as finding that 86.1 per cent of a sample of nurses were overly concerned about the risk of making a mistake.

Another feature which I have observed repeatedly in various hospital settings and have had verbally confirmed in many seminar discussions with nurses is to do with responsibility *and taking clinical initiatives*. Basically nurses appear to *actively avoid being responsible for clinical decisions*. The effect of the ritualisation of procedures is to take away the need for clinical initiative on the part of the nurses. An example of this was nurses on a children's ward insisting on doing a drug round regularly at 9.30 pm. One child who had been fractious all day was beginning to doze off at 8.30 and her mother asked if the child might have her antibiotic syrup then. The nurses said no, as they would have to contact a doctor to check if it was alright and they felt things should be left to the usual procedure. They would wake the child up and cope with the reaction.

Again, Hawker (1983a) cites studies which reveal that the average nurse passively implements the doctors' wishes even when the nurse believes the doctor to be wrong. However, the strategy of avoiding responsibility can be complex and devious, in that the nurse may manipulate and lead the doctor to make a certain decision (which she, the nurse, wishes) but will retain her position as 'not responsible' by subtle ploys. Stein (1978) wrote of this feature of professional relationships in an intriguing little article called, 'The Doctor-nurse Game'. His various analyses indicated that in many instances senior nurses would contact doctors giving selective information about patients which inevitably led to a particular treatment. Effectively, the nurse initiated the treatment but both she and the doctor colluded together to maintain the belief that it had been the doctor's decision. A further observation is that in avoiding responsibility and avoiding challenging medical colleagues, nurses also become involved in the business of withholding information. Searching questions will often be parried with, 'You will have to check with your doctor, I cannot say.'

Such generalisation concerning nurse behaviour must be accepted with considerable caution for the research is very scant. As to the actual nature of relationships which do form and the content of communication between nurses and patients, this is even thinner ice. The reality is that there is probably much more individual variation amongst nurses than doctors. The setting in which they work will produce variability. Compare, for example, the nurses' contact with patients in a small coronary care unit against that in a large general ward working under a full load with many short-stay patients. (Fortunately I do not stand alone in pointing all this out. Hayward [1975], for example, an experienced and senior nurse, has written a very effective text on the necessity for improved communication within hospitals which includes an analysis of the current deficiencies in the approach of the profession. He confirms the basic substance of the critique presented here. Hawker's [1983a] investigation into the communication between nurses and relatives adds further general support to this position.)

What is our conclusion? Despite the very recent influence of the nursing process, it appears that elements of traditional nursing still exert pressure and influence. Where this influence is strong it results in impoverished relationships and inevitably means that the psychological needs of the patients are to some extent unmet and, thus, additional stresses are imposed.

What are the Origins of the Medical Manner of Relating and What Psycho-social Forces Maintain It?

Many people are dissatisfied with the neglect of psychological care in hospitals. These people, and nurses in particular, are seeking to bring about improvement. As we prepare for changes it is clearly important for the people who wish to play a part in developing psychological care to understand why, after centuries of development, the medical profession has failed to see the need for psychological care and why the nursing profession has tended to collude with the medical profession in ignoring the psychological needs of the people it cares for. Such understanding is important because the influences which have been responsible for this situation probably still operate and will continue to obstruct developments unless they are exposed and consciously opposed. The basic idea being considered is that perhaps something shapes and maintains doctors and nurses in the patterns of behaviour that have just been described, rather than the possibility that the people in these professions are abnormally cold and unfeeling.

Table 2.3: Difference in Hospital and Hospice Care

Medical style of Relating Common in General Hospitals	Objectives in Hospice Care
Impersonal, insensitive, detached, authoritarian	Inter-personal closeness, giving comfort through companionship
Withholding information, defensive	Open communication, efforts made to keep the patient fully informed
Lack of awareness of patient's needs	Special attention given to identifying patient's needs
Lack of permission and lack of provision for the emotional component of illness	Staff trained to include emotional care as a central activity

Some clues are to be found in certain differences evident in *hospice* care compared with the general hospitals. In hospice care, staff undergo training to produce behaviour which is visibly different from that in the institutions which they are leaving. Table 2.3 shows some of the differences. These are intriguing because they illustrate the two possibilities before us. Either the staff in hospice care are rather different types of people or the psycho-social conditions of hospice care *free* doctors and nurses from influences which produce the 'medical style of relating'. The converse is that there are certain pressures in general hospitals which mould and trap the majority of the medical and nursing staff in the medical style of relating. What might these pressures be? We will look at each profession one last time with this question in mind.

Influences Which Shape the Behaviour of Doctors

Experiences in training and the development of personal defences. The medical student does not just learn medicine. He or she is trained into a way of thinking, a way of dealing with natural empathy and emotional responding, and a way of relating. In other words, the student is shaped into the norms of a new *sub-culture*, and the pressure to conform is intense. The early exposure to clinical responsibility towards the end of training and in the early years as a house officer are believed by some to have a damaging effect. Both Stein (1979) and Hauser (1981) write on this theme. They illustrate several conflicts that most physicians will experience all their working lives, but which may be traumatically intense during the early years of hospital work, for example, the feelings of compassion, horror even, at the suffering and mutilation associated with severe illness which is heightened by the young doctor's personal responsibility towards a case. In such situations, older doctors will both model and advise detachment. It will be experienced as a 'safe haven' from the emotionally stirring contact with distress.

The young doctor is inexperienced and gets by on basic knowledge. To him, therefore, the dread of mistakes will be high. Senior staff, patients and their families, can all apply pressures which intensify the dread. In the event of a mistake, particularly if it is a damaging one, there is much difficulty to be faced from the people involved, together perhaps with guilt and the uncomfortable feeling of incompetence. Inevitably the young doctor is pushed towards the defensive strategies that were described in the previous section. These are anxiety-reducing and help defuse the tension. For many, the defences become entrenched behavioural patterns without which intolerable stresses would be suffered.

When training is complete and a doctor stands alone with clinical responsibility, there is no doubt that the need for personal defences remains high. To be directly exposed to the fright, anger, dependency and trust of the more distressed patients, and at the same time to be responsible for the outcome of their illness or surgery is a burden that few could bear for long. This is obviously doubly so in very serious illnesses where the doctor's decision can have profound consequences. Jason Brice, a neurosurgeon, recently described some of his experiences in the *Sunday Times*. He talked of the effect on him of deciding whether to operate on aneurisms or tumours in the brain when the operation involved the risk of brain damage and severe impairment.

People say that surgeons are a bit cold, a bit autocratic and un-sympathetic with patients. I suspect a lot of this is part of a psycho-logical barrier we put up to protect ourselves . . . I sometimes feel that the strain of living with the decisions you have made creates greater stress than the operation itself . . . If she had been younger I would have taken the chance and pressed on. It would have been better if I had because the tumour bled and compressed the brain and she woke up with ghastly and gross disabilities. She would have been better off dead.

Without doubt, practising in the isolated and unsupported setting which many doctors face will provoke much emotional upheaval unless there are effective psychological defences, the most likely of these being denial, distancing and the blocking of personal feeling. It seems reason-able to argue that doctors do need defences if they are to bear the burden of clinical responsibility. *However, what is rarely recognised is that the price paid for these defences is the neglect of psychological care.* This is inevitable in that the defences reduce the capacity of doctors to see distress in other people but at the same time the very same doctors, because of their clinical responsibility, are the people in the role of 'managers'. Putting it simply, the psychological needs of the people in distress remain unheeded because many doctors are unable to see them and so do nothing to help.

Medical Mistakes and the Community

The issue of mistakes has figured prominently in much of our discus-sion. So let's ask how did the whole business of medical mistakes turn into the apparent millstone that it has become? Enter the general community — us, that is. Collectively we are the source of a strong pressure on the medical profession which I believe has shaped its development over the last century and, with the promise of new medical technology, is taking an even more powerful grip. The pressure is our clinging to the myth of *medical infallibility* and the consequent expectation of a perfect, mistake-free medical service.

   The psychology of the situation works out in the following fashion. The threat of serious illness and injury looms over us all but in our society it is buffered by denial and a tendency to 'project' special powers onto the medical profession. This term 'projection' refers to a defensive, perceptual response in which an object of perception is experienced as having qualities which the perceiver needs to see rather than actually possess. The suggestion here then is that by and large the general community diminishes the threat of illness by the projection of infallibility onto the medical and nursing professions. Thus, there is a secure feeling because 'casualty' will mend broken bodies after accidents, the physicians and the scanners will spot the threatening tumours and aneurisms, the transplants will replace the failed kidneys or hearts. In short, the doctors will know what is wrong, what to do, and how to do it.

Of course, people do not consciously think like this, it is a *felt* thing. We feel doctors as infallible. This diminishes the threat of illness and death. It is a widely held, comforting myth which allows us to disown responsibility for our own health and pass this on to the fantasised powers of the medical profession.

Now for a very important point. In its development, the medical profession has opted to collude with this myth even though it clearly is a myth. The reality of medicine includes confusions, doubts, misdiagnoses, treatments which fail, treatments which cause damage, procedural mistakes of one sort or another, notes, X-rays and blood tests which somehow go astray, errors in surgery, and poor communication between doctors, nurses and departments. Hospitals are cumbersome, bureaucratic institutions. They inevitably have a high 'mistake rate'. Illich (1976) notes, 'The US Department of Health, Education and Welfare calculates that 7 per cent of all patients suffer compensable injuries while hospitalised . . . the frequency of reported accidents in hospitals is higher than in all industries but mines and high-rise construction.' He goes on to claim that one out of five people admitted to a research hospital acquire damage of one sort or another as a result of investigative procedures or treatment. Of course, the staff in hospitals are well aware of the mistake rate and will be able to identify individual doctors or surgeons as mistake prone, or particular wards will be referred to in terms which recognise high mistake rates ('Oh, Exeter Ward, it's chaos up there.'). However, two sets of needs bring pressure to bear to keep this knowledge within the confines of the professions.

Firstly, the general community *resists* knowing about mistakes. The myth of infallibility is functional as a defence and thus knowledge which conflicts will be rejected. When knowledge is forced into the open there is usually much anger and accusation as we can see from the growing number of court cases and articles hostile to medicine in the press. For this reason, plus the risk of raising anxiety, it is often argued by doctors that people are generally better off if they do not know.

Secondly, the medical profession clearly finds it imperative to protect itself from exposure and works hard to prevent general recognition of the rather more human and fallible realities of medicine. Why this is so important is speculative. Several writers suggest that it is to do with power. Illich has no doubts on this point. In his eyes, medicine is a radical, power-conserving monopoly. It controls large sums of money (estimated at 8.4 per cent of the gross national product [GNP] in the United States during 1975 with a similar figure for other Western European countries including Britain), has ever-growing power over the individual in society (sanctioning illness, judging fitness for occupation, recreations, etc.), governs its own affairs and, like other powerful monopolies, works to remove from the general community any power or knowledge which would rival the monopoly. In short, much of the behaviour of the medical profession is the same as any political organisation which seeks to preserve its own power. Thus, the common defensive strategies (keeping doctor-patient contacts unpredictable and to a minimum, maximising uncertainty by withholding information, refusing to comment on other doctors' work, etc.) may be seen as behaviour which has *evolved to protect the profession from being 'found out' since being found out breaks the myth of infallibility and erodes power.*

Such behaviour is handed on to new members of the profession who find that it gives a more comfortable, defended feeling. The defensive medical behaviour patterns are, therefore, functional defences which are entrenched and very hard to change. Table 2.4 sets out some of these ideas in summary form. As you use it, remember two things. These ideas are to be treated as theory, not proven fact, and the point of developing the theme is to show that the medical style of relating

Table 2.4: Hypothesised Psychological Basis of Medical Behaviour

Objectives and Needs	Strategies and Defences
Accept clinical responsibility but minimise inevitable inter-personal stresses and pressures.	Avoid real relationships with patients by means of detachment, minimising contact by absence and the 'interchangeable' doctor system. Personal defences, e.g. denial, projection of well being, etc.
Preserve the power position of the medical profession and individual doctors.	Maximise autocratic control by use of 'legal responsibility' device, and exclude other professions from decision-making roles. Control patients by withholding
Maintain the image of mistake-free, infallible medicine.	information, refusing to comment on other doctors' decisions and discrediting patients.

does not originate from indifference or malice on the part of individual doctors, but is a way of behaving which has evolved in relation to stresses, needs and objectives.

Influences which Shape the Behaviour of Nurses

The same exercise can be extended to the nursing profession, that is, to assess the needs and objectives of the profession and derive how these have led to the evolution of defensive strategies.

The sparsity of research on the nursing profession makes the exercise rather more problematic for me, added to which two other factors obscure the situation. Firstly, as I argued above, there is likely to be more individual variability within the nursing profession and secondly, the wave of change gathering within the profession makes it difficult to be definitive since needs are changing as the scope of nursing expands.

A good proportion of trainee nurses that I have met in the last year are increasingly psychologically-minded in the conceptualisation of their work, as are many of the nursing journals and conferences. This very much complicates a simple analysis of the type attempted here since it applies a major psycho-social movement. However, if you will at least allow me to present some ideas on the nursing profession as it has been up until recent years, I will leave you to judge the relevance of this analysis to the present day.

From the material available, we have already constructed a profile of the standard nurse of recent years. She had a leaning towards the 'task-oriented' approach, was disciplined, deferred to medical authority and rarely challenged this on behalf of her patients. Rather, she was anxiously preoccupied with making mistakes and although kindly, remained distanced from the people she cared for.

What shaped nursing into this pattern? An important factor must be the inter-personal nature of nursing. The nurse is forced into extended face-to-face contact with the people for whom she cares. Unlike doctors, she is not free to distance herself by absence. She is often in close personal contact with patients, engaged in intimate tasks on the wards day by day. She personally receives the impact of her patients' psychological states. This can be a very variable experience ranging through fright, worry, sadness, grief, depression, anger, frustration, impatience, euphoria, gratitude, affection, trust and dependency. The nurse will inevitably respond with her own feelings, perhaps echoing those of her patients, or at other times reacting to the patients' psychological states. Face-to-face nursing can be a hard job emotionally because relationships will inevitably form and these can produce conflicts and emotionally stirring experiences. Menzies writes, 'The core of the anxiety situation for the nurse lies in her relation with the patient. The closer and more concentrated the relationship, the more the nurse is likely to experience the impact of anxiety.'

Bearing this in mind, we will expect to find that, over the years, the nursing profession will have developed ways of defusing this situation and protecting its members from the risk of traumatic involvement. These solutions will not have been so much thought out as 'felt out'. That is, patterns of behaving will have developed which will leave nurses feeling more emotionally comfortable. What emerges is the pattern I have sketched under the label of 'the typical nurse'. I believe that because of the close personal contact and the inevitability of relationships forming, the nursing profession has defended itself by avoiding direct clinical responsibility. This is the opposite defence of the doctors. The hypothesis is that if there is to be clinical responsibility then relationships will be minimised. If there are to be relationships, clinical responsibility will be minimised. Thus, nurses often appear to push away responsibility and redirect it at the doctors. Traditionally they implement medical orders in a mechanical way and relate to doctors in a manner which shapes and maintains the position of doctors as sole bearers of clinical responsibility. *By so doing, they avoid the conflicting combination of close personal contact combined with clinical responsibility.* (I will remind you of my recognition that in reality not all nurses adhere to this pattern of defence, but we are talking about the general features of nursing behaviour where the profession is regarded as a whole. Also, it is clear that younger nurses are often unsure of their role and so keep to a safe, narrower approach.)

Of course, even though nurses have accepted closer contact with patients, this does not mean open, trouble-free relationships. These are often difficult, thus defensive behaviours have developed. The task-oriented style, for example, offers a means by which relationships may be kept under control and the level of intensity reduced to tolerable levels by splitting a nurse's attention between a number of patients and ensuring that she is busily preoccupied with tasks. The shift system and rotation of duties also produces a distancing effect which is, of course, related to the idea of nurses being relatively impersonal, standard, interchangeable units. Personal defences are in evidence with nurses as well as doctors. The insulating effect of detachment and denial are quite clearly important. In other words, the traditional approach to nursing makes sense if it is viewed as a *solution* to certain inter-personal stresses inherent in the nurse-patient relationship.

Figure 2.5: Hypothesised Psychological Basis of Nursing Behaviour

Objectives and Needs	Strategies and Defences
Accept closer personal contact with patients and the inevitability of relationships forming.	Avoid clinical responsibility, act to maintain doctors as sole decision-making body, perpetuate anxiety at challenging doctors or taking initiatives.
Minimise the stresses and pressures within the relationships.	Reduce the depth of relationships by the mechanistic task-oriented approach, organise nurses as 'interchangeable', maintain an atmosphere of disciplined non-involvement and pressure of work. Personal defences of detachment and denial.
Collude with the medical profession in preserving the image of mistake-free, infallible medicine.	Foster an anxious preoccupation concerning mistakes. Support doctors by refusing to comment on their performance or act as an alternative source of information to patients.
Regulate medical behaviour by covert means.	'Shape' and maintain doctors in the autocratic style, influence their decisions by suggestion and manipulative reporting of observations.

Other aspects we should note have to do with the nurse-doctor relationship. In avoiding clinical responsibility, the nursing profession has had to 'prop up' the medical profession in its acceptance of responsibility, and so has been responsible for strengthening and maintaining medical authority. This has meant collusion with medical behaviour, aimed at the defence of medical power and the image of mistake-free medicine. Nurses have kept their silence whilst seeing the harsh effect of the insensitive medical style of relating. This inhibition has been bolstered by the *use* of an exaggerated concern over their own mistakes and a consequent fear of taking initiatives. But we must remember Stein's point that the nurses do also exert covert control by manipulative tactics. Table 2.5 puts these ideas together. I will go only as far as saying this is how it has been. You must decide if this is how it still is.

Concluding Remarks

As a last word, let's return to the differences between the behaviour of staff in general hospitals compared with that of hospice care. Can we now see a basis for such a difference? One reason which I want you to consider emerges from the material that we have just been through.

People that are dying and know that they are dying do not any longer hold on to the myth of medical infallibility. One of the sources of tension which drives the professions to such defensiveness has gone, allowing a new atmosphere of honesty. Because there is less defensiveness, staff are able to see the psychological needs of the dying people. They are, in fact, *able to see people, and not something called patients*. Both nurses and doctors seem free to engage in real relationships and to offer companionship until the death occurs. The task of this book is to show how this kind of approach can be introduced into hospital units other than those for terminal care — to end the era of psychological neglect.

Notes

1. 'C.M.' in Brand and Keep (1978).
2. Cartwright, A. (1964) cited by Hauser (1981).
3. Korsch, B.M. *et al*. (1968) cited by Hauser (1981).
4. Webb, B. (1976) cited by Ley (1982a).
5. Lipowski, S.J. (1975) cited by Wilson-Barnett (1980).
6. Stevens, D.P. *et al*. (1977) cited by Ley (1982b).
7. Fishbach, R.L. *et al*. (1980) cited by Ley (1982b).
8. Millman, M. (1977) cited by Hauser (1981).
9. Duff, R. and Hollingshead, A.B. (1968) cited by Hauser (1981).
10. Lief and Fox (1963).

3 STEPS IN THE DEVELOPMENT OF PSYCHOLOGICAL CARE

My case claiming a widespread lack of psychological care in the hospitals must rest now. It is time to redirect our attention to more constructive work. What, we must ask, has to be done to clear the way for the development of psychological care in hospitals, who will end up doing the work and what exactly will the work of psychological care involve? In sorting out these issues, we must not lose touch with certain realities, and must take into account the high work load that already presses on some departments in the average general hospital. We have also to consider the present-day attitudes towards psychological care held by doctors, nurses and the community.

Who Gets the Job?

What a luxury it would be if several thousand psychologists or psychiatrists were magically produced and established in the hospitals to start the work. There will be no such event, though, I assure you. The resources of the psychiatric service are spread very thinly as it is. Little possibility exists of substantial help from that quarter even if there was to be a sudden increase in the level of concern held by psychiatrists for the general hospital population. Of course, we must consider clinical psychology. This is a young profession, composed of people with degrees in psychology and postgraduate training in clinical work. It has developed as a specialised service in the psychiatric sector and has recently taken on an independent character beginning to expand out from psychiatry.

Clinical psychologists certainly do have a growing interest in the challenge of the general hospital problems, and a few departments have extended their service into selected units such as coronary care (Wallace, 1982), and pain clinics (Broom, 1982). The current level of input is hopelessly inadequate, though, when you consider the scale of work needed. The problem in terms of development is that there are relatively few clinical psychologists and numbers will rise quite slowly since the production rate is low.

Those psychologists who are already trained have their basic commitment to the psychiatric sector and primary care and although psychologists are expanding into new settings with their service, they do not have the manpower to make much of an impact on the general hospitals. In short, the specialists in psychological treatment cannot provide a direct face-to-face service for the large numbers of general hospital patients who would benefit from psychological assistance. This is not to say that the clinical psychologists or 'psychologically-minded' psychiatrists will not be involved in the development of psychological care. (I must add that not all psychiatrists are psychologically-minded. They are, of course, doctors by training and some still have a medical attitude and think solely in terms of illnesses and physical treatment.) They *must* be involved and will have a vital part to play, but their role will be more to do with training, support and back-up with a specialist service for particularly severe cases. The provision of the basic, routine psychological care for the bulk of hospital patients must be provided by other people. In the model of psychological care which I propose, such a structure is in fact seen as the ideal. That is why I talk of psychological care and not psychological therapy *since the major target is preventative intervention with a widespread impact which encourages change throughout the whole hospital system.*

A curative approach based on treatment given by a number of specialists is more demanding in workload and produces a much narrower effect, added to which, even if a small army of psychologists did become available it would bring with it a danger that the fundamental problems of the hospitals (in terms of psychological care) would remain entrenched. In other words, the basic approach of the medical and nursing professions and the problem of the medical style of relating might remain unchanged simply because there was a specialist department to take care of things — just exactly what has happened in relation to social work, in fact. Such a future will not do at all.

What potential then do the other professions have to take on the work of developing psychological care? Without doubt social workers will be behind any such move and can be used as a resource in the same way as psychologists. Again, though, it is clear that this profession has many statutory commitments and a relatively small work force. It is also the case that despite its intimate involvement with general medicine, social work does not seem to have generated much change. My casual impression, for what it is worth, is that the profession appears to have slotted into a placatory style of co-existence with the medical profession, fearing the retaliatory move of 'no more referrals' should it present a challenge to the existing order. It is difficult then to see how social workers might provide the main thrust of the major developments we have in mind.

From the content of the previous chapter, it must be obvious that there is no point in looking to the medical profession to take on the task. I do not mean this in an unkind way. Even setting aside the issue of suitability and willingness, there are two reasons why doctors should not become directly responsible for psychological care work. Firstly, quite simply, they have sufficient to do already. In some sectors, just getting through the enormous work requirements and maintaining adequate standards is difficult enough. It would be inappropriate to ask more of the doctors, in addition to which the chances of their being able to conduct psychological work of any quality in the context of such pressure of work are low. Secondly, controversially perhaps, I would argue that because of their clinical responsibilities doctors need their basic psychological defences and because of these defences they cannot be effective in direct psychological care. This does not mean that we do not seek changes in the doctors. Considerable shifts in attitude and understanding are vital in order that the medical profession values and complements developments in psychological care, but these will be discussed in the next section.

By now you may have sensed the direction of my thinking. By the process of elimination, we come to consider the nurses. *My own conclusion is that it has to be the nurses who take on the basic work of psychological care.* As a profession they are 'well placed'. They are very numerous compared with all the other professions, and their style of work is such that they maintain extended contact with their patients and are in a physical and inter-personal position to widen their role to include the basic routines of psychological work. I do not mean to suggest that the nursing profession will just take on the job alone, unsupported and without associated changes on the part of the other professions, but the task here is to resolve who is best suited and who can provide the level of input necessary to make the introduction of the psychological approach feasible. For one reason or another, the professions mentioned so far are not good bets. At the same time, there are signs that the nursing profession is already beginning to move in this direction of its own accord, so let's consider the position of the nurses in more detail.

Psychological Care by Nurses

There is no point in making plans involving the nursing profession if the nurses are going to say that they are not interested or that such work is beyond their scope. My judgement, though, is that the profession is interested and quite capable. I draw my evidence from three sources. Firstly, the tenor of the literature originating from the nursing profession indicates a trend of increased interest in raising the quality of nursing care by improvements in nurse-patient relationships, communication, counselling skills and so on. For example, *Nursing Times* (1981) ran various articles in response to the Royal College of Nursing's report, 'Towards Standards'. Amongst other things, this report urged a progressive move towards the nursing process, i.e. the patient-oriented approach to nursing. Various articles in that issue repeatedly stressed the need for developments centred on the nurse becoming more responsible for the transmission of information and being the custodian of inter-personal care. I have already mentioned another publication, *Nursing*, which recently gave the entire content of an issue to the same theme of improving communication with the seriously ill, the bereaved, and the dying. For example, Hacking (1981) is typical of the general theme in the collection of articles when she writes:

> Those caring for the patient have to learn to listen — to find out what he wants, what he is ready to hear and to deal with his questions and remarks appropriately. *A relationship must be built up and time found for the patient to express his fears and feelings* (my italics).

The growing literature expounding the nursing process similarly highlights an increasing emphasis in this direction.

Secondly, drawing from personal experience, I have conducted many seminars with groups of trainee nurses, practising nurses, senior nurses and nursing officers during the last few years, and find that almost to a woman (not forgetting the occasional male nurse) they are in agreement that the hospitals are places of psychological neglect and that they, as nurses, want to do something to alter the situation. The same message has come across from most nurse tutors whom I have met at various schools of nursing. I feel confident that these views do represent the general outlook amongst nurses at the present time.

Thirdly, there have, of course, already been demonstrations of the enthusiasm and capability of nurses in relation to psychological work. The most obvious example is that of the hospices and hospice care organisations. Another example, if I may again draw on personal experience, has been the way in which nurses have taken on the responsibility for basic psychological care at the Kidney Unit at Exeter. This has been described in more detail elsewhere (Nichols, 1984 and Woodhams, 1984). Suffice it to say that during the last five years my work at this Kidney Unit has changed considerably. Initially I functioned as an individual psychological therapist assisting those dialysis patients or their partners who were referred to me by the staff. As time progressed, though, it became obvious to me that much of the work could and should be done by the nurses. They would not be in charge of the more difficult cases needing in-depth psychotherapy, but would be responsible for the routine preventative psychological care for all our patients. It was clear that this would avert many of the common problems associated with training to survive by dialysis. Now it is the sister-in-charge of the Unit who is actually the overseer for this type of care and many of the nurses have become competent assistants. I know that nurses can cope with this type of work because I have watched them do it. In fact, the impetus for this book and the model of psychological care which it expounds are derived from the successes of these nurses working with kidney patients and their relatives. Using these renal nurses as a guide, it has also been apparent that psychological care work generates much job satisfaction and gives nurses an enhanced feeling of professional stature.

Other Professions – Occupational Therapists, Physiotherapists and Speech Therapists

I have indicated that the nursing profession is in the best position to take on the bulk of routine preventative psychological care work in hospitals, primarily because of its numbers and constant contact with patients. However, I in *no way* want to seem excluding. I know from first hand experience that many members of the para-medical professions are intensely interested in psychological work and my hope is that they will contribute significantly. Although I am writing these chapters around the assumption that nurses will accept the main burden of the work I know that they will need much support and assistance. Thus my wish is to encourage occupational, speech and physiotherapists to become directly involved in psychological care wherever possible. I will be very conscious of these professions as I write the next chapters as indeed I have been over the last few years (e.g. Nichols and Rafferty

(1980) put forward a strong plea for speech therapists to expand their psychological work). Medical social workers are, of course, already heavily involved in this work and will be a much needed resource for training and support and, bearing in mind my comments above, it would be a delight to think that individual members of the medical profession would accept training and contribute from time to time as well.

The Basic Principles of Psychological Care

So now let's turn to what the work actually involves. In teaching nurses the basic steps in psychological care it has become helpful to differentiate four separate aspects.

1. emotional care
2. informational care/acting as an agent on behalf of the client
3. counselling
4. monitoring psychological state and referring on

Each of these is dealt with in depth in the following chapters. For our purposes here, I will just introduce them. Note that I will refer to nurses much of the time. Please understand again that this is not meant to be excluding. I wish to encourage people from all the caring professions to develop their interest and skills in this work but the suggestion is that nurses in particular take it on as an explicit component of their routine duties. However, whether it is nurse, doctor, psychologist, physiotherapist, speech therapist, occupational therapist or whoever, the work is the same.

Emotional Care

In the same way that there are certain 'givens' related to illness which have to be dealt with in nursing routines (e.g. if people who are very seriously ill are not turned at regular intervals, difficulties arise), so too it is 'given' that a large proportion of people in hospital are emotionally aroused and, of these, a number are emotionally disturbed. Thus emotional care starts with the effort to understand the nature of these reactions and to glimpse the intrusive power of such feelings. The basis of any response by staff must involve a respect and valuing of the emotional responses. It is important to realise that in many cases, although the emotions may be strong, they are, in fact, *normal and functional*. I say this because we are, so to speak, 'designed' to react with anxiety when there is threat, with anger when there is frustration and deprivation, or grief when there is loss. Serious illness or injury with long periods of hospitalisation can obviously provoke all these experiences and, therefore, such emotional reactions will be triggered. Note, though, that they are 'normal' in the sense of being characteristic of the human being. We should add to this that in times of fright and protracted stress, many of us regress and shift into a pattern of emotional functioning which is similar to that of earlier years. All of these reactions are involuntary and so cannot be stopped by effort of will.

In certain cases, though, the emotional reactions are clearly different in character from these normal patterns. There is a quality which is unusual or abnormal. For example, the threat to a person may appear to be minimal yet he reacts with violent anxiety or, despite nurses and doctors helping a patient in an intensive and kindly way, there is unjustified anger and hostility. Here we can use the term 'neurotic' reaction to imply that the source of such emotion is more to do with the person than the situation, and it is their way of seeing situations which may introduce threat where it does not really exist.

The prime commodity in emotional care is the response which the nurse makes to these emotional states, for this will determine whether she has a facilitating or blocking effect. It is here that one division between psychological care and psychological neglect is to be found. In emotional care, the objective is to provide a relationship and a setting which helps along emotional processes, for they are often important functional experiences for the individual and if they become blocked or internalised there may be damage. At such times there are also emotional needs, by which I mean the need to receive a certain kind of relationship with others. Thus, a nurse trained in emotional care aims to relate in a manner which communicates permission, acceptance and safety, such that the patients involved with her do not feel the need to suppress emotion, or feel ashamed, or believe themselves to be an oddity and a nuisance. With this as a basis, the distressed patients can choose (and it has to be *their* choice) to share their feelings and the thoughts or memories which have triggered them with their nurse. Her role is to provide the patient with a genuine opportunity for expression, the essence of which is the experience of being heard, that is, the nurse has received and understood what the person is expressing because she has listened in an open, non-defensive way, striving to empathise with her patient. It is through such expression of feeling that the work of emotional processing can proceed and because of the interaction with the nurse, the distressed person will also experience a sense of support from a genuinely human encounter.

Informational Care

The actual word which I have chosen as a label for the next element of psychological care has proved controversial. Some colleagues have said it would be better to use a conventional phrase such as 'communication'. The point is, though, that this particular part of the work involves much more than just communicating with people effectively. It requires that nurses understand the reason why the transmission of information in a hospital setting so often proves ineffective, even when staff are making the effort to communicate. It also requires the nurse to realise that transmitting information to seriously ill people is a different and more difficult task compared to that involving people who are not ill, yet it is vital to their well-being. The psychological state of many people who are ill, or of their close relatives for that matter, causes them to receive and process information in an atypical manner compared with their normal mode of functioning. The presence of anxiety and urgency alters the way in which a person listens, remembers, forgets and responds to information. The basic problem in communicating information to distressed people is, therefore, that 'something told does not mean something heard and understood'. To this we must add that when medical or training staff sense distress in patients and their relatives, they often distort information presenting censored and thus placatory versions, part information or even false information hoping to avoid further distress and anxiety.

Because insufficient and inaccurate information creates unnecessary stress and also eventually increases the tension between staff and patients, it has been necessary to consider very carefully the manner in which the average hospital patient is informed. This has led me to suggest a strategy called 'informational care'. The basic idea is quite simple. It is that in much the same manner as nurses carry out routine procedures such as washing and changing dressings, so too they should become *responsible* for maintaining and building up to optimum levels the information that their patients have. Now this is a more active role than simply communicating clearly. The most important aspect is regularly checking exactly what the person does know and identifying gaps, distortions, unrealistic ideas, lack of understanding or confusions and worries to do with insufficient and forgotten information. What the nurse will learn in this work is ways of building up and renewing the information given to people in order to minimise uncertainty and reduce the risk of their being taken by surprise and traumatised by adverse experiences. A pattern which I have observed on many occasions is that staff do not inform patients in advance of possible complications and difficulties in their treatments, even when these are considered to be moderately probable. The staff rationalise this as holding back 'difficult' information in order to avoid upsetting people. In general, though, it is a disastrous policy since people cannot prepare for negative outcomes and then have to discover on their own what these might be, a source of stress which, you may remember, was emphasised in the case history with which we began.

Informational care is best seen as a procedure which has various necessary routines involving checking, supplying and renewing information. It is repetitious work in a sense because people in hospital do listen selectively and forget selectively so it is often necessary to repeat information-giving sessions several times. The objective in all this is to keep people as comfortable as possible by giving them understanding and advance warning so that they can keep some control and plan the rest of their life in relation to possible outcomes. When informational care is put into practice properly it is experienced as a very caring and helpful additional aid which greatly reduces the stress of hospitalisation. Much more of this in Chapter 6.

Acting as an Agent for the Patient

The alternative to technical medicine is an approach to care which is a balanced composite of medical, psychological, social and educational elements. In general, we currently have strong traditions of medical care and also an explicit concern for integrating this with attention to social problems through the activities of the social work profession. As we have seen in comparison, the provision for psychological and educational aspects is weak. This can be expected to improve over the course of time, though, which will then lead us into the problems of co-ordination of the various aspects of care.

I do not wish to make a big issue out of this or divert into a lengthy debate on the issue of who should be 'in charge'. However, while it is clear that the medical profession has *clinical* responsibility, what is not clear is the area of authority they embrace other than strictly medical activities. The traditional use of the possessive pronoun by doctors, i.e. 'my patient, my beds', indicates an assumption of personal and political power which goes way beyond medical activities. For example, one local consultant recently stated, 'I will not have research psychologists disturbing my patients.' That decision belonged to the patients them-selves, but the doctor assumed an authority for which he had no man-date – it was not a medical decision but a social judgement.

The way things go in hospitals at the moment is that the medical profession assumes executive control over most aspects of case manage-ment – arguing that it alone has legal responsibility for medical matters. Referral of a distressed person (say, to a psychologist) is a matter of the doctor taking the initiative, and so depends on his personal ability to notice the need and his own views on the response that should be made to psychological difficulties. Since personal values and non-medical issues are involved, this clearly is beyond the range of the strictly medical. However, someone must have a managerial role and the obvious people are the doctors since they make the central decisions concerning physical treatment. Where things fall down, how-ever, is that the track record of the medical profession demonstrates beyond any doubt that we can place little confidence in the profes-sion's intention to make sure that psychological care and the necessary educational input is provided and integrated with medical treatment at a sufficiently high level of priority. This presents a potential problem of obstruction. One way around the impasse is for the nurses to take on more responsibility for informing doctors and assisting in the co-ordination of various elements of care. They are in a much better position to assess many of the needs of the patients and already have the skill of functioning in a way which does not lead to 'territorial' battles and the loss of trust of their medical colleagues.

The adoption of such a role does not imply that nurses suddenly 'take over'. This would be opposed by the medical profession and lead to a distracting tussle for power which would be most unproduc-tive. A more viable role in assisting with co-ordination is that the nurse takes on the responsibility of representing the patient's case. This task involves actively presenting to doctors information that needs to be taken into account as they make their decisions and making sure that the patient's general needs, beyond the medical concerns, are taken into full account. It also means actively working at the co-ordination of necessary non-medical assistance with psychological or educational matters and making certain that this is not overlooked. That is, the nurse functions with a new sense of responsibility, she has a personal concern to be the patient's advocate and to guarantee the provision of care, rather than to function as a member of a service which simply implements treatment.

Counselling

I will say little about this at the moment. Again it merits a separate chapter. My view is that when nurses have several years experience, they reach an age and a position in life where they are perfectly capable of functioning in a counselling role. Counselling is not, of course, in any way a new activity. What is new, perhaps, is the suggestion that a basic form of counselling should be part of nursing procedures. By this, I mean that nurses will monitor the state of their patients and, where necessary, intervene in a more skilled and informed way than 'trying to calm them down a bit'. The basic skills of counselling are fairly easily acquired with the right training (this is where the psychologists come in) and clearly it will be a major step forward in psychological care if there are several 'nurse-counsellors' available on a ward or unit to deal with difficulties as they arise. This does not mean that they should take on psychological therapy as such. They will have certain helping skills and amongst these will be the ability to recognise when more specialised intervention is needed.

Monitoring and Referring on

Psychological care is not psychological therapy. It does, however, involve knowing when psychological therapy is needed and making sure that the need is met. Put more simply, the person undertaking psychological care with a patient becomes the 'psychological eyes' for the case. She must be able to recognise the point at which care should be supplemented by therapy and when she should be active in engaging the assistance of someone trained as a psychological therapist. There is, thus, a continuing role in monitoring the level of distress, or noting frank disturbance. Given that most of the evidence indicates that doctors in charge of cases are likely to be slow in noticing the psychological plight of their clients, this role becomes a positive responsibility. So too does the need to oppose any tendency towards possessiveness, that is, clinging on to a case when one is rather out of depth with it but at the same time feeling reluctant to let another person have involvement.

The mechanism for referral is one for local negotiation between the members of the medical team and nursing staff. I will go as far as saying the person undertaking psychological care is responsible for ensuring that a referral, or rather a call for immediate assistance, is made. Who actually makes the referral is your own business. We do, however, need to progress beyond the point where the status, anxiety and authority problems of the medical profession no longer *obstruct* rapid and free-flowing action on behalf of the patient.

Figure 3.1: The Elements of Psychological Care

PSYCHOLOGICAL CARE	Emotional care Informational care Basic counselling Monitoring psychological state — referral

Attitudes and Developments

Those of you who have read through this chapter and feel in accord with me and wish to play some part in such developments will almost certainly have realised that all such changes must be underpinned by a basic shift in attitudes. May I then, by way of a conclusion, just list what to me appear to be the vital changes required:

1. The narrow preoccupation with medical treatment must be replaced by a *concern* to provide overall care. The prevailing attitude to date has given an almost exclusive consideration to physical treatment to the extent that the psychological and personal consequences are forgotten or worse, treatment results in psychological damage which goes unattended. The critical factor is that doctors and nurses become openly aware of the situation and worry about it sufficiently to seek changes.

2. Development of a broader outlook which places value upon overall care can only be rational if it is matched by changes in the attitudes held towards seriously ill and injured people. The present attitude includes an element of degradation symbolised in the use of the label 'patient'. Once somebody is labelled a patient, he or she is no longer a person but is something which can be treated in a subtly different manner — an inter-personal perception which allows in much that is unacceptable in the behaviour of medical staff in particular. Thus, the recognition of the person rather than an object called 'the patient' will have important consequences, since it will give greater prominence to personal needs and condition. To underline the significance of this suggestion, I will now cease to use the term patient (as I have done in my clinical work) and rely on other terms which restore attitudes of value and status to the person. The term 'client', for example.

3. The developments in psychological care which I have suggested depend heavily on the nursing profession adopting a modified approach with extended responsibilities. If they are to be comfortable and successful in such work their attitude to themselves must alter. Most

importantly perhaps is an emphasis on *accepting responsibility*. The nurse becomes the person who pursues good overall care on her client's behalf. In other words, nurses take on a more positive negotiating stance with their colleagues, not challenging the medical profession for power but using their knowledge of a client's needs to inform and help steer the management of a case. At the same time, the nurse will take personal initiative and responsibility for the basic psychological care, seeking other professional assistance when it is required.

Doctors in turn must complement this new role by an appropriate maturity in attitudes towards their nursing colleagues. If the medical profession persists with its pursuit of personal power it weakens such endeavours since they depend on trust, collaboration and mutual respect. There does need to be an examination of the difference between meeting personal needs to experience power and authority in the role of a consultant, the 'I'm in charge' syndrome, and maximising the provision of care by encouraging nurses as co-professionals in a trusting, collaborative alliance.

4 EMOTIONAL CARE

A Guide to Using This Chapter

The atmosphere changes now. No longer will I be presenting academic arguments supported by evidence from a string of research papers. I will be writing in the style of an instructor talking to an apprentice. What you will find, therefore, in this and the following chapters, is my understanding of psychological functioning and my views on the best way to go about psychological care. These views are based on first-hand experience in the hospitals and involve a certain amount of innovation in practice. I will not be presenting proof and evidence in a formal manner but rather telling you in quite definite terms how I provide psychological care and how I think *you* should provide psychological care. Because of this change in style you must maintain your own critical perspective. Discuss the ideas and clarify what you find acceptable.

There are several other features to bear in mind. I will not be teaching the skills of psychological care in relation to any specific area of medicine — the basic principles apply to all the specialities. My own experience includes a considerable amount of work with people in renal failure and so several case examples are used from this branch of medicine, but there is no special significance in this. It is also important for you to realise that in order to teach the complete approach to psychological care I assume an ideal environment for the work, particularly in this chapter. That is, I assume you will have sufficient time, a manageable flow of relatively long-stay clients (as opposed to a fast flowing tide of new faces) and colleagues who understand and value the work, expecting you to give it some priority. I have not lost sight of the real world and the comparatively disadvantageous circumstances in which you may actually work. Nevertheless, for the purposes of clear teaching, it is easier to use the example of an idealised setting so that you have a good model with which to compare things.

Remember that although I usually refer to nurses as the people conducting psychological care, the other professions in the hospital service are very much in my mind too. Also, do not forget my abandonment of the label 'patient' which you may find strange at times — it is to symbolise an approach which attempts to consider the whole person, and not somewhat diminished objects called patients.

Emotional Care

If people are emotionally active in circumstances which make them want to hide their emotions or suppress them because of feelings of shame and embarrassment, then they are effectively in a non-caring or even hostile environment. With seriously ill or injured people, there is a high likelihood of greatly increased emotional reactions. These people will usually be in the midst of a traumatic experience which seems socially and physically threatening, is often alien in character and involves separation from the home and supportive network of family and friends.

All of the professions involved in hospital treatment have a role in which emotional care is relevant and necessary, whether it is a doctor confirming to a client that he is developing cancer or kidney failure, a speech therapist beginning work with a stroke victim, a physiotherapist assisting someone with severe spinal injury, an occupational therapist giving attention to an amputee or a nurse admitting a woman prior to a mastectomy. These professionals will all fall short of the target of genuine care unless they either contribute to basic emotional care themselves or make sure that it is provided by someone else in the team. What then are the key elements to emotional care? Is it truly understood, let alone practised, in the typical hospital setting?

I will begin by reflecting on the position of some newly trained nurses who I take to be representative of the new psychological awareness in the nursing profession. The event was a tutorial session a few months ago in which I found myself engaged in something of a heated confrontation. One of the nurses was offended because I had gone through some of the material from Chapters 2 and 3 with them, lamenting the absence of proper psychological care in hospitals. 'You talk', she said, 'as if we have not had any training in psychological care. Half of our work at training school was on the psychological side of things.' I felt a little awkward at this because I did not wish to belittle her experience and training nor antagonise the very people whose interest and help I was seeking, added to which it gave me the uncomfortable feeling that I might be getting out of date. So we chatted on, circling around the complaint for a while. Shortly it became relevant to explore what she had in her mind when she talked of giving psychological care, or to be more specific, emotional care, since we had turned to that as the subject in hand. The issue was how should a nurse respond to someone in her care who had become deeply distressed and was clearly entertaining suicidal thoughts. The outspoken nurse gave her version thus:

Nurse The important thing to remember is that you must listen to people who are distressed and allow them to talk about their problems, even if it is while you are doing some other task. You must not ignore their emotions or try and stifle them.

Psychologist What is the point of encouraging this kind of conversation?

Nurse The point is that it allows people to express their feelings. When they do that, the nurse can see what their problem is about and maybe help them with it.

Psychologist So what objective do you have in your mind with this approach?

Nurse Well, obviously if people are very upset or anxious you want to do something about it, you can't just ignore it. Your job as a nurse is to look after them and deal with problems. Many people need to talk with someone and that is part of our job. We have to help them overcome their distressed feelings and, if they are suicidal, help them see a point to life.

I went away from that exchange thinking that this nurse had indeed received training which pointed her well and truly in the direction of emotional care. Her role concept included a considerable component of psychological concern. But I also felt that her training had stopped short of a full understanding and that, as it had been left, she would not be as effective as she might be in the work. Furthermore, she would actually be rather vulnerable herself in such work since her training had not included any personal preparation.

Basically, the nurse was saying that the emotional comfort of people in hospital is an important objective for nurses to work towards and that they must, therefore, be attentive to the emotional state of the people under their care. The main response by the nurse to emotional distress is that of listening in order to allow feelings to be expressed. During these interactions, the nurse will be vigilant to discover a person's problems and thus ways in which she can help. She will search for ways to respond which will directly alleviate the distressed state, or alter a person's outlook. The general approach in this work appears to be 'as and when required', fitting it in round the routines of nursing. Notice that the underlying concept is really that of an *informal treatment* (in the broadest sense) which depends heavily on the performance of the nurse. She must use her abilities to appraise the difficulties and attempt some resolution to bring about relief to the distressed person. There is nothing wrong in that, you might feel, it sounds like they are doing a good job. Well, we should take a closer look before deciding one way or the other. Firstly, let's examine some of the *assumptions* concerning emotional care which are manifest in the statement of approach conveyed through this conversation. Put briefly, these are:

1. An emotional reaction is regarded as an adverse state, something that the nurse must work to diminish or limit; in other words, there is the feel of the illness/treatment concept.

2. Emotional reactions are usually provoked by 'problems' and thus the means of achieving emotional calm in a distressed person is by firstly identifying the key problems and then coming up with something that helps — often this is taken to mean finding something helpful to say.

3. Emotional care is implemented only when a person is seen to be in distress; it is thus an unscheduled activity limited to 'casualties' and not a specific task routinely undertaken with all seriously ill or injured people.

I wonder what your view of these statements is and whether or not you feel that they represent an accurate picture. My own judgement is that the concepts of emotional functioning and emotional care advanced by the nurse were far too limiting. Firstly, there was little recognition of *normal* emotional functioning. In times of high stress and threatened or actual losses in life, it is *normal and usual* for people to react with strong emotions. Such reactions are part of a process and have a significant function. However, with the approach described, such normal, functional, emotional reactions were basically construed as abnormal. Consequently the orientation adopted towards emotional reaction was of something necessarily needing treatment, something to be 'cured'. In fact, this can actually be the opposite of helpful — damaging even — since the attitude denies 'permission' for normal emotional process and may encourage emotional suppression which blocks important *processes* (the point will be expanded below).

A second adverse feature was the implication that emotional care should be directed to people who show overt signs of need, that is, they have become openly distressed or actually break down. A broader, more realistic view is that all seriously ill or injured people will inevitably need emotional care, not because they are necessarily distressed but in order to help them be more comfortable and to facilitate the natural emotional processes which attend such major life crises. As a parallel to this, of course, those involved in emotional care will be available to assist people who have become overwhelmed and disabled by very strong reactions or actual psychological disturbance. In other words, there are two types of emotion to be held in mind, the normal responses which are part of functional emotional processes and emotional disturbances which have their basis in some psychopathology. Where one ends and the other begins is rarely clear, but one thing is certain. Many instances of obvious emotional responding observed in hospitals are not abnormal and do not need 'treating' in the sense of eliminating a disease.

I find a third aspect that is worrisome buried in this conversation. It is to do with the effect of the last point on nurses or people involved in emotional care. With the 'illness-treatment' theme influencing one's approach, the nurse becomes burdened with the need to 'do something' or say something in order to reduce a client's state of emotional activity. Now this is a heavy burden to bear and certainly one which I would not welcome for myself. It seems to lie behind an anxious statement which I have heard so many young nurses say — 'I did not know what to say, I felt I might say something wrong and make her worse.' The problem is that the felt obligation to do or say something introduces a tension since the nurse's performance is judged by whether or not emotional activity subsides. If she cannot find a way of shifting her client into a less emotional state, she appears to have failed and feels inadequate and guilty. I do assure you that eliminating emotional reaction *is not* the primary target of emotional care. On the contrary, it is concerned with providing an inter-personal atmosphere which facilitates emotional processes by giving the opportunity for their expression. Thus, in some cases, emotional care involves helping a person *into* an emotional response. So you see that it is a great handicap if the basic concept is one in which the continuation of an emotional reaction is seen as some kind of failure on the part of the nurse. It may be the opposite — a sign, as we will see shortly, of her effectiveness.

We have reached the point where some conclusion has to be made as a result of examining the assumptions revealed in this conversation with the nurse. My view is this. The nurse was oriented in the right direction. She recognised the importance of emotional care and saw it as a significant component of her job. She realised that it required involvement on her part and that she had to work verbally in a rather intimate relationship. However, she worked with the idea that emotional reactions are something to be 'dealt with' and diminished by means of discovering the problems which are presumed to act as the cause. In other words, she was including emotional activity in her general medical-illness scheme of things. This, I believe, is a significant mistake which will reduce her ability in emotional care and cause her considerable personal difficulty.

So now to the business of putting forward the alternative ideas. From now on this chapter will be set out as a short 'teach-in', giving the basic elements to prepare you for emotional care work.

Personal Preparation

Attitudes to Emotion

In the normal course of our education we are taught little about emotional functioning, either at home or at school. There are some fortunate exceptions but most of us are launched on the world with little to guide us other than the stereotyped views from our native culture as expressed within our family subculture. While there is no convenient way of assessing the precise outcome of this situation, what is obvious is that the level of understanding on matters to do with emotional functioning varies greatly from person to person. Very many people are quite ill at ease with the experience of emotion, either finding great difficulty in recognising their own emotional life or feeling greatly perturbed by the emotional life of others.

In the former case there will be a defensive style, repressing personal emotion and denying awareness of it to conscious experience. So, for example, a man may deny that he is anxious in a particular situation and believe that to be the case, whereas the language of his body and behaviour states very clearly that he *is* anxious. Such a characteristic leads an individual to struggle very hard to hold back emotion and if this bid fails then there is a sense of shame and failure. In the latter case, face-to-face contact with emotional expression in others gives a feeling of agitated discomfort and so the need is to escape it or, if that is not possible, stem the flow of emotion in the other by one means or another. Sometimes people are uncomfortable with one sort of emotion but not others. For example, a woman may find it easy to deal with depressed feelings in *any* of her friends but want to rush away from their anger.

In considerable contrast it is possible to find people who are fully in touch with and accepting of their own emotional life. They have the facility of expressing this to others without inhibition. More than that, they do not find emotional expression in other people to be threatening and may even have a 'feel' for what is going on inside others. Thus, our lesson in emotional care starts with an unsurprising assertion. We all have our own characteristic patterns of reactions to our own emotions, ranging from inhibited, shameful and blocking through to open, allowing and accepting. Similarly, we all have our own characteristic patterns of reactions to emotional expression by other people, ranging from threatened, denying, rejecting and suppressing to at ease, approaching and encouraging.

The differences between us will in part be related to experiences in our formative phases. One person in a recent training group recalled having been punished and shamed in childhood for emotional expressiveness and taught to strive for emotional inertness. Such a style was modelled and rewarded by his parents and key figures in his schooling. Another member described how as a child she had to deal with the traumatic exposure to her mother's frequent severe depressions which eventually led to a successful suicide bid. Both these people found that their adult personalities were influenced by a powerful need to hold back their own emotions, and they experienced considerable discomfort with any significant show of feeling by others. As the work of the training group progressed and they both relaxed a little, they were able to take stock and identify that for years the whole business of emotion and personal feeling had been a difficult struggle. Both, in their own ways, had actively fought against any (in their eyes) 'weakness' in letting emotion through. In effect, they had blocked off an important part of their lives as people, stunting development as mature individuals.

Personal Questions to be Asked

Where is this taking us? Both these people were in medically-related professions and both wanted to take on some activities to do with psychological care. However, they were still hampered *themselves* by inhibitions and fears to do with emotion. (Indeed, part of their desire to get involved with this kind of work was probably the fact that they had gone through some very damaging experiences in childhood and, as adults, still felt a need for healing care which they expressed by turning in concern to the care of others.) Because of this, without further personal development they could never be very effective in the work of emotional care since these difficulties would intrude. In particular, their behaviour in the more demanding areas of emotional care would be influenced by *their own anxieties and needs, rather than those of the client*.

In contrast to some of the mechanistic roles in medicine, in this type of work personal development is of considerable significance. Simply learning procedures and having an enthusiasm to get involved is insufficient. It is important that people intending to take on this work have themselves developed to a point where there is reasonable freedom from personal difficulties and inhibitions to do with the expression of human emotion. Thus, for you, the very first steps in training work involve your development as a person. It is necessary for you to assess your position when it comes to dealing with emotion. How capable are you in identifying your own emotions and allowing expression of these without anxiety and shame, or a sense of being weak such that an apology is required? How capable are you of communicating your emotions directly to others, as opposed to acting them out while verbally denying them, or even attempting to hide them completely? I do not mean this in a trivial sense, nor is the implication that we should all be disinhibited and give vent to emotions in any situation and with any person. I am talking of a developed capacity to accept rather than deny feeling and a capacity for self-disclosure and sharing with appropriate people in appropriate situations without tenseness. Clearly this has to be developed as a situation-specific skill, the opposite skill being necessary at times. For example, the inhibition of emotional expression is important during complex surgery, important planning committees or emergency situations.

In the same way, you must also ask the question, 'How do I respond to the emotions of other people — am I at ease with them or do they make me feel tense/guilty, and do I cast around for some means of stopping them?' This effort made towards self-knowledge will prove of considerable value. In the short term, it will allow a perspective on one's state of readiness for work of this type and also throw into relief targets for necessary personal development. In the long term, for many people the very act of thinking and talking in this way and reflecting on one's properties as a person in relation to certain ideals actually begins to produce slow change and development of a positive type.

I will not claim that self-help of this nature is easy. Most of the people who function as counsellors or psychological therapists have been assisted in the endeavour by formal training courses which include much work of this type and make it so much easier. Nevertheless, I have to be honest with you. In any other activity, 'the workman is as good as his tools', the point being that in psychological care work *you* are the tool and your 'cutting edge' is partly determined by your progress in the kind of personal development that we have been discussing.

Having raised the issue, I must sadly leave you in the lurch with it since it is way beyond the scope of this book to encompass the topic in depth. Use what resources you have. Study your behaviour in relation to emotional functioning. Involve people with whom you have

Figure 4.1: Some Characteristics of a Person Thoroughly Suited to the Task of Emotional Care

1. Reactions to His/Her Own Emotional Responses

Attitude Emotion and the flow of personal feeling are valued and respected as an essential part of human behaviour.

Understanding There is recognition that certain experiences are bound to evoke powerful emotional reactions and that, in most cases, these are signs of a normal process to do with preparedness, adjustment and change. It is understood that the reflexive denial and repression of emotional response is an abnormality; so too is the proneness to frequent and overwhelming emotional reaction.

Awareness The person has achieved development to the point where there is an awareness of the flow of personal feeling with the ability to identify and 'own' these feelings without needing to deny or block them.

Expression There is an ability to express emotion and be emotional with 'appropriate others' without anxiety or shame. The ability is experienced as normal, mature and advantageous. There is also recognition that certain circumstances require the temporary suppression of emotion where it would obstruct other important activities.

Self-knowledge This person has some idea of his/her 'trouble spots' in relation to personal emotion. That is, there will be awareness of which emotions are easy to express and accept and which are difficult and what type of situation or people create inhibition.

2. Reactions to the Emotional Response of Other People

Attitude and understanding The positive attitude towards personal emotions will be extended to encompass the emotional expressions of other people. Emotion is valued as a significant and inherent part of human functioning. It is seen as a *normal* component of the overall reaction to illness or injury.

Exposure (a). Absence of negative reactions: when in face-to-face contact with the emotional reactions of others, there is an ability to accept the situation:

— without horror and an anxious need to escape
— without a need to encourage the other person to suppress his reaction and shift him to an emotionally neutral state in order to meet a personal need for safety and comfort
— without a sense of hurry to resolve the issue involved and produce emotional calm based on the belief that active emotional responding is something that has to be stemmed and thus needs 'treating'
— without a feeling of being trapped or paralysed by the other person's emotion
— without a feeling of guilt that one is personally responsible but powerless to do anything
— without a need for inter-personal distance for fear that one's own emotions will be stirred and revealed

(b). Positive reactions: there will be a sense of supporting and sharing in an experience which involves the other person's need to discharge emotion without any 'curative' response from the listener, together with the recognition that the person's reaction may be an aspect of complex emotional processes which could continue for some while. There is, thus, a patient acceptance of the present state, with a concern for immediate comfort rather than a drive for the urgent termination of the reaction.

There will be an ability to be close and empathise with the feelings involved, to communicate this involvement together with the knowledge that feelings can be shared in safety, with freedom from comments that would evoke defensive feelings.

Self-knowledge This person will have an awareness of the different effects that exposure to various emotional reactions has on him/her, some probably being easier to deal with for the individual than others. It will be accepted that exposure to the emotions of another can be troubling at times and the use of support and discussion on a regular basis will be felt as comfortable and advantageous.

close relationships in giving you feedback on your most characteristic ways of dealing with emotion. If you have the chance of using time in a discussion group to take up this theme then exploit the opportunity. I will, before moving on though, offer an aid. If your thoughts turn to this subject in any depth and you feel you have some work to do towards personal preparation, what is the ideal? What should you aim for? Here is my version of the ideal to use as a basis for further thought and discussion (see Figure 4.1).

To keep this all in perspective, remember that we are talking of ideals here. I cannot say that I have met too many people who are quite so well-rounded as this — which, to impart a confidence, is to my satisfaction, since people without any hang-ups at all always seem a hint insufferable to me. Nevertheless, most of the people working in this field have struggled some way along the path towards these ideals and I hope that you too will see the need and take up the challenge.

Understanding Emotion

The Basis of Personal Feeling

It would be foolish to get involved in the work of emotional care without a reasonable understanding of emotional functioning. This section serves, therefore, as an orientation to the topic. It is a rather hotly debated area with some fierce disagreements, and I have to warn you that it is my view which you are getting and that not all psychologists would accept it.

Much of our behaviour is determined by what we see and how we react to what we see. In fact, we are in a constant state of reaction to the world about us and also to our inner world of thought and fantasy. This flow of reaction is something which involves our whole body. Our reactions are, at the physical level, a constant shifting of body state to various patterns appropriate to the perceptions of the moment. It is this sensing of the body state which forms the basis of what we call feelings. The concept of feeling is rather broader than that of emotion, although the two words are close in meaning and are often used interchangeably. It is common for people to confuse the constant, ever present flow of personal feeling with major emotional reactions. For example, on various occasions in group therapy sessions, I have asked members what their particular feeling was at a specific moment in conversation. Some have said, 'I'm not feeling anything.' What they actually meant was, 'I'm not anxious, angry, tearful or depressed' — in other words, they have no obvious major emotion. The reality is that under normal circumstances it is impossible to be without feeling since the word refers to the experience of one's body state and its meaningful relationship to the events of the moment. It is, though, frequently the case that we are not immediately aware of our feelings because our attention is elsewhere. Also, not everybody understands how to identify feeling and it takes a little guidance in the means of getting in touch. Basically, it involves sensing the overall state that your body is in — reading the message of the body, we might say.

Gendlin (1978) has developed this idea and introduced a technique called focusing which sharpens people's ability to identify the 'felt sense' of their body. His basic point is that if we require to know exactly what we are feeling we have to learn ways of inquiring within. Our body state *is* our feeling, we thus have to search out the nature of our body state at any one time to identify feeling. If, therefore, the members of my group had stopped momentarily and 'read out the feeling message' of their overall body states, they would have been able to discriminate the various sorts of feelings typically generated in group sessions, viz interested and alert, or tense and on guard with a sense of something difficult about to happen, relaxed and uninvolved, on edge with a protective concern, bubbly, at ease, agitated with something to say which is difficult to get out, and so on.

The point is that being alive and being human inevitably involves a constantly changing flow of feeling as our bodies, thoughts and overall conscious experience take in the succession of stimuli to which we are sensitive. Of course, the complete experience of personal feelings involves more than just physical response and changed body state. As writers in existential psychology suggest, feeling is a synthesis of other functions which can involve changes in the quality of the experience of the world, but it is beyond our range to develop this point further here. Sometimes feelings may be present on a long-term basis, related perhaps to certain circumstances which prevail for a lengthy period. An example of this would be the experience of threat to one's sense of wholeness as a person if cancer was identified in the testes or breast.

So, in summary, as we take in a constant flow of perceptions we react totally, with our whole body and our whole experience. Sensing the consequent body state is the basis to feeling and emotion.

The distinction between emotion and feeling is vague and not, I think, one which we should divert to investigate. It is probably easiest if we adopt the convention of regarding emotion as a term used to imply strong feelings, that is, there is a physiological impact on body state beyond the usual and we become aware of changes in our physiology, general behaviour, verbal expressions and thinking. There may also be new behaviour which is not necessarily under voluntary control, like crying and angry outbursts. In other words, while in an emotional state, daily behaviour is more obviously dominated by global shifts in body state which we label anxiety, depression, euphoria, grief, anger, etc.

I want to stress the point that the concept of 'feelings' is often used loosely and disparagingly in Western culture, the inference being that they are an indecent sideshow within us which is rather embarrassing or, for men particularly, something to be grown out of. A variant of this is the asceptic atmosphere of the hospital which creates an atmosphere wherein feelings are often greeted like bacteria. Thus, anxiety-inhibitors and anti-depressants are handed out with the same urgent sense of getting rid of something threatening as are antibiotics. Such attitudes betray a gross misunderstanding and conceptual distortion. Feelings are a product of the core processes of reaction which direct our behaviour. We behave through our perceptions and consequent feeling reactions. They are an ever present, central feature of living. Our normal functioning is such that (if I may use a metaphor to make the point) we are 'designed' to have feelings as a fundamental part of our system of responding. If we wished to build a computer simulation of human functioning, a significant portion of the programming would be in the provision of feelings.

Conclusions. If you are going to offer emotional care you must be at ease with the idea and experience of human feeling and the ways in which it is expressed. Above all, you must realise that in the majority of cases which you will encounter in the general hospital setting, the feeling reactions of others are *normal*. Do not, therefore, be frightened by them and do not become involved in efforts to stifle them or suppress them with drugs without very careful thought as to the appropriateness in the individual cases.

Emotional Processes

From your training in whatever profession you have been drawn to, you will have noticed that human physiology is staggeringly complex and elegantly economic. Each function interlocks with the others to give a functional harmony. In terms of current biological assumptions we have evolved in this way by a remorseless process, selecting out the most effective changes. Few features can be demonstrated that are redundant, without function, or inefficient. In this context, our

emotional life has an enigmatic quality. At first sight, emotional reactions are cumbersome obstacles to efficient function and would be
better swept away. After all, we could argue for a moment, they do not
actually do anything of real use for us. Or do they?

I have described above the view that what we call feelings are in part
the sensing of body state. The various patterns of body state, ranging
through the relaxed-resting state to high levels of tension and vigilance
or attraction and sexual arousal, etc., are in reality states of *preparation
and adaption* to the needs of perceived circumstances. The obvious
point is that personal feelings reveal a continuous process whereby the
combination of a person's physical and psychological resources can be
directed and energised to provide the most appropriate and most
effective response. Consider a person reflecting on forthcoming exams
who realises that time is short, the ground to be covered is great and
the threat of failure is real. He responds with the feeling of nervous,
tense urgency. His focus of attention narrows more to work, his sense
of urgency fuels a far greater capacity to work, study, stay awake and
keep going than normal. Other activities are displaced and seem less
important because of the nervous energy. These are unpleasant feelings
but they are *functional, part of an adaptive process* which serves to
optimise the person's efficiency in a situation of perceived threat.
Without them, his behaviour would remain unchanged and the exams
would come and go with predictable outcome. In the same way the
emotional reactions which you will observe in your career in the
medical or medically-related professions, are often processes which have
a function and are to do with a person's preparation for a taxing event
or adaption to a stressing change. *Because these processes are functional, the essential attitude towards them is that of facilitation and
provision of any assistance that will allow their completion.* Take very
careful note of this point because it is central to a full understanding
of emotional reactions. The states of apparent emotional upheaval
which attend life crises such as illness or the death of a relative should
not be seen as if they were illnesses. They are changes in a person's
whole state which indicate a process of change and preparation.

To avoid introducing any confusion, I should make two qualifications here in order to accommodate the idea of abnormal reactions.
Firstly, while it is normal behaviour to react to what we see, many
people experience excessive difficulty because they see threat where
there is none or expect loss when it will never happen. That is, *the
problem is not how a person is feeling but what they are seeing*. As I so
often hear myself saying in seminars, 'Given the way she sees the

situation she *should* be anxious. It would be abnormal if she were not, the real problem is the way she sees it all.' Unless people have a physical disorder which creates an anxious state, say thyroid trouble or other hormonal disturbances, where people react with excessive emotional power, the safest assumption must be that the presence of such strong feeling is a normal response to what they are seeing in the situation — but their perception may be inaccurate and distorted. Secondly, a proportion of people enter the experience of illness already overly sensitised to certain elements of personal threat by prior experience, and thus their emotional reaction is amplified by factors originating from the past. This is likely to be the case with so-called neurotic or anxious personalities. With these two qualifications in mind, I will leave the topic of abnormal reactions until later on.

Your basic ideas on the nature of emotion are extremely important. They will determine the stance you take towards the people you work with. I have been stressing the notion of valuing personal feeling as a normal and important aspect of human functioning, arguing that the idea of emotional reactions as some state of disorder or illness which must be treated is quite wrong for the majority of cases in a general hospital. Instead, the reactions are best seen as processes which have a function. Our next step is to come down to earth a little and make sense of all these through a couple of case examples. These will attempt to convey the way in which anxiety and the grief/depressive reactions can be accounted for within the terms of this conceptualisation.

Case 1: Productive Anxiety. A youngish woman, Paula by name and 34 years old, was employed as a medical receptionist. She was divorced and due to remarry within three months when, to her great distress, her GP advised an urgent consultation with a surgeon because she almost certainly had a well-advanced cancer in her right breast. The GP's fears were confirmed. The surgeon, a considerate man, spent some while with Paula and talked through the implications. He could see no way out of the problem other than a mastectomy. He could not be certain whether he could limit this to a simple mastectomy or not. If the cancer was extensive then, in his view, a more disfiguring radical mastectomy would be the only safe option. He appreciated her situation and offered the reassurance that he would minimise surgery to what was absolutely necessary. A date for admission was offered, with the operation scheduled to take place two weeks later.

During these two weeks Paula was in a state of considerable anxiety. She found herself distracted by a procession of tense, worrying thoughts.

The normal routines of her day were difficult to concentrate on and social interaction suddenly became an ordeal. At night, she was restless and lay awake for many hours with her heart thumping and an alert tension denying her sleep. She spent considerable time contacting people that she knew had experienced a mastectomy, and she also made appointments with several consultants in alternative medicine to sound them out on ways of reversing cancer other than surgery. In the end she felt that the actual threat to life, since the cancer appeared to be advanced, did not give these approaches sufficient time. The risks seemed too great. On the day of her admission to the hospital, Paula was in control but still gripped by a powerful feeling of anxiety. She anxiously questioned the anaesthetist (being aware of the risks of general anaesthesia) and the surgeon when they called in to see her, stressing again how fearful she was of the outcome of the surgery and pressing the surgeon to cause as little change as possible. Her anxiety conveyed itself to the nursing staff too, who were concerned and offered reassurance.

How should we regard the anxiety that gripped Paula during these times and kept her awake late into the night before her operation? Firstly, we must recognise that as a normally adjusted, average human, she should have been anxious. She, like all normal people, responded with the characteristic changes which we call anxiety, when she perceived threat. What threat was she in touch with? There were several elements. In the first place there was the risk of continuing illness and death within a year or two after suffering the agonies of treatment and the illness itself. Secondly, the surgery would destroy (for a while at least) her sense of being a complete person. She would be disfigured to a greater or lesser degree and in her fantasy of the future would loathe the remains of her breast, feeling that she would always want to hide it and apologise for it. Both of these were direct physical threats but the latter brought with it profound psycho-social threats. Paula had used her body as a way of presenting herself to the world. She had a good shape and was proud of it. Her initial approaches in developing relationships with men were dependent on her physical attraction, and she valued an active sex life both for its own sake and as a means of securing relationships. Her self-image was thus under threat and her known safe route to securing relationships looked as if it was to be closed off. Thirdly, and worst of all, her impending marriage also seemed under threat. The relationship had, to a certain extent, been built around Paula's physical attractiveness and the importance that she had in her partner's eyes as a sexual partner. Now, she agonised, this would no longer be possible. The most frightening fantasy was of revealing the wound to her boyfriend. The marriage plans might well founder, maybe he would pull out, maybe she should pull out. In this thought there was buried a last frightening implication. Perhaps she would end up on her own, stripped of her impact as a person (in her judgement) and with no secure relationships. These were Paula's perceptions. For two weeks the thoughts and images ran endlessly through her consciousness.

It would be ridiculous to say to a person in Paula's position, 'Don't be anxious.' She is anxious for a good reason. She realises that the situation she faces threatens her both physically and socially. She has responded as she is 'designed' to respond and needs understanding, support and companionship with her anxiety.

But let's take a closer look at the outcome of her anxiety. I want you to see that although it is uncomfortable and she would dearly wish it to go away, *it is adaptive and does have a function.* Her anxiety is, amongst other things, a state of raised vigilance and increased energy to tackle the threat. It has led her to strive to master the situation by rapidly finding out about the effects of mastectomy, seeking various alternatives to the operation and, within the limits that he could move, influence her surgeon's approach. In other words, she has adopted a confrontational stance, which is the positive, adaptive outcome of the emotional reaction. While this has been going on she has also been involved in what some writers call 'the work of worrying'. She has created in fantasy the various outcomes and experiences that could well present themselves to her in reality during the months to come. She will now not be overwhelmed by surprise if any of these actually become reality. She is braced and has to some extent rehearsed the experiences in advance. In other words, the anxious worrying has been a sort of preparation. It has been painful but it has had a function. It is in this sense, therefore, that we should talk of functional emotional processes.

Case 2: The Work of Grief. I will preface this case description with a fragment of theory. People have the capacity to become attached to other people – we call this bonding. It is a complex emotional and perceptual event that most of us are acquainted with through personal experience. When such bonds are broken through some separating event, a powerful emotional response takes place which is termed grief. The feelings involved range through despair, anguish, anger, intense sadness and even sensations of physical pain. With these feelings there is usually a flood of thought, memories and images to do with the lost person. During grieving, attention is focused on what has been lost to the exclusion of other interests, but as the months go by, this process seems to lead to an erosion of the emotional bonding. The images of the lost person no longer have such a powerful capacity to trigger emotion and other people or aspects of life begin to acquire more significance again. Janis and Levanthal (1965) describe this as the work of grieving. Their belief is that when a person is heavily bonded to another and that bond is severed it is not possible for the bereaved person to make new bonds immediately because the old ones are still active and have a blocking effect. In grieving, a process occurs which progressively weakens the blocking effect of the old bonds. The apparent turmoil of thought and memory centred on the lost person functions to slowly erode the power of the emotional attachment. The repetitiveness of so-called reflective grief exhausts the response. With the completion of this process, the person is again free to make new attachments.

Rachman (1980) talks of a similar idea which he terms 'emotional processing'. Whenever we experience psychological trauma such as an incident with a profoundly shocking or frightening impact, or the loss of someone to whom we are attached, it is a normal characteristic, Rachman observes, for the event to intrude in our thoughts with great frequency and to trigger the associated emotions over and over again. (Some of you may have experienced the, 'I can't get it out of my thoughts' effect after an accident, for example.) After a period of this unsettling activity, the impact of the event lessens in that it no longer has the power to produce the emotional response. The emotional processing is complete. When, for one reason or another, this period of emotional processing is blocked, atypical patterns of extended grief result. There may even be episodes of emotional disturbance with phobic or obsessional features.

With these thoughts in mind, the following case example should make more sense. The case involves another woman, Sue, who went into renal failure at the age of 38. At the time she was a nurse in charge of a children's unit. Sue was happily married but without children of her own since early on she had decided that her career was of central importance to her. She had never regretted the decision and had progressed steadily in her field to become well respected and highly skilled. The kidney failure was unexpected, following a short but severe viral infection. She could not believe it at first but as she recovered from the panic and physical agonies of severe uraemia, the awful truth bore down on her. The nurses caring for her reported that after a short spell of being rather gracious and kindly, she became angry, often snapping at the nurses for no apparent reason. Her mood changed again a day or two later and she became withdrawn and tearful, not in a hysterical or overt way, but spending long periods alone in her room weeping, turning away company and responding little to the attempts by the doctors, nurses or relatives to comfort her. She ate little and was not much interested in caring for herself. In dialysis sessions she adopted the approach of stoical endurance, keeping her eyes shut much of the time rather than learning about the techniques and beginning her training towards self-sufficiency. She was clearly very down and the senior registrar handling her case thought she was clinically depressed and wanted her to take anti-depressants. Some of the staff began to be offended by her rebuffs and entered her room only when it was necessary. So what was going on?

If we remain loyal to the idea that her reaction was part of a normal emotional process which would make sense if we knew what she was seeing and thinking in this situation, then our thoughts must turn to the notion that this was a pattern of behaviour rather similar to the grief reaction. Who was dead or departed though? The answer was clear, in Sue's inner world *part of her had died*, although she would not describe it quite like that herself. Her existence was centred on her role as a nurse, where she dealt with very dependant, young people and their anxious parents. This included a vision of the future with her career extending until retirement age. Much of her sense of worth and strategy of living was locked up in this 'core role'. Now, as a realist who understood the basic problems of living by dialysis and the gamble of renal transplantation, she was well aware that her career had been cut dead. A most important, central part of her life was gone, the very basis of her self-image and self-worth. Her feeling was of anger, protest and a despairing loss. She had begun to grieve for this part of herself. Thus the slow emotional process that would take many months to complete was underway. The daily experience of the dialysis unit compounded the loss. Each hour she had to relate to people still in possession of the role which she had loved so much. This triggered resentment which she knew was unreasonable and the reversal of roles led to feelings of being humiliated and diminished. It was as if a part of her had been amputated.

From this case study there are two lessons for us. Firstly, that grieving is a response which can occur in relation to *any* major loss. We can be bonded to aspects of our physical, social or psychological selves, to key roles or even objectives in the future. If these bonds are powerful and stable, their unexpected severance will be traumatic and probably trigger the grieving reaction. Secondly (as with Sue), such reactions do have a function. Through this process with its turmoil of thought and feeling comes the eventual weakening of the bonds to the lost object of attachment and thus the freedom to develop a new life. The aim with people who react in this way should not be to 'knock the depression out' or to 'get her over it as soon as possible' but to help her into and through the process, to facilitate its completion.

Making People Comfortable

In the last two sections, I have advanced the view that emotional reactions in people facing the trauma of serious illness or injury (1) are to be expected, (2) should in most cases be conceived as normal behaviour, and (3) should be valued as processes which enable adaptation to threat or transition through major life changes involving loss of role or body parts. It has been recognised that the occurrence of such reactions is primarily determined by the way in which people perceive their situations. Some will experience severe threat or loss, others will actively deny contact with such perceptions (usually a short-term defence which collapses) and a third group will perceive the situation in alternative, less threatening ways, and so appear fairly self-contained. Much will depend on a person's position in life and whether 'core roles' are threatened (it is a useful exercise to ask yourself how *you* would react at present if you were involved in an accident that led, say, to the loss of an arm). It must also be remembered that the general atmosphere in hospitals creates a situation where very many people are highly active emotionally but struggle desperately to hide this from staff and relatives.

The reason that so much space has been allocated to the development of this theme is that the work of emotional care is based on a basic premise, namely, we are not treating emotional illnesses but rather facilitating emotional processes and supporting people through the period of time when such processes are ongoing. At this point, however, there could well be some confusion. *Am I saying that we should leave people to bear the full impact of these sometimes painful emotional experiences because they are important processes?* By no means — emotional care has the same target as, say, basic nursing care. That is, to make people comfortable and bring them to a condition which is most likely to promote rapid healing and a return to health. In these terms there is nothing wrong in assisting people with some kind of sedation or sleeping aid if they seek it. The impact of strong emotion can be exhausting and alarming in itself. Clearly, any resources that genuinely improve a person's condition and make him more comfortable should be exploited. However, it is important to retain the perspective that *assistance with drugs is in order to make people more comfortable and not as a treatment to combat emotion because it is being misconstrued as an illness.* This approach would not only reveal a staggering ignorance of the phenomena involved but would compound the atmosphere of denial and have a blocking effect on the emotional processes involved. It would be a case of medicine making things worse, not better.

The Emotions of Illness

What can you expect to meet if you get involved in the work of emotional care? There is little point in my constructing a detailed and tedious list of emotional reactions related to illness. It would be unrealistic anyway since, as a life experience, illness and involvement with the medical and medically-related professions can be painful, harrowing, frustrating, depriving, frightening, severely threatening, depressing, humiliating, intimidating, boring, annoying, intimate, evocative of profound relief and gratitude, safe, relaxing, nurturant with great human warmth, comic, inspiring and much more. In other words, the whole range of human feelings will be encountered. Most commonly you will be dealing with fragile people working hard to contain feelings of anxiety, anger, grief and depression, who may also show warm feelings of trust, affection, gratitude and dependency. In the majority of cases there will be no mystery about why people are feeling as they do, assuming, that is, you develop contact and through careful listening begin to see their world through their eyes. In many cases you will understand quite clearly because you would feel something similar if you took their place. Perhaps it will be helpful to use another case example here to show that sometimes the character of a person's reactions can be surprising, but it does make sense when their position is made clear.

Case 3. Eddie was another dialysis trainee, 43 years old and a draughtsman by trade. He was about three months into his training and had reached the point where he was receiving instruction in the art of needling — that is, placing two cannulae into his fistula prior to a haemodialysis session. The trouble was that when Eddie was in the Unit everybody knew it. He was angry in a subdued way all the time but would suddenly flare up into terrible tempers, openly shouting at the nurses. Occasionally objects were thrown. He seemed genuinely angry with the staff, but for no obvious reason. He received the same treatment as everybody else. The nurses found his behaviour hurtful and annoying and saw it as being unreasonable.

The psychologist was involved in this case and after several sessions was able to explain to the nurses what was happening. Briefly, Eddie had been the son of a harsh, critical man who endlessly undermined Eddie's sense of worth by belittling his achievements and driving him on to do better by sneering at his efforts. He had emerged into adulthood as a man who was phobic of failure. He instantly abandoned anything at which he could not do well, and drove himself to his limits in everything that he did. He had taken on his father's critical attitude. The handicap induced by kidney failure is severe loss of energy and a certain degree of intellectual slowing. This had led Eddie to be increasingly critical of himself, increasingly impatient of all his new limitations. He turned his despising condemnation onto himself. Presenting this weakened self at the haemodialysis training unit was an agony. When he had to tackle subtle and complex skills such as venepuncture, his needs were to master them instantly. When he could not do so, an uncontrollable anger surged through him for when he looked at himself he could only see failure. Although this anger was meant for himself, he could not aggress against himself effectively so it spilled over in his interactions with the nurses.

Basic Steps in Emotional Care

Now at last we can get down to the issue of what is actually done. To illustrate the elements of emotional care I will develop an extended example and 'talk you through it' as if you had to do the work personally. What is to come could apply equally to a doctor, physiotherapist, speech or occupational therapist, but for convenience it will be written using solely the image of a nurse as the central figure. The illustration will be an idealisation in that I will assume a development in this particular ward to the point where the nurses offer psychological care to all the people passing through it and in the case of the more seriously ill who are making a longer stay, have an allocation of time and a suitable place for emotional care work.

Your client is John Rayner. He is 42 years old. Two days ago he sustained a moderate myocardial infarction. His condition has now stabilised without evident disrythmia and he will be resident in your

ward for about two weeks. John works as a self-employed plumber in
a style typical of the so-called coronary prone personality, that is,
building up long hours with little rest, taking few holidays and driven
by a restless need to keep on striving towards some private objective
of achievement and perfection. There are two children in his family
together with Ruth, his wife, who runs the office end of the business.
You will find him a little tense, wary of what is happening to him and
rather close to tears at times.

Laying the Foundation

John does not know you as a person. He needs to feel secure with you
and to achieve this, you must spend a little time with him, time during
which you are not fussing with one or another of a dozen duties but
when you sit on his bed and look at him and talk with him. The
content is not vital but what is important is that he can sense what kind
of a person you are and he can feel that you have the capacity to relate
to him without nervousness on an open, honest basis. He must sense
your caring intentions and discover you to be someone who does not
put him on his guard. With this in mind, you should make several brief
visits simply to find out how he is doing and to exchange words with
him about whatever seems a sensible topic. On one such visit you
should let him know that you will be talking with him at greater length
soon on how he is feeling personally as a result of his coronary.

Initiating Emotional Care

Your entry into emotional care work with John must come as a gentle
invitation with plenty of scope for him to take his time, delay his
response or even refuse. You *offer* care, never force it. At the same
time, note that you take the initiative and do not wait for 'something
to come up' to precipitate your action. Some people, however, will beat
you to the offer because they have an urgent need to talk out some of
their feelings and they begin before you have a chance to issue an
invitation, but John is more defensive. In casual ward conversation he
is adopting a denying strategy, saying that he is alright and is already
planning how to sort out a couple of incomplete jobs. At the same
time, the message of his manner is that he is unsure and has taken a
heavy blow which has shattered his confidence.

The invitation will be your version of the following. 'Part of my
work is helping people with the personal and emotional side of their
illness. Many people coming into the ward find it stressful and have
anxieties and often times of depression. I do not know whether this

applies to you, John, but at this point in your treatment I would normally put aside half an hour to meet with you in private to check how you are getting on and how this has affected you personally. Is this something you would like to take part in?' If he is comfortable with the idea arrange a meeting within the next day or so to do just that.

What you are doing here is giving John permission to have a personal side to his illness and validating it by showing that it merits separate attention but dealing with it as a normal part of the care in the ward. Part of the reassurance necessary at this phase is to communicate the idea of normality, that strong feeling reactions are to be expected and are part of the normal pattern of illnesses such as coronary heart disease. The more you can make this just a part of the routine and relax about it yourself, the better. Observe John's reaction to your invitation carefully. If he seems bothered about it, rather than arranging your first session check back with him later, saying that you felt he was a little unsure about the suggestion of talking over the personal side of things and would he rather leave it for a while.

Beginning the First Session

We will assume that John gets on with you and feels positive to the thought of someone with whom he can talk through his reactions to the heart attack. You have organised a time and the first 'session' is imminent. Incidentally, a word about time and setting. Since we are talking of ideals, I should say that the least optimum conditions for this kind of work is perched on a bed, in uniform and in an open ward. The optimum conditions (in my view) are to make use of an interview room, office or individual bedroom, to be out of uniform and to have an agreement not to be interrupted. We have to accept reality, though, and if people are in bed, in plaster with traction, or linked to monitors or dialysis machines, such conditions will be unobtainable. But give thought to making your client as socially comfortable as you can.

Just before beginning, let's pause a moment and think about you. Why are you doing this? What is your motive and in what frame of mind are you meeting John? These are important questions and we should establish this as a ground rule; never lose sight of yourself and your own needs in this kind of work. Monitor your state because there may be times when it would be best to leave the work to somebody else. A meeting is about to take place in which John will have the opportunity of reflecting on his feelings and the circumstances that prevail upon him. He may be very closed up about it, in which case it will be a fairly desultory session. He may be able to just describe some of the thoughts and feelings he has experienced, in a flat, held-in way, but it is also a possibility that in talking of his experiences, emotions which have been held back will begin to well up. You must expect his emotions and be at peace with them. To use an analogy, surgery cannot be undertaken without contact with blood and in the same way, it is not possible to be involved in emotional care without face-to-face contact with the emotional experiences of others. If, for example, John should break down and shed some tears and this makes you want to say, 'don't cry', or feel guilty as if something has gone wrong and it is your fault, *do not go any further* – you are not ready for it yet. Your own needs will start to predominate and your tension will block the very events which need to be facilitated, added to which you will, frankly, be something of a fake because a situation is being created which you, rather than John, cannot handle.

Assuming that this moment of self-inquiry reveals nothing to make you hesitate, let's get you to meet with John Rayner now – he is expecting you. If you have the use of a room, take him to it or, better still, meet him there. You should sit near him, looking at him in a relaxed manner, ideally out of uniform, not behind a desk and without pen and notepad. Hopefully you will have already established the reciprocal use of first names. If the session has to be a visit on the ward then do everything you can to create the atmosphere of two equal people meeting in some sort of privacy.

Task number one is to lead him slowly to the targets of the encounter, so be very clear what these are. You know that there is a high likelihood that he is experiencing considerable emotional upheaval as he appraises the significance of his heart attack. Your intention is to relieve the isolation of this emotional processing and offer a situation wherein he can express his feelings, live them in the presence of another (which may not be possible with family members and certainly is not possible in the busy routine of ward life) and experience care through tension-free acceptance. He will probably find this a new situation and be unsure of his ground, needing to approach it in easy steps. Your opening remarks, therefore, are important because they will carry the guidelines which he will be searching for. Avoid patronising put-downs such as, 'It's time we had our little talk', or officious professional-to-patient openings like, 'Now, John, I would like to ask you a few questions.' I would not want to suggest any sort of script or a standard opening – you must develop your own style with a view to leading him in the right direction, relaxing both himself and yourself and giving it the feel of a normal part of the work of the ward. However, here is a typical opening exchange which does have a gentle, directive quality. (Bear in mind that John comes across as being rather tense and wary and will probably not prove an easy talker to start off with.)

Nurse Well, John, I'd like to check on how you've found these last few days since your coronary.

John I've been glad to be here. I got a bit wound up the day it happened, didn't know what had hit me — you do mean me to talk about the personal side and not my chest pains, don't you?

Nurse I'd like you to talk about whatever is on your mind, but you're quite right, this isn't really for dealing with the medical side of things. I was wondering what it's been doing to you in terms of how you've been thinking and feeling since you came in here.

This type of beginning gives John a sense of direction and allows him to choose his own pace. He can start by dealing with past experiences and past feelings which allows a little distancing and also enables him to test out your reactions. It will be quite useful to get him to talk out in full his reactions to the last few days (rather like an abreaction) as an exercise to get both of you used to working together and dealing with the emotional aspects. Later on, after his early disclosures, one or two prompts may help if he becomes blocked. For example:

Nurse If, in your imagination, you could tell someone who is shortly going to have a heart attack about the difficult side of it, the things that have really troubled you, what would you say?

Or,

Nurse I've never had a heart attack although I've nursed many people that have, so I see it from a different angle. From your experiences, what are the aspects that have a lot of personal impact that I might not know about?

This kind of conversation may well be an important learning experience for John. He will either flourish and develop his capacity for this type of communication or shrink back to become defensive and closed off. Thus, your job in this first encounter is to ensure that events foster this learning. It is the way you handle the session and your reaction to what he says which will determine his progress. Your key role is that of giving supportive validation towards feeling-based communication, in other words, he receives confirmation that these particular types of self-disclosure are valid and exactly what the session is about. Your primary means of achieving this is by listening with undivided attention, reflecting back what he is saying from time to time to show that you understand and accept it, together with giving occasional encouragement and assistance if he gets blocked. Beyond that, you have no brief at present since we are confined to purely emotional care and not counselling. Any urge you may have to 'cure' needs to be resisted – your objective is to allow feelings, not obstruct them.

Later Stages of the First Session

Assume that John has taken quarter of an hour or so recalling his experiences and feelings of the last few days. He seems to have settled to the task and is talking easily. He is fairly matter of fact, though guarded. As he talks of his feelings he clearly has no real contact with them in the sense that he is not giving himself the time or the opportunity to sense these feelings and let them stir him now. He is holding them at bay. In formal psychotherapy it would be part of the therapist's task to direct such a client in ways which would develop greater contact with his feelings and free him from the defensive denial or repression that was taking place. Here, however, this is not the case. You are not involved as a psychological therapist. The objective in emotional care is not to activate people into greater emotional responsiveness, it is to care for them on the level at which they are functioning. In other words, try not to become exasperated with him and hold back any need to prod him or stir things up. You must remember he is not in a strong state and will be much better without additional sources of upheaval. Never forget, therefore, that you are offering him an invitation to talk with you – he has no obligation to do so – otherwise the meeting could be threatening and counter-productive. The chances are, though, that if you work with him maintains the character described below, he will feel increasingly able to make contact with his feeling reactions in your presence.

As the initial session proceeds, it may be helpful to bring John closer to the here-and-now, to his state of feeling in the present day. Again, a gentle invitation such as:

Nurse So how are things for you today, what is your feeling at the moment?

And a little later on,

Nurse If you can't get to sleep tonight and are lying awake thinking of what has happened and what is going to happen, what will your thoughts be and how will you be feeling?

I have mentioned several times in this chapter that your general approach in this encounter is of great significance. It is through the medium of your reactions that people such as John learn a new attitude and a new ability with feeling-based communications. By no means all of your clients will need this kind of initiation. Some will be thoroughly at ease with this type of communication and will not need you to guide them, although they will need to feel they can trust you. In my own experience, though, the proportion of clients like John is quite high so perhaps we should press on to specify in more detail the elements of emotional care in order that you have something to guide you.

The Core Content of Emotional Care

Making the Situation Safe

The foundation of emotional care is that your clients feel safe with you, by which I mean they sense that they will not be attacked, embarrassed, humiliated, judged inadequate or devalued. This atmosphere of safety will come from the character and tone of your reactions to the disclosures which they make. The overall message conveyed in your replies must be that the disclosure of personal feeling, the worries, regrets, anger, sadnesses, black thoughts and so on are appropriate within the context of the session and that the situation harbours no threat. Part of the sense of safety will come from the realisation that you respect the emotional upheaval provoked by illness as a normal event which makes you neither tense, embarrassed nor despising.

People will often begin a series of meetings like this in a wary state. It is a little foreign and they are wondering what you will think of them. But on the whole, they will not feel the need to be defensive or shy away in embarrassment unless you introduce such an atmosphere. So consider what you say in terms of whether it makes for safety or threat. Never, for example, directly challenge, contradict or devalue a person's experiences and the feelings associated with them, since that will drive him into a defensive position. Even kindly meant challenges may have the opposite effect to that intended. For example:

John My wife is such a worrier, sometimes I feel more bothered about her than I do about the heart trouble itself.

Ineffective Nurse It's silly to be worrying about things like that, your job is to get well and you won't do this by getting bothered about other people and things you have no control over. She'll be alright, I'm sure.

Comment Basically this is a rejecting communication which begins by construing John's feeling of concern for his wife as 'silly'. It does not teach him that feelings are accepted and valued — it teaches him to be wary because revelations of inner feelings may result in statements from the nurse which are belittling. In other words, the situation is made unsafe to John.

Effective Nurse Well, let's expand on that for a while because it's obviously very important to you. When you say you feel very bothered about her, what are you actually referring to? Do you mean you feel nervous, angry, protective or what?

Comment In contrast, this response carries the message that the disclosure is of importance as it stands, worth spending time on, worth elaborating. The interest by the nurse and her readiness to see such experiences as acceptable make the situation appear safe to John.

By taking up the things that a client says, acknowledging them and encouraging an elaboration, you are declaring them valid. This is the necessary source of safety. With a prevailing atmosphere of this type, wary people like John will reach a position where they feel more secure. Their experience is that, 'I am free to talk of my feelings, that is what is wanted. She understands and accepts how I feel, I sense her support and sympathy. I do not feel devalued or humiliated, it is easy to talk with her.' In this light you can see why so many of the communications from medical and nursing staff in, say, a ward round situation, are grotesque devaluations of personal feeling. I quote from a recent event:

Consultant How are we this morning? Nurse tells me you have been a bit upset.

Client Yes, I've been feeling a bit depressed for the last two days. I keep wanting to cry.

Consultant Absolutely no reason for you to be depressed, my dear, everything is going well, it's all healing up nicely. Just a bit of post-operation blues, I expect. You'll have to try and get things like that out of your head. I'll get nurse to give you some pills to shift it.

Giving Permission for Emotions and Emotional Expression

Have you noticed in your work, or general living for that matter, that when people become emotional they will usually apologise. A mother, on hearing that her child was deaf, broke down and cried in the presence of her GP — and then apologised. A man I met a few weeks ago who had gone into sudden renal failure was very emotional and when talking about the effect this would have on the way his wife regarded him, burst into tears — and then apologised to me. It's natural enough, of course. In our society a show of emotion is considered as embarrassing, something which should happen in private. As we have seen, though, a significant proportion of your clients will be in a state of emotional reaction. For them the difficulty is that in the typical hospital sub-culture with its emphasis on uniformity, the atmosphere of

Figure 4.2: The Elements of Emotional Care

Making the situation safe (without threat)
Enabling a client to get 'in touch' with feeling reactions
'Giving permission' for the expression of feelings
Communicating understanding and empathy
Communicating acceptance
Sharing personal feeling with the client
Support
i.e. facilitating emotional process

asceptic routines, the growing technology and above all, the wide social distance maintained between professionals and 'patients', the sense of the inappropriateness of emotional reaction is amplified; there is little place for human feeling. Put another way, in the average hospital setting there is no natural permission within the sub-culture for this expression of feeling. For you, this presents a tide to swim against because emotional care work requires that the opposite conditions prevail. A clear sense of *positive permission* for the expression of human feeling is vital.

Without doubt, this is a difficult and complex objective for professionals in a hospital setting. It presents various potential problems, not the least of which will be in staff relations. For example, it will be difficult not to feel hostile when a client with whom you have established an atmosphere fostering permission for emotional expression is treated roughly by an insensitive colleague *because* they have shown emotion. (The risk of inter-professional division as a consequence of this work is obvious and will have to be monitored with great care since it would be to no-one's advantage if, say, the nursing profession changed with great rapidity in the direction of psychological care while the medical profession lagged behind. A divisive tension could be created since the traditional behaviour of the medical profession could not be allowed to damage and retard progress of this type.)

How then is 'permission' given? Again, the important factor is the character of your reactions and communications in the presence of your client's emotion. This is why I earlier placed such stress on personal preparation. You cannot create a permission-giving atmosphere if you do not feel permission for your own emotional life or are ill at ease with that of others. Let's return to your encounter with John Rayner to find some concrete examples. Your first interview with him has gone well enough. He is relaxed, happy to talk, clearly getting something out of it but still keeping the issue of his feelings at arm's length.

You are happy to work with him at this level, trying to guide him gently in his first experiences of emotional care and using the flow of conversation as a way of making him feel safe and supported. Attention has turned to his feelings of the day and John has mentioned for the first time that he feels very down at times. So let's eavesdrop on your future skilled self and see how it's done.

John I do have some awful thoughts sometimes, like last night and when I woke up this morning. I haven't told anyone and it would really upset my wife. I expect you'll think it's stupid.

(He is giving you a warning — there is something he needs to reveal but in doing so becomes vulnerable.)

Nurse Take your time, John. Just say what you feel comfortable saying and then I'll be honest with you and tell you how I feel about it.

John I find myself thinking . . . gosh, it's so stupid . . . I find myself thinking that now I've got heart disease the best part of my life is over. I don't mean I want to do myself in, but yesterday I thought maybe it's best if I have another coronary and that finishes it. I'll never keep the business going like I need to, and I was top of the squash ladder, really strong for my age and, I hope you don't mind me saying it, pretty good in bed. It all seems to be gone now. I keep remembering my Dad in his wheelchair — I don't want to be like that.

(At this point tears trickle down John's face and he cannot continue talking.)

Nurse She says nothing, puts her hand on John's hand and simply gives him a tissue. She does not fuss or shuffle around in tension but waits a little while in silence still looking at him in a relaxed way. She is at ease with his emotion. She cares about it but it is not her fault so she does not feel guilty — it belongs to the situation that John is in.

John I'm sorry, I didn't mean to make a fuss like this.

Nurse Are you embarrassed?

John Yes, you must think I'm a complete fool.

Nurse I can see that you aren't used to sharing your emotions with other people, John. You seem so condemning of yourself, using words like 'stupid' and 'fool'. Is that how you actually see yourself at the moment?

John Well, perhaps not, I know what you mean. I don't really mean it quite like that, I got a bit flustered.

Nurse You were saying that you felt finished and would be happy for it all to end.

John That's right. Not all the time, you know, but sometimes I get low, can't seem to shake it off. Can you understand?

Nurse Yes, I can. It feels like a terribly sad experience that you're going through.

(There's a silence for a minute or so – John is lost in thought.)

Nurse What are you thinking?

John Just about what the doctor said. Then I was wondering what you thought of a grown man crying.

Nurse Alright, I said I would give you my views, so here they are. You have had a severe shock and things are going to change a lot for you. It's been frightening and the future looks frightening too. So it's bound to stir up some intense feelings including, as you've found, wishing yourself dead. It will probably be months or even longer before you feel emotionally strong again. That's how it is for many of the people who have heart attacks. I'm pleased that you've been able to share this side of your illness with me. I don't suppose it is easy to tell your wife. (Pause) How are you feeling at the moment?

John A bit choked up to be honest.

Nurse Would you like to leave it there for today or go on and tell me a little more about the sad experience when you woke up this morning?

John Well, I don't know really, have you got the time? It's a relief to talk about it.

You can see what is happening here. John is, in effect, asking questions and you are answering them. It is all about, 'what do you think of me now that I have told you my depressed thoughts and shown you my emotions?' It is a critical moment. You could well have ruined things if you had become anxious at John's distress and tried to rush in with placatory platitudes in order to stem the tears. It did not happen that way, though, and the situation was used to good effect, giving him time and then showing him the way towards a positive attitude to his own emotion. *You introduced the element of permission.* Then you gave the responsibility of deciding whether or not to continue to John. He clearly felt safe, he clearly sensed the permission and he opted to continue. Some of the later contacts with him will similarly involve depressed feelings, tears and anger. He will again need your calmness and your reaffirmation of permission to have and express such emotion.

Facilitating Emotional Expression

The Means. We are pursuing the case of a man who does not find the actual process of introspection and verbal disclosure of personal feeling easy. Apart from these acquired inhibitions from earlier years, John has a limited (I should say undeveloped) skill in working out how he is reacting — in Gendlin's terms he has poor contact with the 'felt sense'. As we have noted, people vary greatly in their expressive ability. Some will not need help at all. Many will struggle though, and you cannot leave them to flounder. After all, the main point of these encounters is to give an opportunity for the expression of feeling. The skill of facilitating the expression of feeling is something that psychological therapists spend many years acquiring and cannot be picked up by means of a few quick tips. Like any craft, you must spend time and more time developing a feel for the material you use and slowly elaborate your knowledge and repertoire of abilities. Thus, dealing with reality, I will try and illustrate the notion of facilitation and lodge it in your mind as an asset to strive for — through discussion with more experienced people and plenty of practice.

Several incidents during the contacts with John had in common the feature of a rushed and impoverished expression of feeling on his part — he seemed to be glossing over important issues. In these instances, assistance into further expression of feeling would obviously be worthwhile as long as he remained comfortable with it. An example of this is illustrated in the next portion of transcript. Let's assume that you are not a beginner but are well trained in this work and have considerable experience. This is probably how you would handle the following situation:

John (Talking of the ward round of yesterday morning) When the doctor said I would have to find another sport, that I couldn't go on with competitive squash, it really got to me. I was in quite a stew for an hour or so. Funny, isn't it, that it seemed to bother me so much, but it's only a game, I suppose. (Pauses) Anyway, then the wife came up later and we had a look at a few invoices . . .

Nurse John, hold it a minute there, because you've mentioned feeling really bothered but I'm not sure what you were actually thinking and feeling. You've rushed through it. Go back to that bad moment you had and let's go through it again.

John Well, it was afterwards, really, they had gone on to Bob in the next bed. I suppose it just came home a bit. My heart turned over — you know.

Nurse Alright, try and bring back what you were picturing in your mind and the actual feelings it stirred up.

John This is going to start me off again.

Nurse If you're not comfortable going through it then leave it for now.

John No, I do feel better when I get things off my chest.

Nurse What was in your thoughts at that time?

John Going back into the club, I think. I've been playing squash there for five years. I'm doing well – was doing well – in the squash league and I play for the first team.

Nurse What did you imagine, I mean, what did you actually visualise which upset you?

John Going in and having them see me like this. Well, they won't see that much difference but they'll know about me, and all I will be able to do is sit and watch – a has-been. That's what got to me, turning up like a cripple.

Nurse And this makes you feel . . .

John Angry. Really wild, like I could smash something.

Nurse Can you take it a little further, John, pause for a moment and picture that situation again? You're angry at something or someone. Do you know what?

John It's this feeling of being out of it, a write-off. I have to be at the top of things – can't stand being second best. It was the same with the business. I don't know – I can feel it now, like needing to shout and punch something – punch myself I suppose.

Nurse You feel angry because your body is letting you down, do you mean?

John Not exactly. In here you get the message that it's almost your fault that you've had a heart attack and that if you'd done things differently you'd still be fine. They only tell you after it's happened though. No, I feel as if I'm to blame, really. I've knocked myself out of everything that matters.

You see how by catching things at the right moment and then getting him to go back and put a microscope on a particular incident this led him into a greater awareness of what was happening at that time, and helped him identify the feelings involved and express them. Notice also that you do not challenge these feelings or comment on them. You work at helping him express them and elaborate his contact with them. The more he makes contact with this anger and works his way through it, the sooner he will be free from it. You are helping the process develop.

This skill is heavily dependant on noticing that a person is clearly feeling a great deal but that this is partially blocked from expression. Your client must be gently led back to discover the source of feeling in more detail, perhaps feel it then and there in your presence. But again, note very carefully, this is not about pushing someone into emotional activation for its own sake. You take him as far as *his* limits allow, no more. If he is pressed, a tension will grow and you will have made a bad mistake.

The Reason. A short reminder on why you should put emphasis on facilitating emotional reactions. They often signify important ongoing psychological processes of adaptive preparation and adaptive change. The processes can usually be aided by direct and frequent expression of the feelings involved to another person and, when there is blocking, assistance in the expression of the feelings. This promotes the 'working through' of the process. An example of a rather more advanced form of this work is a specific form of therapy known as guided mourning. Mawson *et al.* (1981) described how people locked into a state of morbid grief which had persisted for twelve months or more were assisted by therapy sessions in which the therapist encouraged them to face those thoughts, memories, photographs and possessions of their lost partners most likely to trigger the powerful grieving feeling. This was done over and over again in the course of several therapy sessions. It inevitably produced a great flood of emotion. However, in comparison to a control group that did not have these facilitating experiences, the people accepting this therapy were measurably less disturbed by grief two weeks later. Guided mourning serves as a rather more dramatic illustration of the value of facilitating rather than inhibiting emotional processes. It is a psychological therapy, though, and not part of emotional care so I would not suggest you adopt such an approach.

In your work of emotional care, one of the major objectives is to create a situation which encourages and supports emotional processes so that a person may settle more readily into a stable adjustment to the *consequences* of illness or injury. But again, I will plead caution. The facilitation of emotional expression is not just stirring people into emotion. That in itself is aimless, punitive and counter-productive. So, go very cautiously with this aspect of emotional care, or you may do emotional damage.

Communicating Empathy and Acceptance – Sharing Personal Feeling

These elements of emotional care merit separate attention although they will inevitably be components of those already dealt with.

Empathy. A person with good empathy accurately identifies what another person is feeling. Sometimes this is achieved without actually being told, because there is an ability to read non-verbal behaviour and sense the sort of impact a situation is having on a person. For you, presumably at a beginning level, it is a matter of listening very carefully to the statements of the client and trying to project yourself into his experience. It means forgetting the need to perform as a counsellor and say the right thing, and relaxing into the work of picking up what the client is seeing and thinking and then identifying the feeling – trying to get inside his world. If you can do this, you will in many cases echo his feelings within yourself, almost like resonating in sympathy. Letting your client know that you do have empathy is important. It bridges the gap, producing a closeness and the necessary feelings of safety. You can do this from time to time by repeating back a recent statement together with a little elaboration. Following the last words of John in the previous section, one might have said, 'Yes, I understand, I can pick up an awful feeling of bottled-in rage – frustrating because it's difficult to really vent anger on yourself and get rid of it like you would if you were cross with another person.'

I will give you another illustration. Hopefully you will cope with my momentarily jumping to an entirely different case. This is of a session with a woman who has developed multiple sclerosis. She is white-faced and shaky as she talks of the future.

Woman It's not knowing how long it will take or how far it will go. I could be incontinent and barely mobile within a couple of years . . . (she cannot continue for a while – she sobs bitterly and the psychologist holds her hand) . . . the children, how will I protect my children, they will have to watch me get ill, and weaker, and die. That's awful. What a burden for them.

Psychologist (Near to tears himself but not fighting it since this was a moment of intense empathy and closeness, they were sharing the emotion of the situation.) I can sense how painful your need is as a mother to protect your children from this distress. Putting myself in your place just now – it makes my throat ache too – so much sadness and fright for them to bear and such a need in you to protect them.

Returning empathy is rather like being a mirror. You take in and sometimes take on the emotions of the moment and reveal this to your client.

Acceptance. There is little more to say on this since it falls within the material covered in the earlier section on making your client feel safe. Your position is of one who values and respects the reactions of the individual. In emotional care whether these reactions are based on correct or false perceptions (provided this can actually be decided) is not a central issue. The important thing is that given the way your client is experiencing the situation, his reactions are accepted by you and given value. This should be communicated frequently in your exchanges. However, I am not saying that if a person is responding to a perception which is an obvious distortion of reality that you should leave him that way. If you remember, we are being disciplined in this chapter and are dealing purely with emotional care. The business of leading people to alternative perception comes in the work of counselling which has been split, rather artificially perhaps, from emotional care for the purposes of clear teaching.

Sharing Personal Feeling. Many medical schools teach that the ideal conduct for a doctor is of concerned detachment. A lengthy process of indoctrination is fostered to produce young doctors who have the ability to remain emotionally switched off and uninvolved. This atmosphere can spill over to the other professions to a certain extent so that a whole department or ward can appear resolutely detached and preoccupied with stifling personal feeling. Where professions do experience feeling, it is common for them to mask this feeling from the population of hospital clients (although again we should note the wind of change in the philosophy of nursing care and the fact that the detached, feelingless nurse is becoming synonymous with a bad nurse in the new climate of nursing schools and nursing literature).

In the specific context of emotional care work, it would be a bizarre posture to adopt if you set out to hide your own feelings and remain stonily detached. At the same time, over-involvement such that you become caught up in your client's situation to a degree which disturbs you is also unacceptable. Somewhere between the extremes of personal detachment and over-involvement there is a middle, optimal approach. Obviously this will differ in character from the so-called medical manner of relating, the most obvious difference being that one does exchange views and, on occasions, share thoughts, experiences and feelings. There does need to be restraint, however, since the object of meeting with a client is for him to express *his* feelings and thoughts, not to spend time listening to yours. Nevertheless, a little self-disclosure on your part prevents you being construed as a neutral professional (which fosters inhibition) and builds a sense of mutual trust. Also, by occasionally sharing your feelings about the issue being dealt with, either verbally or by actually showing the emotion, you reduce the asymmetry that typifies a relationship between a 'professional and his patient'. In so doing, you make possible a genuine trusting relationship which can be used to achieve the aims of emotional care.

Let's be clear about what is being suggested here. Certainly the work of emotional care is professional work and you should never lose sight of the fact that you are engaged in professional duties during the session. The relationship which develops with your client needs to be of a genuine, human quality, but at the same time under control and limited. This is not in any way equivalent to developing an open friendship or forming an alliance. It is possible to have a sense of human closeness and remain within the limits of your role, pursuing the targets of good, emotional care. This contained relationship will be to your advantage when you are engaged with the same client in the other areas of nursing or professional work which form the main proportion of your working day.

Thus, when it feels appropriate and when it complements the aspects of emotional care which have been dealt with above, be free in mentioning your own reactions, perhaps disclosing what you feel when you project yourself into the client's position, or what you feel in the here-and-now, listening to him. There may be times when you identify very strongly with your client's emotions and find yourself very moved by them, near to tears perhaps. In most cases it will be productive to be open and just simply share the emotion rather than desperately fighting it off or steering the subject onto neutral ground for your own safety, not the least reason being that you should not ask your client to be more open in emotional expression when you are still stuck with powerful inhibitions yourself.

Support

Support is really a product rather than an activity. If there is a consistent and readily available provision of emotional care as just described, then it will inevitably be supportive. The awareness by a client that his experience and feelings are known and understood by another person, the availability of that person to spend time with him in the immediate future so that the client may continue to talk through difficulties, discharge feelings and experience acceptance with sensitive caring, provides the basis of support. Notice that it is not a particularly active role. Being supportive at the emotional level does not mean taking over a person's problems and solving them, or adopting some kind of psychotherapeutic approach in order to give treatment and diminish stress. It is primarily that you offer your time and are capable of spending this time with the client in the ways shown here, that is, absorbing what he says, understanding, empathising and gently assisting him with the task of confronting and expressing feeling. In so doing, you guarantee that your client is not isolated with his feelings and thoughts – you remove the stress which comes from being alone with heavy emotional burdens.

Let me just expand the point in relation to the care of the dying. As you can see, emotional care with dying people cannot in any way hope to alter the basic situation. Death is inevitable, there are no long term issues of adaptation and rehabilitation. In these terms there is, therefore, little to actually be done. It is, however, of extreme value to provide a caring, supportive, companionship throughout the period leading to death. The availability of someone with whom it is possible to share *all* types of thought and *all* types of feeling, with whom one can grieve or protest or just take the nurturing experience of feeling closeness and concern, is the basis of support for dying people.

Ending a Session

We must not forget that you have been left in the middle of a session with John Rayner. You have many other things to do and have nearly used up the 30 minutes allocated to the first meeting. How should you end?

It is quite a good idea to establish the length of a session at its start. That way, you will not be found in the middle of an important exchange surreptitiously looking at your watch and worrying about the time. Be firm and be definite. I usually give an estimate of time and later signal the end of a session in advance by saying something like, 'We will have to finish in five minutes. Is there anything else you would like to mention in the time we have left?'

On most occasions, finishing will present no problems. Just do it easily and naturally. If it has been a relaxed and fairly inactive meeting you can simply bid one another goodbye, ideally reaching an agreement on when you will next meet. On occasions, though, it will not have been a relaxed event and your client may have been through some distressing or disturbing material with you, expressing much emotion. In this instance use your last five minutes to bring him back into the here-and-now and effect a sense of completion if possible. Let's return to you and John for a moment to illustrate this. You set aside 30 minutes for the first meeting and time is up. In the latter part of the session, John slipped out from behind his defensive screen and talked of his sense of loss as he identified the changes that would occur following his coronary. It was probably the first time in his life that he had systematically talked of his feelings in this way. It was not easy and clearly he was very emotional at times. An appropriate way to end would be like this:

Nurse We must finish in a moment, John. I have to do some observations. How are you feeling?

John Well, I'm sorry to have taken up your time like this . . .

Nurse It's part of our work, we believe that it's important.

John It's still kind of you to take such an interest. I appreciate it.

Nurse So how are you feeling then — you'll be back with the others
in the ward soon. Is it going to be alright?

John I'm feeling alright now — sort of relieved. I think I'll just stay
on my own for a while, though.

Nurse Good. I'll probably have 20 minutes or so with you at the
end of the week, but if you need to talk anything through before then
you will let me know, won't you?

Deciding the Pattern of Contact

The first meeting with John Rayner is now over, the work of providing
him with emotional care has begun. Tomorrow you will be asked to
provide care for an older woman admitted three days ago with pericarditis. Should you deal with them both in an identical way in a fixed
pattern of contacts or will there be differences?

The obvious fact is that people coming into a hospital differ in every
possible way. Their length of stay, severity of illness, social background
and back-up, personality and the actual nature of their psychological
responses to the situation are just some of the variables. From your
point of view *they all need emotional care* but the extent to which this
is a major commitment for you will vary in relation to each person's
needs at the time (and your own availability). Some people will remain
genuinely stable and self-contained throughout their stay, and your
work need be little more than occasional brief meetings to enquire how
they are getting on at a personal level and, in so doing, reassuring them
that the concern which you have for them persists. However, during the
course of an illness there can be changes in circumstance which destroy
confidence and so you must be prepared to handle their altered needs
should the atmosphere change.

On the other hand, a sizeable proportion of the seriously ill are
bound to be in great emotional upheaval. We know this from the
research reported in Chapter 2. In these cases, early contact with
frequent meetings are the ideal, particularly when 'crises' occur. For
example, a woman taken into a kidney unit had spent eight weeks
training to self-sufficiency in continuous ambulatory peritoneal
dialysis. Her first three weeks had been an appalling time for her, what

with the shock of unexpected kidney failure and the tremendous disruption to her life. However, she had some good care and made real progress in coming to terms with her future. By the seventh week she was considered competent with her dialysis technique and was looking forward to going back to her family. In fact, to be honest, she was desperate to return home. Disaster struck, though, in the form of a persistent fungal peritonitis. This did not respond well to antibiotics and she had to transfer into the haemodialysis unit for a period while attempts to contain the infection were pursued. It looked like she could not go home for another two or three weeks at least and might have to abandon CAPD and start afresh with the six-month haemodialysis training programme. In this case, several of the staff including myself joined to make very full and necessary provision of emotional care. There were informal contacts with nurses each day and I met her on a scheduled basis once or twice a week. We rode this crisis out with her and were able to respond similarly when a transplant attempt failed some two years later.

Then, of course, there is your situation to consider. The pattern of working followed by nurses allows frequent unscheduled contact, perhaps dropping in to see a person briefly once a day with occasional longer sessions. In contrast, a speech therapist, say, will often work on an out-patient basis with weekly scheduled meetings. Basically you have to work within the confines of your role. The most important thing is to be flexible and 'read' the needs of your client, altering the pattern of your contacts accordingly. The same applies to where you meet. All my examples so far are idealised. They talk of 'sessions', implying periods of uninterrupted work in the privacy of a separate room. You may not have this facility in which case improvisation and flexibility are the essential qualities needed. The main thing is to find a way to offer the core elements of emotional care in good time and with sufficient frequency to meet the needs of the individual case, within the limits of your environment and work pattern. There are no rules, you must be the judge.

Formal Versus Informal Structuring

This is a point about which I have some strong feelings myself. The debate goes rather like this:

Nurse I don't like this idea of making appointments to see people as you suggest. I think you can talk with people much better if you do it informally. I find that 'patients' talk to me a lot when I'm giving them a bath.

Second Nurse It's easier when you're helping them with something like dressing – they chatter away and tell you their problems.

A Dozen Other Nurses at a Dozen Other Training Sessions Yes, it's much easier to talk when you are bathing them or doing something. Making it formal means it would be harder.

Psychologist You are disappointing me. You haven't really understood some of the basic principles. Can't you see that all you are doing is expressing your own anxiety about coping with the work and then building defences and escape routes? It's the old, trusty, nurses' defence against responsibility – the flight into fragmentation of roles and task-oriented nursing.

If you are bathing someone then your attention is divided. There will be distractions and interruptions to do with this task and you will not be able to look at your client, or they you, and you will not be able to think about what is happening. This is *downgrading* emotional care to a casual, non-professional, superficial and unimportant event. Such encounters in the bath tub would never guarantee that emotional care work was conducted consistently with all clients, and would never give a setting where you could work systematically at making things safe, giving permission, elaborating the expression of feeling, empathising and so on. Lastly, it would lead to chaos. Who would be working with whom? Who would assess the emotional needs and progress of an individual client?

No. Emphatically no. This is not the way to do it. Emotional care is a subtle, skilful, professional activity. It does not need people who are so insecure about the work that they must build in major defences of this type. In the bathroom consultation the nurse is dressed, the 'patient' naked – there is marked social asymmetry. The nurse can deflect the conversation whenever she feels pressed by using some distraction to do with the bathing or ending the bath. She can hide her own reactions. Worst of all, she can jolly along and trivialise the whole event. By combining tasks, the nurse reduces her accountability in the situation so that she is not really seen to be engaged on specific psychological tasks at all. Would other extensions of professional activity be attempted in such a defensive way – venepuncture, for example?

Now, what I will confirm is that social settings such as bath times do create a special caring, rather regressed atmosphere. The nurse is literally much more like a mother. These times should be used as a complement to the structured psychological care work. They are important additions, *but never substitutes*. When you arrange a session of emotional care work it must have your full attention and its value must be confirmed by giving the work its own time. So, if your concept of emotional care is such that you see a chat about problems during bathtime as sufficient, you have failed to absorb the key ideas and, sadly, you are not competent in psychological care.

Having said this, I do realise that emotional care work can be a new and rather intimidating venture. That is why you need support, training and a place where you can work through your own anxieties to find confidence.

Relatives

In certain areas of medicine, research shows that many immediate relatives are clearly disturbed emotionally by events. The ideal, of course, would be to extend emotional care to them too. Perhaps twelve per cent of my working time at the kidney unit is spent with relatives. The obvious problem, though, is the availability of time. This is an issue for discussion and practical compromise, I guess. It is pointless over-extending staff as the quality of their work will fade as they tire.

Beyond these comments, I think that I must declare the issue of whether to extend care to certain relatives and how these are selected as beyond the brief of this book, but it is something to keep in mind and debate in your ward or department. The approach to the work is exactly the same as that undertaken with clients and does not need separate treatment.

Your Own Reactions, Objectivity, Feedback and Support for Yourself

On occasions, one or other of the nurses that I work with will say something like, 'Can I talk with you about John Rayner (or whoever) for a few minutes, I'm struggling a little with him at the moment.' I find these extremely reassuring requests because they carry a message, namely that the nurses *are able to notice when they are over-extended*, either because they are trying to achieve an objective with a particular client but have lost the direction and feel powerless to achieve this, or because they have become troubled at an emotional level themselves in relation to a case. *This capacity to keep a watch on oneself is important and you must work hard to develop it.* I'll expand this point with a few notes on the various aspects involved.

Losing Objectivity. Inevitably some people will prove very difficult for you to work with. From time to time, you may feel yourself having considerable problems, perhaps resenting something about your client and feeling a growing anger during the contacts. Once in a while, you are likely to become intensely identifying with a particular client and thus drawn into their perception. Then you too are vulnerable to the extent of being paralysed by their despair and sense of defeat. It happens to us all and it can be very uncomfortable. Similarly, most of us in this work have discovered the hard way how easy it can be to lose objectivity (or at least neutrality), and edge into accepting the client's beliefs concerning relationships and verbal transactions, without checking the alternative perspectives with the other people involved. While working specifically in emotional care (not counselling) the effort towards acceptance of a person's feelings is not, you will remember, to be confused with attributing the status of fact to what they are seeing and saying. In accepting and valuing a person's reactions you do not assume accuracy of perception. This is very important indeed where other members of the family are involved or indeed, other members of staff.

Recently, I had a couple of meetings with a woman who had lately gone into kidney failure. She became very distressed during a weekend visit home because she felt her family did not need her and were glad to have her away in hospital. Her conviction was a powerful force and I had to work hard to retain a neutral view and keep myself mindful that, 'this is how she sees it now, when she is stronger she may see it differently, the family may see it differently.' As it turned out, she did change her perception quite markedly within a couple of weeks. Meanwhile, I had met her husband to check his view of things and discovered that he could not understand why she had changed, but possibly they had run around her too much and left her with no feeling of function in the home. It was very helpful for me to have access to his view to help bolster my own neutrality. She felt rejected by the family, they did not feel rejecting to her. Thus, I was able to accept her feelings as reasonable in relation to her perception but I did not challenge this perception directly in order to retain a good level of safety and support. Our conversations did, however, lead her to reflect and check through the issue herself, with a positive outcome.

A side effect of losing neutrality and being 'sucked into' your client's view of things is that you may unwittingly become the victim of manipulation. Your client may not realise his or her own motive so it is not necessarily a hostile or reprehensible tendency. Nevertheless, it will cause you difficulties in professional relationships if you appear to be drawn into your client's beliefs.

Two types of 'professional reflex' will insulate you from these danger areas. You need to develop them. Firstly, wherever possible, diplomatically check alternative views of a situation with whoever else is involved. This is not to obtain the 'right' version but to establish the alternatives in order to maintain neutrality. The very act of doing this will help you resist crossing the threshold into absorbing your client's views as a statement of reality, and will endlessly teach you that one person's perception of a situation can be enormously different from another's. In this type of work, there is little point in chasing after the accurate perception, which is often mirage-like anyway. What is important, though, is working to understand and, where productive, communicate the alternative perceptions to each party. This point will surface again in the next chapter which deals with informational care and communication.

Secondly, *regular case discussions and feedback* are essential. A psychological therapist who does not discipline himself to regularly discussing his work with a colleague is doing shoddy work. This applies similarly with counsellors or those giving psychological care. Without the feedback of another experienced person, there is no good way of discovering that your self-monitoring is accurate. In one's analysis of a case, it is easy to allow personal needs to influence the handling of it without awareness of this happening. One can, for example, lose sight of one's level of involvement and any tendency towards being manipulated that may have crept in. It would be wrong, however, to see discussions with other professionals in terms of having *mistakes* pointed out. That would put us all on the defensive and this is a much more positive exercise than that. You seek the view of another on the way you are dealing with a case in order to extend your perception and glimpse possibilities which would not otherwise have been available.

Good, constructive feedback from a colleague is invaluable in helping you assess what is happening to both you and your client and in determining the future direction to follow. It is unprofessional to work without such feedback, although once you have a good level of experience it is not necessary to do this with all cases. Arbitrarily, I will commit myself and say that a minimum of one out of ten cases should be discussed in depth. In the beginning stages, though, when supervision is necessary, each case should be discussed although, to be realistic, not always in great depth. Probably the most effective way of doing this is for a group of people working at psychological care to meet once a month to share case experiences and comment. Another task for you, therefore, is to ensure you have someone to do this with. If necessary, phone up your local clinical psychologist — you could do worse.

Support for You. Once you do have a setting in which you can talk through some of your case work with another person who is engaged in similar duties, then there also exists the opportunity of support for you. You will need it. At times there will be some rather powerful feelings within you as a direct consequence of the emotional care work. Occasionally, a case will pull you down, make you feel inadequate and ineffective. Sometimes you will feel that you have handled it badly and have a restless feeling of irritation at yourself, or a client will make you feel angry and resentful. Again, this is an experience and a need common to all people who work in the psychological field. Thus, it is a professional responsibility to ensure a support figure for yourself. You may not need one very often but then again, if you never need one there is something odd about you and your work. In your support sessions you can switch roles for a short while and express *your* feelings to your support figure, from which you will gain the same benefits as your clients gain from you. We call it 'caring for the carers'.

Referring On

An important part of psychological care is monitoring the state of your clients, and judging whether the help that they need is within the scope of your role and the limits of your ability. When a client's needs exceed either of those, the appropriate act is to refer the case on to someone in a better position to cope. Because this is a significant and separate aspect of care, I will give it a short chapter of its own later.

Concluding Comments

In a way this chapter has had an air of artificiality about it. For one thing there has been the underlying assumption of an ideal environment and work pattern to allow emotional care time and space. Also, the examples given are of *just* emotional care. In a balanced scheme of psychological care, other aspects would have been intermixed and many encounters of the character used in these examples would, therefore, have involved some basic counselling content too. However, these aspects have been excluded deliberately to allow clear teaching and to show what we need to attain in the progressive development of caring medicine.

5 INFORMATIONAL CARE

Keeping people informed, communicating with them in an appropriate way on a regular basis, should be easy. Of all the hurdles to overcome with ill people in a hospital setting, surely this must be one of the simplest ones? After all, the topic of communication now makes frequent and prominent appearances in the literature of the nursing and para-medical professions. Trainee doctors are not excluded from exposure to such material either, since some medical schools go so far as to include tutorials in interview and communication skills in their curriculum; so we must examine what is done and how effective it appears to be.

At the risk of being repetitious, I would like to adopt an approach similar to that in the chapter on emotional care, beginning by taking a recent issue from a nursing journal devoted to the theme of communication and establishing what ideas are presented and how well they stand up to scrutiny.

Nursing (July, 1981) comprised twelve articles all constructed to teach the importance of communication in a hospital setting and to discuss the basic skills involved. These articles talk gently and encouragingly of the following principles. In communication, one must convey a feeling of having time, patience and involvement. The language must be appropriate and a basis of trust developed. The communicator must be familiar with patients' needs, be able to pick up cues, give the right kind of information at the right kind of pace and possess such conversational skills as reflection (expressing back to a person the ideas they have just spoken) and clarification. Listening skills need to be well developed in the professional 'communicator' such that inner feelings on the part of the client are allowed expression without blocking or interruption. Then there is the important non-verbal component which also receives full attention. The way one touches another, looks at them, the posture and position adopted and the gestures made, all contribute to the skill of communication. Why do these authors place so much stress on efforts at communication? Primarily because they see it as a buffer against the incubation of fear and confusion, allowing a person to collaborate and follow treatment through in a more relaxed manner. In other words, effective communication is a positive contribution to recovery. The series of articles ends with a set of five principles which I summarise as:

1. Each 'patient' is unique, bringing differing needs and abilities and, therefore, requiring an individual approach.
2. Communication skills are as necessary for the 'ordinary patient' as for those in specialised areas.
3. The type of communication must be assessed in relation to a person's particular state and needs.
4. Essential communication skills must be identified, taught and converted into the norm of professional behaviour.
5. Communication makes demands on the professional. The primary demand is involvement and because of this there must be support.

This and many similar publications are without doubt very positive and useful contributions to the growth of communication skills within the medical and medically-related professions. There is little doubt that training within the profession is sensitising many people to the importance of communicating information to seriously ill or injured people. As you will have probably guessed though, there is, of course, some bad news too. The bad news is this. At the time that I write, if you or I were to be admitted to our local hospital, it is still highly likely that we would find ourselves the victims of poor communication and kept short of the type of information that really matters. Here are some typical examples of what seems to remain commonplace in the average hospital (note the dates which do not encourage the view that this is how things *used* to be).

1. Extract from the *Sunday Times*, June , 1983. A woman is describing her recent experiences in childbirth: 'I never wanted to be treated like a VIP but it was the most important and frightening thing that had ever happened to me and I felt that they just couldn't be bothered.'

At each of her dozen or so ante-natal checks, she was prodded by a different pair of hands. Finally, on the basis of an estimated date, doctors concluded that she was overdue. An induction was recommended and she was told that she was risking her baby's life if she refused.

'I was flat on my back for 20 hours with electronic monitors, drips and then emergency oxygen, because the speed of contractions was causing distress. It terrified the life out of me.'

After a difficult forceps delivery, performed, says Beverley, by a nervous junior doctor, 'My baby was cleaned up, wrapped and handed to me briefly. Then everyone just filed out of the room without a word.

The drip was turned up so high that I was still contracting after the delivery. I found out after that they couldn't just turn it off, it had to be turned down gradually, but no-one would explain why I was in such terrible pain.' The bruising was dismissed by midwives as, 'what motherhood is about'.

2. Richards (1981). Another woman relates her experiences after an accident in the home:

A brief visit from the surgeon dismissed the idea of an operation but revealed that I was to be admitted, and I finally reached the ward six and a half hours after entering casualty. By this time I was unable to take in what was said to me. I was put on complete bed rest and eventually gathered that I had broken the first lumbar vertebra. But it was not until the consultant appeared a week later that the injury itself and some of the possible consequences were explained. I was told that it was a serious injury — the vertebra was completely smashed and I was lucky not to have any nerve damage. I was also told it would be about six weeks before the fracture was sufficiently consolidated for me to move. Three weeks after admission more X-rays were taken of my back. The registrar showed them to me shortly before the consultant arrived, and explained that although the bones were starting to knit together it would be another two or three weeks before I could be moved.

When the consultant arrived late that afternoon, my first impression was that he had enjoyed a good lunch! He glanced at the X-rays, decided they were too dark to see and then announced that I should get up the next day. Having arrived late, he was in a hurry and unwilling to be engaged in discussion. It is, in any case, extremely difficult for a patient lying flat on her back to initiate a conversation, when she is separated by a blanket cage from the group of doctors and nurses talking amongst themselves at the foot of the bed. As common sense and reason, as well as all my earlier information, were against the possibility that my recovery time should suddenly be reduced by half, I decided not to take it seriously.

The next morning I was distressed at the arrival of a brisk physiotherapist announcing that she had come to get me up. Suddenly, all the pent-up anxiety about the possible consequences of things not properly explained focused on what I felt sure was an ill-considered decision. I wept profusely and refused to move until the decision was explained. I was left alone for some time, but later, when I tried to explain my anxiety to the staff nurse on duty, she reproached me as if I were a five year old, at the same time accusing me of childish behaviour.

3. May, 1983. The experience related here was conveyed to me by a young woman who came to see me just an hour before I sat down to write this paragraph – an odd coincidence. She had just been discharged from the local hospital where she underwent minor abdominal surgery to remove an abcess.

I was put in a cubicle after a nurse had taken details and waited three hours before a doctor came. He could barely speak English but he said I would have to go to theatre to have it dealt with. The nurse put me in a bed in an empty side ward at midday. She did not know how long I would have to wait but thought they might want me at about 4 p.m. No-one would or could tell me what was happening. I waited without any further information until 11 p.m. when finally I was told I would be taken to the theatre. I had assumed that the operation would be done under local anaesthetic but suddenly it came out that it was to be a general anaesthetic. I felt very worried – maybe they had mistaken me for someone else, or misunderstood the problem. Nobody would tell me anything definite, it was really quite frightening and frustrating. Looking back on it I feel so angry towards them.

Of course, it is by no means always this bad but clearly there is an odd situation here. Many people qualifying in nursing and the medically-related professions do not know of the importance of clear and regular communication. The objective of good communication seems to be valued and every so often, as described, relevant journals make powerful appeals for improved efforts and improved performance in communication. Yet recent research and the continuing stream of impressions from the present day suggest there is still something going wrong in terms of implementation.

In Chapter 2 we had a look at some theoretical issues accounting for the development of 'professional behaviour' in medicine, which include the psycho-social explanation of why the professions were inclined to be defensive and maintain poor levels of communication. These factors still operate to a varying degree and undoubtedly hold back progress. Even so, when good intentions do exist, things still do not seem to go well.

Let's assume for a moment that we could spend a while in a hospital department where the staff are highly enthused with the ideal of com-munication. They go about work in the usual way, simply trying a little harder with communication. Would we find that the common shortcomings brought to light by various investigations were eradi-cated? Probably not, and indeed this is quite likely to be a transitional state that exists in a good proportion of hospitals today. Many profes-sional staff in hospitals now seem keen to achieve better communica-tion yet there are still obstacles which seem to block the breakthrough. That is, *positive motivation alone is not sufficient, there are practical problems to be overcome before standards of communication truly improve.* Accordingly, it should be helpful to take a quick look at some of these practical problems before launching into a detailed account of the approach which I have called informational care.

Hayward (1975) summarised some very relevant findings given in a Ministry of Health report concerned with communication in hospitals. Blending these with some points of my own, a set of answers can be derived in reply to the question, 'given good motivation towards com-munication in hospitals, where do things still go wrong?' There are five main points:

Inadequate comprehensibility – doctors and nurses often give information to people which is non-usable because it is not in a form which the individual can understand. Various factors influence the chances of good understanding being achieved. Prior knowledge of medical terminology and concepts is clearly important, as are actual intelligence and language or vocabulary differences (that is, the com-municator may have a different style of using language compared with the recipient). When there are major discrepancies of this type, a session of well-meant communication may leave the recipient little better off. This explains why Ley (1982a) reports some of his own surveys revealing that approximately 50 per cent of people interviewed after being given medical information did not understand what they had just been told concerning the diagnosis, aetiology and prognosis of the complaint involved. In psychological terms, this is sometimes referred to as egocentric conversation, that is, the conversational con-tent means a lot to the communicator but not much to the recipient.

Unfavourable context – information may be well presented and comprehensible but that in itself does not guarantee good reception and retention. Anxious people are usually poor listeners with a reduced capacity to take in information or question the person giving the information in order to achieve clarity. Thus, if attempts at com-munication are conducted in a social context which adds *social* tensions

to the anxiety inherent in the situation of illness itself, then comprehension and retention are likely to be reduced. In addition to this,
requests for repetition, consolidation and discussion of the information are harder to make. The terse, socially awkward atmosphere
of a ward round is a typical example of heightened social tension. In
such a setting, the ability of the listener to absorb, understand and
retain information is inevitably reduced. In short, some of the cus-
tomary settings for communication in the hospital are likely to *reduce*
many people's abilities to make use of the communication, the standard
ward round and examination consultation being the two most suspect
situations.

Inappropriate form and quantity — in many non-medical settings,
information which is of significance is recorded in writing as it is ex-
pounded verbally. The decisions of a committee, a pilot obtaining
meteorological information and air traffic details, are good examples.
The information is written down because it is vital and the 'vehicle'
of spoken words alone is inadequate. However, if we were to conduct
a random set of observations upon the transactions within the consulting room or ward round we would find very few people being given
a written summary of the information they have just received. The
information is presented verbally, without diagram and without a
written record to assist the person to remember it. Quite often the
information load may be high, possibly too high, and then without
aids forgetting is inevitable. The reliance on verbal information,
delivered episodically in unpredictable quantity but with predictable
lack of additional aids, is a major hindrance to medical communication.

*No one person has responsibility for co-ordinating and relaying infor-
mation* — in the average hospital the allocation of responsibility to keep
people informed is haphazard in the extreme. Information is presented
piecemeal, sometimes by doctors, sometimes by nurses. There is no one
person who has a special responsibility to check what has been told and
what is known, and who then works to bring a client's level of information up to an appropriate level. It is the 'luck of the draw' which nurse
or doctor you will see, whether or not they will tell you anything
useful, and whether this confirms or contradicts what you have already
been told. Such disorganisation can only be resolved by having particular people assigned to the role of co-ordinating communication and
guaranteeing minimum standards by regular contacts. As long ago as
1963, a Ministry of Health Report, 'Communication between doctors,
nurses and patients', recommended the notion of personal responsibility for giving information. It does not seem important to specify the

profession but the issue is that *someone* should have a clear role in giving information in each individual case.

Added to this problem is the variable quality of communication between doctors and nurses or other professionals. I say variable because each team will have differing strengths in this aspect of professionalism. In some less fortunate examples that I have encountered, the nurses would have been delighted to spend time with people in the wards building up their level of understanding and information, but were impaired because they had no means of getting clear information from medical colleagues themselves. Incidentally, this was not all the fault of the doctors — the nurses had played their part in creating the situation.

Information is 'censored' — because of a reluctance to tell people bad news, there is a general tendency to shelter them by giving only the more favourable bits of information. It is easy to talk of the hopes rather than the fears in a doctor's mind, and it is easier to give estimates of outcome based on things going well rather than the (in many cases) equally likely outcome of things going badly. The motive is benign but the impact can be destructive. When information is 'filtered' to allow only positive aspects to be exchanged, if a case then goes badly, this information will be experienced as misleading, or misconstrued as incompetence on the part of the staff. Either way, it erodes confidence and is another nail in the coffin of high quality, open, honest communication.

Equally, I hope you can see that enthusiastic communication 'binges' are not the real solution. The vital requirement is a change in approach and that requires a basic change in attitude on the part of hospital staff. What are these necessary changes?

Sharing Information: a Contrast between Two Philosophies with a Plea to End ESO Medicine

At this point, some of you may well think that I have gone over the top. I want to highlight the differences between two philosophies of medical care. To do so I will run the risk of offending more traditionally minded readers by stating the characteristics in very strong terms — something of a gamble, but it's worth it.

Unrepentantly and to the annoyance of some colleagues, I hold the view that a stay in hospital should be a *collaborative* venture, that is, the so-called 'patient' will work at the best level of understanding possible to aid the staff in what they are doing, and the staff will work with the person to share information to the highest degree possible, making available the knowledge which allows collaboration. Lastly, the staff will share information with each other. Hardly exceptional, you might think, obviously this is the sort of attitude required in a caring institution. In reality, though, as those of you who work in large general hospitals will know, and as Chapter 2 demonstrates, it does not work quite like this in many of them. There is a wide degree of variation between two extremes. In Chapter 2 I referred to these as caring versus technical medicine. Here, to make the point rather more firmly, I will use slightly different terms. One of the extremes I will term 'collaborative medicine', which emphasises caring and information sharing. The other extreme which was prevalent in the earlier part of the century and clearly still exists in pockets today, is a complex of attitudes which I will describe as 'ESO medicine'.

No doubt you will be curious as to the identity of the abbreviation. It stands for Experts, Servants and Objects. This particular label is used to signify a social system wherein experts (doctors) administer to objects (patients) through the agency of servants (nurses and other para-medical professions). The experts do their own thing and keep their own counsel. Quite often even the servants do not know what they are planning and thinking and the objects certainly do not. There is inevitably resentment and tension from the servants (nurses) to the experts (doctors), and the objects (people) are often wounded by not being given sufficient information to prepare themselves for what is to come, and by discovering significant changes in plans which have been introduced without their prior knowledge or consultation. I will make no claims as to the relative prevalences of the collaborative and ESO approach to medicine. You must judge for yourself. My guess is that many of you will find your own hospital department somewhere in between but will 'know of' an ESO ward or unit. Now to enhance our understanding, let's take on the exercise of considering how ESO medicine can be converted to collaborative medicine (since clearly with my interests, that is the required direction of change).

In developing away from the destructive social order of ESO medicine, the key change has to be towards collaboration and the effective transmission of information is the platform on which genuine collaboration exists. If psychological care is to be introduced during the next few years, a corner has to be turned which involves a significant change in attitudes since psychological care cannot co-exist with ESO medicine. The two are mutually antagonistic. The professions have to mature away from the position wherein full access to information is regarded as a privilege limited to the medical profession and where, for defensive purposes, the medical profession assumes control of the flow of information in order to secure safety from criticism. The ultimate objective has to be an approach which fosters tension-free collaboration between the professionals and users of the hospital service. The core behaviour underpinning this approach inevitably has to be the implementation of procedures which keep staff and clients optimally informed, as opposed to episodically and partially informed, according to the personal whims and patronage of individual members of the medical profession. As Illich puts it, 'information should be a shared property'. I do not want to claim that these ideas are especially original. Ley (1982b), for example, cites trial schemes in which people acted as co-authors with their doctors in writing medical notes. It worked very nicely.

Caring by Informing

After that brief interlude of political exhortation (in which I do hope I did not tread on any sensitive toes), our attention must return to the individual in hospital. The problem for any one of us in a hospital is how to make sense of what is happening and how to build up enough knowledge and information to gain an accurate appraisal of the immediate future with its various medical possibilities. If a member of staff checked what we knew, corrected it, updated it, amplified it as required and actually went and found out answers to questions for which answers were not immediately to hand, we would experience this as a very caring regime. Worry would not be banished but the anxiety generated by *needless* uncertainty would go, and the experience of someone functioning in this way for our benefit would have a very supportive effect. There would be a sense of collaborating with the staff to deal with problems together.

An illustration of this was evident in the case study given in Chapter 1, the case of Alan and the arthrodesis, if you remember. I stressed how isolated he had been with his failing arthrodesis. *He* did not know what was happening. The consultant did. Now this consultant was not an unkind or inconsiderate man but he was reared in the style of ESO medicine which meant that this whole idea of caring by informing was foreign to him. Allow me to re-run a little of the story, telling it as if informational care was being practised. (I will deal just with the phase when he had been sent home after six months in hospital − he was in pain, but still clinging to the idea that time was all that was needed for the bone to fuse. He was, however, becoming rather desperate.)

Instead of the once every six to eight weeks contact with a brief appointment for a physical examination and X-ray, there would have been recognition that to a person in pain, frightened because his operation was not following the expected pattern, two months was far too long a gap to be left without checking on how he was coping and what he believed was happening. He needed contact at least every two or three weeks with someone informed about his case. This member of staff would have gone through and repeated the various thoughts on what might be happening with his hip joint, looked at the X-rays with him again and shared the medical speculations on the future outcome. Honest and frequent communications such as the following: 'The pain is not a good sign and it means that fusion is incomplete – you can see the gaps on the X-ray – we are powerless at this stage to do anything about it at all except encourage you to be patient and comply with the physiotherapist's instructions. Don't give up hope yet – sometimes these wounds do fuse after a long while of not knitting so we are not stringing you along pointlessly. Ideally we will have to give it nine months in plaster, you have done six. We will go on with X-rays every six weeks and watch it carefully with you. It is in my mind that we may well need a second operation to repack the joint with bone chippings taken from elsewhere. If you like, I'll tell you about that now so that you don't get the wrong idea, and I'll just jot down a couple of notes for you to take away as a reminder . . . Being practical I'd say the chances are 50/50 that a second operation will be needed. If on the next X-ray there is no improvement then I'd say more definitely that a second operation will be necessary, but I'll not commit us until the full nine months. I asked you last time to bring a list of any questions or worries you had – do you have it with you? Are you finding the level of pain tolerable – enough to go another six weeks?'

Two or three weeks later that doctor, or another member of the team, for example, a well-informed nurse or physiotherapist, would meet with Alan again to check his understanding of the situation, go through the plan again, discuss any matters arising and check on his general level of morale. This pattern would continue until the medical problem was resolved in order to maintain, correct and update Alan's understanding. With contact of this nature, Alan would have felt cared for and seen that his situation was under control. Also, he would have felt that, inconvenient though it was, the best path was in fact being followed. However, 'normal' hospital routine and behaviour prevailed, allowing (not causing) a situation wherein he felt completely out of touch with his doctors and was bitterly convinced they were not concerned (did not even believe) that he was in so much pain.

This was not, of course, the case — they were aware and it did bother them. Unfortunately, though, the transfer of information was often little better than, 'mmm — I think we will have to give it another six weeks.' The gap between the ideal and the actual in this history indicates that the staff involved could not see how important staying in touch and keeping clients fully informed might be. They were kindly, but unwittingly uncaring. As one of the medical team actually said when the need for this type of back-up was pointed out, 'Where are we going to find the time for these gossip sessions?' I have to tell you that the inability to understand how to care by informing and the failure to invest 15 minutes every two or three weeks in this work made it necessary to provide many hours of psychologist time for Alan, a good number of consultations with his GP, an admission to a casualty department and it certainly created the circumstances in which Alan was risking his life in his own attempts at pain killing and sedation. Furthermore, because the same information-depriving approach had prevailed in the run up to the operation and the following months, Alan's reactions were adverse and the resultant disturbed behaviour probably contributed to the failure of the arthrodesis in the first place — a heavy price indeed.

In case you feel I am being unreasonably critical, please understand that my motive in taking us through the less admirable aspects of this case example is *not to condemn, but to demonstrate in maximum clarity how the absence of informational care risks creating great anguish and causing much greater consumption of professional time in the long run.*

Basic Steps in Informational Care

There is no great mystique involved with the work. It looks after itself if certain vital principles are observed. These are:

1. An identified person is assigned by the director of the medical or nursing team to take *basic responsibility* for providing and maintaining the level of information which a client holds. There is no set level of information required, rather the target adopted is to maintain reasonable levels with adequate understanding in relation to the individual's abilities. This does not imply that one member of staff monopolises the transfer of information, rather his/her job is to check that the client has been, and remains, well informed and to make up any deficits.

2. The work of assessing a person's knowledge and expectations must be emphasised to the same degree as actually giving information, that is, prior to and after the communication of significant information, it becomes standard practice to check what a person knows, how accurate and complete this is, and what expectations they generate from this material. Since the objective is to maintain optimum levels of accurate information, it is necessary to monitor what people actually do with the information they are given. Simply to deliver information without linking this to prior levels of understanding and failing to check back on another occasion to see what and how much has been retained, is a particularly effective way of being ineffectual.

3. The task of giving information should be professionalised (but not, emphatically not, dehumanised). Like any other skill, venepuncture, for example, there is a right way and a wrong way to go about the task. Thus, people involved in giving information should be trained in the role and approach it with a professional attitude. It is quite unacceptable that it be left as an unco-ordinated, amateurish free for all, conducted by people who, although trained in their own field, are actually untrained in the skills of communication. The training is not hard and basically requires the adaption of well known communication skills to the special needs of ill and injured people within the hospital environment.

So now we can turn these general principles into specific aspects of practice. The rest of the chapter will be a briefing on how to run a programme of informational care for the individual client. As we launch into it, let me remind you of one of the findings given in Chapter 2. Ley (1982a), in his extensive review of the research literature on medical information, notes:

1. 'It would appear from survey evidence that the majority of patients wish to know as much as possible about their illness . . . in fact, patients probably want to know more about their medication than professionals would wish to tell them.'

2. 'Those health professionals who do not believe that patients should be informed about such matters as a diagnosis of cancer, the risks of treatment or the risks of investigation, predict that the provision of such information will lead to the following consequences.

a. undesirable emotional reaction

b. reduced compliance

c. anxious over-concern

d. more frequent reporting of the side effects of drugs'

A small number of investigators have attempted empirical tests of these assumptions and in general *found no support for them*. In other words, do not fall victim of the well tried excuse for poor communication efforts, namely the belief that people are better off if they do not know more than is absolutely necessary. It is a myth valid for defensive purposes only.

As in emotional care, the first steps in the preparation for informational care involve *changing you*. This time it is a greater depth of understanding that we are after. It is clear that a tremendous amount of 'informing behaviour' in hospitals is inappropriate in style and dramatically unsuccessful. The professionalisation of information-giving depends on knowing what you are trying to do and why — so often this understanding is the missing ingredient. We must begin by considering two general aspects. Firstly, there are certain psychological characteristics of people *receiving* information in a hospital environment to think about. Here my thoughts are directed to the average person in hospital who fits the description 'seriously ill or injured' and also the close relatives. Secondly, we need to consider certain psychological characteristics of people *giving* information in a hospital environment — primarily doctors and nurses — although you will have realised by now that in the overall scheme of psychological care this will include other professions, these being the social workers, psychologists, physio, occupational and speech therapists who might become involved in psychological care with a proportion of cases.

Important Psychological Characteristics of People Receiving Information in a Hospital Environment

Communications to the ill and injured must take into account the high probability of psychological changes having been induced which alter a person's ability to receive information. Consequently, you cannot go about the task of giving information in an everyday fashion and reasonably expect to have much success. Both the hospital environment and the traumatic circumstances are likely to create the following sorts of impediments.

1. *Dislocation and confusion* — when you have worked in a department or ward for a few months it becomes thoroughly familiar. The geography, social structure, conventions and routines become totally absorbed. Then it is hard to see it as unfamiliar and unknown and all too easy to *project* familiarity, i.e. you experience your clients as finding it familiar and homely as you now do. This projection of

familiarity is misleading. In the first few days of admission (particularly an unexpected admission) or in the first few days of an internal transfer, say, from a ward to an intensive care unit following a kidney transplant, the known world is dislocated and substituted by an unknown (and sometimes alien) world. Then results a state of *confusion* in relation to people, places, routines, norms of interaction and behaviour. This applies especially to those experiencing a first admission to a hospital. As Heatherington (1964) describes:

> When the patient goes into hospital for the first time he has to make a sudden adjustment to a new kind of life. He has to fit in with a new timetable involving a modified sleeping schedule, he may have to adjust to a strange diet, and he has to get used to sharing a dormitory with complete strangers. He may see strange and frightening apparatus being wheeled about on trolleys; he may experience real pain or discomfort for the first time in his life. He may also meet death or disfigurement at close quarters for the first time. He may have to submit to the authority of nurses, some young enough to be his daughters, and will have to submit to the dictates of doctors, many of whom may be his own age or younger. The patient may not know all that is expected of him in the hospital ward. He does not know the rules. Can he smoke or not? Is it 'done' to speak to the man in the next bed? How does he get hold of a newspaper? Is he allowed to get out of bed to go to the lavatory? To whom should he speak about worries concerning his family at home? He may not know who is the appropriate person to ask: indeed he may not have a very clear idea of who is who in the ward. He tends to confuse the consultant and the junior house-physician, the sister and the probationer-nurse. At first he will not have learned what the various uniforms mean. Just because he sees more of the house-physician than he does of the consultant, he may view the former as the doctor-in-charge.

When we absorb information in our everyday world, we are usually absorbing the relatively familiar into the already known. A newly admitted client, possibly of high intelligence and verbal skills but without prior experience of medical environments and language, cannot necessarily do this. A good number of the people will be disoriented and confused in this way, struggling to make sense of what is happening and why, not knowing who is who and what can be expected of the staff. In this state, the ability to make use of medical information is likely to be diminished since it cannot be readily assimilated into aspects of life that *are* familiar to the individual. People need time to learn the language and conventions of hospitals, to incorporate them into a 'known' world.

The extent to which this confusion disables people is enormously variable. Those with past experience of hospitals will have learned how to learn about new hospital environments, the uninitiated are likely to be more handicapped. In general, though, I cannot tell you what proportion of people are affected nor how long such effects persist. All I can do is warn you that you must expect this as a difficulty with new or newly moved clients and build in compensatory elements (specified later) to your informational care work.

2. *Socio-educational gulf* — hospitals are effectively a separate sub-culture. They (necessarily) use a set of concepts and corresponding vocabulary of their own. To participate within this sub-culture, one must either know the language and concepts or have ready access to an accurate translation into familiar terms. The temptation in casual communication within hospitals is to give a short measure in the translation to save time, which means overtly simplified explanations that do not give genuine understanding. What translation, for example, would the wife of a seriously injured man admitted for intensive care in your hospital receive of the following: 'In ITU supported by a ventilator, with cardiac monitoring, an intravenous drip and penile catheter.' For the average citizen, unless there is a good translation of these terms which actually takes into account the level of knowledge, intelligence and verbal ability of the recipient, much of what is told will be meaningless and wasted. The only people to benefit will be the staff who will feel some job satisfaction with the belief that they have kept people informed.

3. *Adverse psychological states* — it is not possible to give precise laws concerning the relationships between psychological state and the ability to listen, absorb and retain information. There is copious research, though, which confirms the obvious, namely that emotional arousal and psychological shock produce an impaired ability to take in new information. A relative in an anxious state of 'information hunger', people who are dazed and frightened with the impact of unexpected entry into hospital, people who are very tense and inhibited during a consultation, victims of illness who are emotionally distraught, angry, driven with a constant fear or an anxiety to resolve problems, people shaken by the disappointment of a medical failure — in all these instances together with the many other forms of emotional reaction

you must expect disruption of the usual processes involved in information absorption. People are less able to listen with full attention, their
attention is fragmented. They become preoccupied and distracted by
an idea or experience of the moment which diverts attention, they find
they cannot follow the full flow of an explanation through, nor take
in details. Later they may be remarkably blank about what has been
said. Even short-term elevation of anxiety can have this disruptive
effect. You can observe this in yourself no doubt (do you remember
how you were affected by anxiety in an oral or practical exam?). Thus,
people in states of emotional arousal require special techniques when
information is being relayed to them.

Other factors may also influence a person's capacity to take in
information. The illness itself may cause deficits, for example, there
is intellectual deterioration accompanying uraemia, while injuries to
the head will often produce confusion and amnesia. Similarly, certain
drugs take the edge off people's intellectual abilities. So do keep this
aspect in mind before you ever begin. Is the person you are about to
inform functioning in a way which impairs the ability to receive
information?

4. *Selective listening and forgetting* – if your experiences follow the
same path as mine then you will be impressed by the power of this
effect. We have established that people in hospital harbour some sense
of threat and often add to this an urgency to return to their own world.
Their listening and remembering, therefore, is interspersed with fears,
fantasies, hopes and strong personal needs. The effect of varied psychological states of this nature is analogous to a filter. Certain information
is easier to listen to and retain than other types, and some information
has a high loss rate for an individual compared with other types. Before
expanding this, I think a short case example will be of help to you.

Case Incident

Tony was a self-employed electrician. He was 34 and had two young
children. He was an extremely self-sufficient man, priding himself on
his ability to deal with the problems of his work on his own, running
his business efficiently and independently. He was ill with influenza
in the month of March last year. He worked on despite being ill, there
being an important job to complete. Two days later he complained of
pains in his back but he continued to work on, clearly finding it increasingly difficult. Then he noticed blood in his urine and became alarmed,
so decided to call in to see his GP. A month later he was taken into a
kidney unit in complete renal failure.

As with most people, the shock of the transition was tremendous. However, Tony was very tightly held in, bringing all his powers of self-reliance to deal with the situation. The nurses described him as brooding, silently angry, spending much time sitting thinking in his room.

After two weeks of conventional peritoneal dialysis, he began training with the bag system of peritoneal dialysis, CAPD. His information on this was standard, being given an overview of the training scheme and the outline plan for conversion to home dialysis in five to six weeks. The staff were reluctant to give exact timing because various obstacles can delay training. Things went well, the habit of self-sufficiency driving him to master the techniques and learn to overcome the snags quickly. However, after a week of training an incident occurred in which he exploded into violent anger. The sister in charge of the unit was chatting about his progress when it came to light that he was expecting to convert to home dialysis at the end of two weeks after the start of his CAPD training. The sister said that this was not possible, it would be at least four. 'But,' he said, 'the nurse told me I would be going in two weeks – you people just change things to suit yourself. The organisation here is disgusting.' (Actually, he said a great deal more, in increasingly vehement terms, but we will not go into that just now.) The poor sister was somewhat taken aback. Only the day before at a review discussion it had been agreed that he would be ready in about three weeks time, making a total of four. She 'knew' no-one had told Tony two weeks. Correspondingly, Tony 'knew' that someone had.

In retrospect it is easy to see what had happened and why it had happened. Tony found that the situation of being in hospital, dependant on others and not knowing much about dialysis treatment, was like being in a cage. He could not exercise his self-reliance – his great defence against anxiety. He was profoundly ill at ease and desperate to get away. He drove himself to achieve this end, learning all he could by talking with the nurses and other patients and fixing in his mind the objective of early conversion to dialysis at home. He found out that one trainee had completed training on the bag system in two weeks and decided that he could manage this too. However, he failed to take sufficient account of the differences in their respective positions, namely that his fellow trainee was converting to CAPD after five years of haemodialysis and was thoroughly well experienced in the ways of life on dialysis, the sterile techniques, dietary principles and so on. Tony, meantime, could expect at least two weeks on conventional peritoneal dialysis and then a training period on CAPD, the *average* length of which was four weeks assuming no complications. He had certainly been told this. It became a clear case of something told does not mean something heard, understood and remembered. One source of the discrepancy between Tony and the sister came from an earlier conversation which Tony had shortly after starting the CAPD training. He had carefully questioned a young nurse helping him with a bag change.

Tony Do people sometimes finish training and go home after two weeks?

Nurse Well, I think some do if they get on very quickly and know what they are doing.

Tony How am I getting on, do you think?

Nurse (sensing both Tony's anxiety and the pressure he was exerting) I think you're doing very well, really, for someone who has only been trying this technique for a few days.

Tony I must get back to my business as soon as possible − do you think they'll let me go at the end of two weeks?

Nurse I don't know, really. It's not for me to say. I should think you might be able to if you keep up like this. You should ask sister or the doctors tomorrow. I'll mention it to them, if you like.

Tony did not hear the qualification in this last reply including the suggestion that he should check with other staff. The next day he told his wife, 'The nurse said I might come home after two weeks.' He fixed this objective in his mind and several days later he 'knew that he had been told that it would be two weeks'. He had blocked out the information given to him as he started the training.

You can see what was happening here. Some of Tony's questioning was manipulative. Through non-verbal means he was signalling the kind of answer he needed to hear. He was then responding only to selected elements of a statement − he was hearing what fed his hopes and soothed his agitation. This selected-out material was remembered with greater ease than the rest. Before long, he 'knew' that certain things were said to him, although in reality this knowledge departed considerably from the original information. There are very few of us who do not function like this from time to time, we hear what we want to hear and memories include certain modifications − it is, should we say, a very human trait. Be that as it may, it is also a very prevalent hazard to effective communication in a hospital setting where there is the catalyst of anxiety and strong personal need.

As you begin to work in this general area, one idea must be burned into your consciousness − *something told does not mean something*

heard, understood and remembered. The information which you give
has to run the gauntlet of the following active distorting processes:

1. The client is *searching* for certain types of communication and
information, for example, reassuring predictions.

2. The client has *powerful expectations* of certain types of information related to angry, depressed, anxious and hopeful fantasies which
will distort the reception and recall of information received.

3. *Blocking* response – an active rejection of information without
conscious awareness that this has happened. The individual simply has
no memory of the communication.

4. Straightforward *forgetting* because the person is either overloaded
with information or because of comprehension problems.

Information Drift

One of the disruptive aspects to communication in the hospital environment is the multiplicity of sources of information – medical staff,
nursing staff, social workers, relatives who have conversed with these,
other people resident in the ward, and so on. Information from differing sources almost inevitably means variations in the theme of important information. The variability together with manipulative inquiring,
seeking alternative views and simple gossip can lead to the erosion of
precise information and a progressive drift away from accuracy, not at
all unlike the party game which predictably goes badly astray.

Important Psychological Characteristics of People Giving Information in a Hospital Environment

You will remember, I hope, from Chapter 2 that the most obvious
failure of information exchange between the medical profession and its
clients is the *lack* of information exchange. The very prevalent habit of
withholding information was accounted for by illustrating how for
purposes of (1) defence against criticism and the exposure of errors,
(2) the maintenance of an absolute power position in relation to the
users of the hospital service, and (3) minimising involvement with the
distress of ill people, the ploy of holding back information has evolved
as virtually standard practice.

To this must be added additional factors including the difficulties of
effective and consistent information exchange resulting from the high
work load carried by the majority of doctors. I imagine that this particular problem has received a sufficient airing already and, since this

book is primarily intended to convey the elements of good practice in psychological care, we must limit any further comment concerning the basic approach of the medical profession to noting likely behavioural characteristics and remaining mindful that these characteristics may be antagonistic to good psychological care. Obviously, our present concern with the provision of information has to take into account this habit of withholding information. However, the idea in this chapter is to assume that a positive motivation to provide good communication and optimal information exchange *does* exist, then to examine what is likely still to go wrong.

Thus, imagine again that we could visit a unit where the doctors and nurses, without further preparation or thought, simply decided to try harder with the business of communication. What would we be likely to discover as the main obstacles to their success in actually giving their clients information? Consider yourself in the following situation. A young woman has been diagnosed as having suffered an episode of illness which has been positively identified as multiple sclerosis. The disease is expected to develop and then she is likely to deteriorate badly over the next two or three years. She does not know this yet, she is sitting facing you and you have the job of saying something in reply to her question asking what the diagnosis might be.

What motives does this fantasy situation stir up in you? Unless you are unusual, there will be a feeling of awkwardness and a need to minimise the impact of the bad news on her. You will probably experience a wish to placate, to reassure, give hope that the next episode will not happen for a long time, maybe never happen. That is how most of us feel; *our* needs are strong in such a situation too. Of course, the young woman does not want, nor will she profit from hearing the outcome of the investigation blurted out in an insensitive way. However that may be undertaken, we will leave the issue of how best to convey such news until later. At this point, I want you to register that for most of us, situations of this type create strong feelings which direct our behaviour. Our 'instinct' is to shelter people from bad news, to offer hope and reassurance as a buffer against distress. Put more directly, our own anxieties in this situation are likely to direct a predominantly evasive and placatory style of communication. An example catches a doctor from our fantasised unit where the effort to communicate is running on goodwill and instinct alone.

Doctor Well, we have had your tests back now and we can't really be certain what is going to happen. So there is no point in worrying too much at present. Certainly you have had some form of nerve disorder which was responsible for the weakness in your legs and arms. There is a chance that your illness might have been an episode of multiple sclerosis. At this stage, though, it is best we think of it as inflammation of the spinal cord. Now, please don't worry yourself unduly. Isolated episodes can occur like this and nothing more happens for years and years. We will just have to see. Still, I'm glad to hear you've picked up a bit over the last week or two.

You will see that the doctor is working hard at slipping in a little information and then negating this by qualification and reassurances. In fact, although this is an invented piece of transcript, it is based on experiences described to me by a young woman, the only difference being that her doctor actually refused to mention the term 'multiple sclerosis' to her, although in a confidential consultation with her mother he gave a positive diagnosis of the disease. Ironically, the family already had experience of it and the woman, together with her parents, had already decided that this was the nature of her illness. The general effect of the doctor's attempt to shelter her was simply to create annoyance and mistrust.

The vital point derived from this example is that the doctor appears kindly and seems to be trying to shelter his client. This was certainly the case, but there was another underlying motive – he was also looking after his own anxieties by avoiding contact with the potential distress of his client. *He 'feared' her distress and so gave a watered-down version of the diagnosis.*

When we are anxious we will avoid the sources of that anxiety if it is possible. Most of us find it difficult to provoke distress and fear in others. It makes us anxious and our natural tendency, therefore, is to avoid actually doing this, hence the great debate in medicine concerning 'whether to tell or not'. This is no real debate, in fact, and as Ley (1982a) stated research clearly shows that the vast majority of people want full, honest medical information (backed up, I will add the plea, with emotional care). However, the resistance to this view and the projection that the truth will be destructive, goes back to the fact that *we, the professionals, are the people with a problem as much as our clients. Many of us find it hard to endure their reactions to distressing information and so resort to the various evasive strategies of holding back information, 'filtering' information and giving placatory, reassuring statements which create false hopes. In short, one of the most common characteristics of those giving information in a hospital environment is that of being governed by an anxiety about creating anxiety.*

In a similar vein I should mention how individual psychodynamics influence information exchange. Much written here is in the manner of generalisations. Obviously I cannot qualify everything said to take account of the vast range of personal psychology to be found in hospital staff. One law can be given though. You *do* have a personal psychology and it *will* affect your approach to information-giving. Therefore, the better you become aware of your own characteristic fears, identifications and projections, the easier you will find it to professionalise information-giving without losing your humane rapport. How, for example, do you react to a client who makes you feel guilty or who has a challenging, accusing, rather awesome persona? Would you distort information to cope with your needs in such encounters? How do you respond to clients whose illnesses evoke in you fears for your own future? Various of our case examples come to mind. They are likely to provoke powerful and threatening thoughts of identification:

'I might become like this and need to have my breast removed.'

'I might develop multiple sclerosis like this and lose my job.'

'She reminds me of my wife — she could develop this.'

Such thoughts may not even be entertained consciously, but because they have a genuinely threatening impact, many of us will want to push them away, to deny the risk. We may remain unaware of having done so, but if we analyse our conversations with clients there we will find evidence of *our* denial.

'Don't worry about it, I'm sure that your husband will not react as badly as that.' (To the woman facing a mastectomy, by a male doctor who worries in case his own wife develops a tumour.)

'We will not use the term "multiple sclerosis" at the moment, better to think of it as an inflammation of the nerves.' (To the person diagnosed as having multiple sclerosis from a doctor whose mother developed the disease.)

With such communication, there is a very high possibility that we are expressing our own denial and own hopes without being aware of doing so.

Lastly, in the fantasised ward which we are visiting there is likely to be a general failure in everyday practice to check on what a person actually knows, what he is capable of understanding and what he has been able to remember. In other words, there is a proneness to be out of touch with the person being informed, whereupon the likelihood increases that the wrong type and quantity of information will be given at the wrong time. Of course, if you are involved in emotional care work it will eliminate much of the risk, since you will be in much closer contact with your clients and be better placed to judge how much they can take and what kind of material they can assimilate.

Thus, taking an overview, it is important to realise how your schooling in your professional work and how your own needs as a person will shape your tendencies in giving information. If you have no knowledge of yourself in this area you will be like a boat drifting in a strong tide — without knowing that the tide exists.

The Basic Practice of Informational Care

Informational care depends heavily on a system of co-operation between the staff involved with any one client. Unless the system of co-operation exists, then consistent and high quality information exchange will always break down. Let me, therefore, list the properties of the setting which I believe will foster good informational care. Were you to have the luxury of being employed in such a setting, this is what you would find.

1. You will actually be assigned as the person *co-ordinating* informational care for specific clients. Other nurses, doctors or para-medics will similarly be assigned to other cases. It will be clearly known who is working with who.

2. It will be agreed by the medical staff and sister-in-charge that your role will be that of an 'agent acting on behalf of your clients' in terms of providing and acquiring information.

3. You will be expected to monitor the level of information and understanding achieved by your clients and carry the responsibility of maintaining this, either by personal intervention or by arranging for one of the other staff to provide the necessary material.

4. You will have good support in that the medical staff in this ideal ward will be well aware of the damaging effects of information deprivation. They will be positively motivated to assist you in your responsibility with your various clients (and will expect a reciprocal assistance from you in relation to their own informational care work). They will comply with requests to give additional or repeat information either to you or directly to your client as seems best.

5. The medical staff will recognise that as the medical decision-makers, they have a vital responsibility in keeping *you* informed of their general thoughts, intentions, changes of plan and treatment strategies, that is, regularly updating you on what is happening. Wherever possible, this will be *in advance*, not in retrospect. The effort to

inform other staff on the part of the medical team will form a highly significant contribution to the system. In recognising this, the doctors will *work* at keeping you informed and you will not have to pursue them for information or find yourself being treated condescendingly as if you were party to a considerable favour. All staff will work to contribute and make available their information to facilitate the programme of care. The task is not onerous – many other types of organisation achieve this.

6. You will have time allocated for this work (it will not be a heavy demand) in order that you will not have to combine the regular duties of this work with the other aspects of your nursing role.

Such is the *ideal* setting. Maybe I'm depressing you. I know that very few of you, if any, will actually find this kind of atmosphere in the hospitals of the present day. However, it helps to specify the ideal since progress towards truly effective programmes of informational care will depend on co-operation and integration and you are the people to bring about these changes. As the nursing and other professions expand their commitment to psychological care, it will begin to happen – attitudes will change. They are already doing so, in fact.

Giving Informational Care

May we work now on an exercise which draws these principles together? Assume that we have to design a programme of informational care suitable for clients newly admitted to a typical hospital unit. How should this be conducted? I will present one last case based on my own work with people in kidney failure as the background to an extended example. By the way, if you feel that there is an over-emphasis on kidney failure, it is worth pointing out that the actual identity of the illness is unimportant since the basic approach will be the same for most areas of medicine. Should you in your own work actually care for surgical cases, diabetics, accident trauma cases, leukaemia victims, people with eye disorders or whatever, you will readily be able to adapt the main substance of this example to suit your own type of work. However, for the next few pages, you work in a kidney unit.

We have been advised by the consultant nephrologist that one Carol Morris is likely to need dialysis treatment within about six months. The date is vague, however. The situation is as follows. Carol, a 31-year-old mother of two young children, complained two months previously to her GP of pain in her kidneys and blood in her urine. The doctor gave her antibiotics, took a urine sample and asked her to return in a week. She was not able to report much improvement on her second visit. A blood sample was taken. The blood analysis revealed levels of urea and creatinine which alarmed the doctor. Her kidneys appeared to be failing. He told Carol that she had a serious kidney condition and that he wanted her to see a specialist straight away. This was her wish too since she was feeling pretty rough and was becoming worried. The nephrologist saw her three times in all and diagnosed a rapidly progressing glomerulonephritis. Appropriate drug therapy was given in an attempt to contain the disease and improve her blood condition. It was, however, just a holding strategy. The expectation was that the kidneys would continue to deteriorate and dialysis would be needed some time in the next six to nine months, the earlier date being more likely.

The consultant, as a contributor to the Unit's scheme of informational care, conveyed this information to Carol in a gentle but non-evasive way. He asked her to begin domestic preparations so that she could reside in the Unit for about eight weeks (assuming no complications) at a time to be decided according to the rate at which her kidneys deteriorated. He gave her a brief outline on the nature of dialysis and the various events to come, including her training for independent dialysis using the continuous ambulatory peritoneal dialysis (CAPD) method. The meeting ended with the doctor telling Carol that the nursing staff at the Unit would be advised of her position and would make contact *in advance* of her admission. With that, he formally advised the sister-in-charge to expect Carol to join the CAPD training scheme within the next nine months.

This is where you come in on the story because the sister has just asked if you will accept the assignment to deal with Carol's psychological care. As your supervisor in these matters, I said yes before you could get a word in. Our attention here is solely on the informational care aspects of your work with Carol, although in reality you would offer emotional care and counselling as required.

We must begin by planning out the informational care programme. The first job is easy, sketching out the framework of contacts. These are best planned as different phases, viz:

1. *Pre-admission contacts* — normally two sessions of about an hour's duration will be needed, one early on in Carol's waiting period and a second when she is getting near to admission. (NB: There is a very great deal to explain in circumstances of kidney failure. With other

types of illness and treatment 15 minutes may well suffice.)

2. *Admission contact* – this will occur as soon after admission as is possible for us and suitable for Carol (she may be too ill initially). The length of the meeting will vary with circumstances.

3. *Post-admission contacts* – here we must operate on an 'as and when required' basis related to Carol's general progress, medical problems, informational input from other staff, etc. On average, we should allow 15 to 20 minutes once or twice a week.

The general objective of these meetings is not to monopolise information exchange. We expect all the medical and nursing staff to 'care by informing'. *Our job is to monitor the level of understanding and information and maintain it at adequate levels.* We need Carol and her husband to understand what has happened and what is going to happen, thus enabling them to follow the progress and problems through and collaborate with the staff. We want to insulate them from the destructive experiences brought about through inadequate information, thereby minimising anxiety, confusion and anger. The tendencies towards information drift must also be opposed. Lastly, we must make sure that they are not vulnerable in that they could be traumatically surprised by complications and changes in plan of which *they* have no prior knowledge. Obviously, you cannot go through the book – this forewarning has to be limited to common problems. Everyone knows, for example, that Carol has a 50 per cent chance or more of contracting peritonitis in the first three months and that this might require a period of emergency haemodialysis, so setting her training back. *She* should know this too, since advance information allows preparation (information should be a shared property).

The work in these various phases is basically the same, therefore we will take as the main illustration the pre-admission contact period. These particular meetings form the foundation of preventative informational care. In an hour you can do much to prevent months of worry and doubt. You begin by writing to Carol inviting her to attend the Unit with her husband during the interim period before admission. Your letter explains that they will be shown around the Unit and meet with some of the staff and people training in dialysis. After that they will have a meeting with you to receive more information.

Your job in this first session is to check what they have retained from the consultations with the nephrologist and then set about consolidating and amplifying this knowledge as seems appropriate. You will carry in your mind the following objectives. Firstly, the Morris's will be given a further explanation of the work kidneys do, why Carol's have failed and how peritoneal dialysis works to simulate kidney function. This will be kept basic but adequate since they will be exposed to much new information on this visit. Simple reading material will be given for them to study in their own time. You will then explain and write down the broad outline of events which will take place during Carol's first week of treatment. The initial event will be the minor operation for the insertion of the peritoneal catheter. Levels of pain, location of the operation, type of anaesthetic and her feelings after the operation will be detailed. You will go on to say that shortly after the insertion of the catheter, Carol will receive 36 hours' continuous dialysis with 60 litres of dialysate fluid being passed through her abdomen during this time. The sensations produced by this treatment will be clearly described. You will continue by illustrating the events after this initial dialysis − how Carol will change to dialysing nightly for a week, with 20 litres of dialysate being passed through her abdomen during each eight to nine hour session, after which dialysis will be decreased to alternating nights. You will explain that as well as improving the condition of the blood, this concentrated dialysis is also meant to create some stretching of the abdominal wall in order that two litres of dialysate fluid can be run into the abdomen without discomfort.

Lastly in this first meeting, you will give Carol and her husband brief details of the conversion to the bag system. They need to understand that there is much more to learn than may be covered in this first meeting, but you do not want to give them too much information at once. They will be learning steadily for three months or more. These two people have no background in medicine and they may need patient coaching with some of the ideas. It is vital that they be given time to formulate questions and express anxieties.

We have allowed about an hour for this visit, during which time they will be faced with a great deal to absorb. Thus, we must be mindful of the objectives of caring by informing and the need to 'professionalise' the work. We wish them to understand and retain meaningful, usable information and must, therefore, use language which they can follow, progress at a pace which suits their capacity to learn and avoid creating an atmosphere wherein they become inhibited and pretend to understand instead of feeling free to question when they do not. Above all, there must be an ever present awareness on your part that 'something told does not mean something heard and understood'. To counter the various obstacles against effective information exchange, I suggest that you use an approach to communication which I will term *monitored information exchange*. It is very simple. Information is broken down into manageable packages and with each package you go through the following cycle − initial check/information exchange/final accuracy check. Use the mnemonic IIFAC to remember it by, that is, I (initial check), I (information exchange) and FAC (final accuracy check). The activity during each element of the cycle is as follows:

Initial Check (1) − check what is already known or expected in relation to the information package being dealt with. Do not just ask clients if they have previously been told something − have them actually state the information back to you so that you can assess it for accuracy and completeness.

Information Exchange (1) − where there is some knowledge, correct and extend this as is necessary in order to achieve an adequate level of information. Where there is no knowledge, start at the beginning. Use diagrams and make simple notes for the clients as you go along. (*You* make the notes − being under some load, your clients may well make bad notes.) In long sessions use a tape recorder and give them the cassette to take away and play through at home, or on the ward, for that matter.

Final Accuracy Check (FAC) − once you have delivered a package of information and dealt with questions, *check again* − do not just ask your clients if they understood − have them repeat back the information and assess its accuracy. Coach them again in the elements which have been blocked, forgotten or misunderstood.

Now, perhaps, we should eavesdrop on some typical moments in this work.

Case Example A

Carol and her husband have completed their viewing of the Unit and you have settled down with them in the office for their 'pre-admission briefing'. In your letter of appointment you asked them to confirm their attendance, and say whether or not they possessed an audio tape player and would bring a cassette in order to record the briefing. They gave affirmation to both of these and brought with them a one-hour cassette which is running on the Unit machine. You also have notepaper to hand for written material (ideally you will be able to give them a small file with pre-printed dialysis literature which the Unit will inevitably have) and a notebook so that everything may be kept together. 'And who will pay for this?' do I hear? Put it this way, if Carol survives ten years she will have run through many thousands of pounds or

Figure 5.1: IIFAC — The Basis of Good Information Exchange

I	Initial information check
	↓
I	Information exchange (suitability, quantity, aids)
	↓
FAC	Final accuracy check

dollars in medical expenses. Clearly the Unit budget can stand the price of a few files and notepads. We should not, taking counsel from our past, sink the ship for a halfpenny worth of tar.

You have made sure that they are both adequately relaxed and capable of giving attention to the content of the session. Do not press on regardless if they are not. There is no point in giving information if people are not in a state to receive it. Another time will have to be found for them. Assuming everything is favourable, give them the following orientation. All clients of the Unit have a special relationship with one nurse (or social worker, physiotherapist, etc.) who looks after their personal needs and acts as a counsellor. This person is also responsible for keeping them fully informed. Introduce yourself as *their* nurse-counsellor. Then go on to start the first session thus:

Nurse I am going to go through the important aspects of kidney failure and give you some information on how dialysis treatment works and how you must be made ready for it. I will also be giving you a diary of the events occurring in your first week after admission here. I know that you've been told some of this before but I don't know which aspects and whether you've been able to remember it all. What I'll do is split everything up into convenient parts and before we go through each one, I'll ask you what you've been told and what you remember of it. This makes it easier for me to start off at the right place and do a good job. Don't worry at all if you've forgotten things that Dr Thomas told you or if you don't find them clear — it's going to take some time before you get it all straightened out and at this phase it would be ridiculous of anyone to expect you to have remembered much because it's all so unfamiliar.

Thirty minutes later the briefing is well under way. Carol and her husband are moderately at ease and seem to have coped with the basics of kidney function and dialysis. Now you will move on to the next unit of information, that is, the insertion of the abdominal catheter. As always throughout informational work, use the IIFAC cycle (initial check/information exchange/final accuracy check).

I (initial check)

Nurse Right, so we've gone through how they decide when you need to start dialysis. You understand that eventually you'll have a date to come in here, but no-one knows when this will be because we can't say exactly how long your kidneys will take before they stop working completely. So, do you recall what will happen first when you come in?

Carol Well, obviously I have to go onto those machines that we saw in the long stay area.

Nurse Do you need any preparation?

Carol Dr Thomas said I had to have an operation.

Nurse Yes, that's correct. What have you been told about the point of the operation? Do you have any details like how big it is, where it will be done and what kind of anaesthetic will be used?

Carol Oh dear, I think you were right when you said we'd forget things. I know the doctor explained some of it to me but that was three weeks ago. I have a plastic tube inserted into my stomach for the peritoneal machine to work. He said it would be a small operation, I think. I don't know much more – is it done in the main hospital?

I (information exchange)

Nurse Alright. You have the most important piece of information so let's go through the details now. I've brought along the plastic catheter for you to look at. You understand that the dialysis machine pumps fluid in and out of your body cavity – it does this through one of these tubes. Take a look at this diagram. Here, you see, the tube just lies in your body cavity against the intestines – it doesn't go into any organ at all – and the fluid is pumped in so that it surrounds the organs. The operation you will have is to place the tube in position in the abdomen and stitch the outer end into your skin.

Firstly, you'll be given a drug to make you relax – a pre-medication, it's called. This will be an hour or so before the operation. Then you'll go into our procedures room, which is like a small operating theatre. I'll take you along for a look at it before you go. You don't leave the Unit for this operation. Once you're settled, you'll be given a 'local' anaesthetic. Normally this is the only part that actually hurts at all. You'll have four or five injections of the anaesthetic fluid under your skin near to your navel. The first one will sting, nothing too desperate, rather like a dental injection. You'll feel the fluid stretching your skin. After that, the skin stops feeling pain and the other injections will not sting so much. It's very important to remember that this injection just stops you feeling pain, it doesn't stop you feeling pressure and skin sensations and, of course, you'll stay awake for the whole of the operation. When the area is numb, the doctor will make a two- or three-inch cut in the skin and muscle — don't forget, you'll feel no pain but *will* feel his movements. He'll then feed the tube through the cut to meet the lining of your abdomen which is called the peritoneum. This is very tough tissue and to get the tube through, he'll ask you to tense your abdominal area. He'll then push down on the tube. It'll seem like a heavy push to you and there will be a feeling like something suddenly giving as it goes through. I'm told it's an odd experience but it doesn't hurt and no damage will be done.

Lastly, he'll continue to feed the tube through and then stitch your skin up around the dacron collar at its end. The wound will be cleaned up and you'll go back to your room for your first peritoneal dialysis. In all, it should take 20 to 30 minutes once he begins the anaesthetising. Have you got any questions yet or is there anything you'd like me to go over again or explain more clearly?

Carol Show me where he makes the incision.

Nurse Probably just here, to the left and just below the navel.

Husband She gets a bit nervous with injections — she might faint on you.

Nurse The drug Carol will have before the operation should make her relaxed and happy. If she's still tense, though, she can ask for more. We'll check carefully . . .

FAC (final accuracy check)

Nurse Right then, let me see if anything I told you was unclear or if it was too much to take in at once. Imagine that I'm one of your relatives. Explain to me what the operation is about and how it's to be done.

Carol I can't do it as well as you.

Nurse Don't look at it that way, as if it's an exam. I just want to check how clear *I* was to you and make sure that you've the right information to take away.

Carol Alright. I would tell her that I have to undergo a small operation to have a plastic tube called a catheter inserted in my abdomen. This is to let fluid in and out. The operation starts with a local anaesthetic . . .

Nurse What about the pre-med?

Carol Oh yes, I have a relaxing drug first then a series of local anaesthetic injections in the skin to the left of my navel. These might hurt at first but they take effect quickly and I won't feel anything.

Nurse Not quite — the injections just stop you feeling pain. You'll feel everything else.

Carol Right, I remember. After that, an incision is made . . .

You must work away at this final check, teaching again any 'foggy patches'. Satisfy yourself on the quality of your information. *Be professional, care by informing properly and checking your own work.* Note that if you have given sufficient visual and auditory aids there is no special need for your client to remember everything at this stage. In this particular case, Carol has notes and a tape recording. Remembering it all is not important as long as she plays the tape through to reacquaint herself with the material and glances through your notes. Failing to understand or getting it wrong *is* important, though, and this is what you must eradicate in the final accuracy check. Despite your efforts, by the next time you meet Carol, the forces of selective listening and recall, information drift and so on, may have blurred some of your information and you will almost certainly need to rework some of the material.

Interlude

Let's just take a moment between examples for a couple of short anecdotes which demonstrate the opposite of informational care, and show how thoroughly professional people are often bungling amateurs at the task of communication and information exchange. These are both events which occurred during the months that I have been writing this book and whose accuracy I have checked.

1. Mrs W (a nursing sister as it happens) elected for minor surgery to remove a varicose vein in her leg. The surgeon came to see her before the operation, briefed her on what he planned to do and went away secure in the knowledge that 'she had been told'. Sadly, half an hour before his visit, the staff nurse had given Mrs W her pre-medication drug. After the operation, Mrs W asked the nurse, 'Did Dr S come and see me before the operation or was it a dream? I haven't the least idea what he said to me if he did come.' Had the surgeon checked on her state to receive information and checked again after the information exchange, he would have gone away thinking, 'She has not been told — I left it too late.'

2. Mrs N developed shingles on her face; it spread to her left eye. She arranged to see an eye specialist privately since the local hospital could not give immediate assistance. On meeting the specialist, he discovered her eye to be substantially damaged by the shingles with raised pressure and iritis as complications. He said, 'I will admit you and see what I can do but don't hold out too much hope.' While he

talked at length on the condition of the eye, he gave no more information on the actual events to come in hospital. Then followed two days
of near terror for Mrs N who was highly anxious concerning any form
of medical attention and was left alone to face the full range of horror
fantasies concerning operations on the eye. On admission, her nurses
knew little more about what would happen than she. They made no
attempt to find out either. One of them did say, however, that maybe
she would be given an injection into the eye the next day. Mrs N spent
the night awake in an anxiety state. Nobody meant her any harm, of
course. They were, to be frank, just clueless about how to care by
informing. Incidentally, the woman was 70 and had a history of heart
damage. There was a real risk that the induced anxiety could have put
her into heart failure.

Case Example B

I want to illustrate two aspects of informational care which merit special
emphasis. Firstly, there is the idea of *preparing people for likely complications*, and, secondly, *your role as the person who finds things out
on behalf of your client*.

Carol has come back for her second pre-admission briefing with you.
Part of your task today is making sure that she understands the
common problems resulting from the insertion of the peritoneal
catheter and subsequent dialysis. Her family will cope better if they
have contingency plans and do not become drawn into inflexible beliefs
that suggest a reliable timetable of events.

I (initial check)

Nurse Have you any information to do with common problems after
the operation and during the first few weeks of dialysis?

Carol No, none at all. I didn't know that there was any, to be
honest.

I (information exchange)

Nurse Well, to be equally honest, it would be unrealistic to expect any
side of medicine to be problem-free. We have our fair share of difficulties in renal medicine. I want to tell you about them so that if you
do run into one or the other of the common problems then you won't
be surprised, or feel that we've let you down. I'll write them out as a
list and tell you about each one. Firstly, the end of the catheter may
become obstructed either because it has slid into a poor position and
is blocked by the intestines, or because the end has become clogged

with omentum (tissue which sometimes grows round foreign matter). This is in no way dangerous but will mean that the catheter has to be re-positioned in a second similar operation. The chances of needing a second operation are about 50 per cent. Very occasionally there have to be three attempts before things are right. Sometimes there are diffi- culties with the other end of the catheter, where the dacron collar forms a joint with the skin. This can leak and the dialysate fluid seeps out during dialysis. Again, this usually leads to a re-positioning opera- tion. Also, about one in five of our people develop infections at the site — these will be treated by antibiotics.

Another very common problem is peritonitis. What happens here is that bacteria or fungal organisms manage to get inside the abdominal cavity and the lining (the peritoneum) becomes infected by them. Even with apparently fastidious sterile techniques this can still happen. We would love to be able to prevent it but at the moment it's not possible. If you develop peritonitis, you'll have a very high temperature, severe abdominal pains and will generally feel unwell. It's not pleasant, I'm afraid. It's treated by strong antibiotics run in with the dialysate fluid and you'll also be given painkillers. So you see, Carol, when you make your plans for going home after training, you must be flexible and bear in mind two things. Your chances of getting peritonitis during training are about 50 per cent, that is, one out of every two trainees develop it. If it occurs it will *delay* your training. Occasionally people with resis- tant forms of peritonitis have to convert to haemodialysis for a while. This interrupts your training and will delay your change to home dialysis by maybe six weeks or more. Fortunately this doesn't happen to many people. That's about it, I'm glad to say. Do you have any questions?

Having completed the information exchange, you will, of course, monitor your success in communicating these facts with the FAC (final accuracy check). The task, you can see, is quite simple. Instead of a conspiracy of silence or adoption of the myth, 'the less they know the less they worry', you draw people in on the event by sharing informa- tion in order that they can make advance preparations. They will worry, naturally. It is, after all, a worrying situation to be in but it will be productive worry, preparing themselves emotionally and allowing imaginary rehearsals for the events should they ever occur. Whenever you can, do give advance information. With surgical cases, for example, tell people in advance of the type and severity of pain they will have to deal with. Do not try and protect them by hiding information. All you are doing is making them more vulnerable, but *do* make sure that the advance information is complete and includes an indication on how likely problems are dealt with.

The second aspect to be emphasised is the function I have termed 'acting as an agent on behalf of your client'. Once again, the principle is exceptionally simple. Your job is to keep your client informed at an optimum level. If he asks something or it becomes clear that a piece of information is important and you do not have the information, take positive steps to obtain it. This is why goodwill on the part of medical colleagues is important.

For example, it is now three weeks after her admission and Carol has indeed contracted peritonitis. In times of crisis like this she will be frightened and will need regular short visits from you to keep a good check on what she knows and is expecting to happen. You have looked in for one of these brief visits:

Carol The ward round was rushed this morning and I didn't get much chance for questions. How long will it be before I can go back onto peritoneal dialysis?

Nurse I don't know at the moment. I'll ask Dr Thomas at the meeting this afternoon how he thinks the peritonitis is responding to treatment. I'll ask him to give me his estimate for the best possible and worst possible outcomes in your case.

(Later)

Nurse Hello, Carol. I've just looked in for a second. Dr Thomas thinks that at the worst you'll have to stay on emergency haemodialysis for another week. Yesterday morning's specimen was quite encouraging, though, and his most optimistic guess is one more haemodialysis session then back to CAPD. So, somewhere between two days and a week. I've written that down for you to show your husband.

Overview

If you were the master of a trawler you would have in mind the central task of getting to where fish are located, catching them and transporting them to a place where you could find a buyer. There would be no rigid rules or procedures. You would be flexible and organise your affairs in relation to the weather, disposition of fish, crew availability, market state and so on. In a similar vein, when you take on informational care work with your clients, you must work intelligently in relation to the adopted task, following a course with each individual which keeps them informed throughout the various stages of their illness. The work cannot be rigidly timetabled or rule bound to any extent — it must follow the flow of medical events. Maybe Carol will develop peritonitis, maybe she will not. A few weeks after changing to home dialysis, she might be offered a transplant and even if this is initially successful, it could fail at any time. Each new medical event needs information and, since it will bring with it a variety of outcomes, there will be a need for preventative advance information. Your own clients, like Carol, will need to know of the likely procedures and complications confronting them, the physical experiences, social disruption and the most/least favourable estimates of outcome. It is, though, *your responsibility* to organise the interventions. You must think for your clients, bear the burden of decision and conduct your task with professional thoroughness at all times. Each person's needs will differ and you must be pragmatic and thoughtful. If you are good at your job, you will be making a major contribution towards your clients' well-being and they will be cared for in a more complete sense.

6 COUNSELLING

The third element of psychological care you may remember from Chapter 3 was declared to be counselling. This is an activity which lies somewhere between the relatively non-intervening approach of emotional care and the in-depth, highly interventionist approach of formal psychological therapy. No-one, of course, is going to expect you to become overly involved with your clients to a point which approaches psychological therapy. It would not be appropriate since you presumably are not trained for it. However, competent workers in psychological care *will* have basic counselling skills, and psychological care will for them be an intermixture of emotional and informational care together with basic counselling. Our last major task then is to throw some light on the nature of counselling.

We have, at the beginning, to deal with a problem of ambiguity to do with the term 'counselling'. As used in this context, it refers to a way of assisting people with human problems which do not lend themselves to instant solution by simply passing over information or structured guidance. In other words, the focus of concern is on personal dilemmas, basic conflicts, relationship struggles to which there are no immediate answers or dependable codes of right and wrong. However, it is not unusual to hear, for example, of legal counselling, careers counselling or sexual counselling, activities which are all very much concerned with giving information, advice and being fairly directive. It is, therefore, important to develop a clear picture of the different forms of counselling and not to confuse the styles. Can we find an agreed definition of counselling to help in this confusion? I will compromise and give you a composite definition drawn from a variety of sources:

> Counselling is a technique concerned to help people help themselves by the development of a special relationship which leads a client into a greater depth of self-understanding, clarifies the identity of problems and conflicts and mobilises personal coping abilities.

The 'Basics' of Counselling

You may already have noticed that this is not a long chapter, whereas counselling is clearly a large topic. The explanation for this discrepancy is that there already exist some very effective books which devote themselves to showing how the definition given above may be turned into reality. Frankly, there is no point in my treading over the same ground at length. It is important that you go through one or more of these texts (detailed later) and also seek some live, face-to-face training. However, we must at least dispel the mysteries of counselling and resolve exactly what is done and said in a typical session of counselling associated with the psychological care of a physically ill person.

A counsellor and client engage directly in conversations centred on the issues which the client finds problematic. Examples of these would be the woman who finds herself distracted with self-blame when, after years of assistance from a gynaecologist, she still fails to become pregnant, or the man who knows he should make the effort to maintain social contact after a stroke has affected his speech but he wants to hide away. With such difficulties, the target in counselling is to enable clients to achieve a new understanding of themselves and to see new perspectives in the situations they face. In other words, there will be personal education. At the same time, the client will experience being truly listened to, feeling truly understood and will benefit from a supportive relationship.

In my hospital work, it is a not infrequent experience to hear staff of one profession or another saying something like, 'that person needs counselling'. A little investigatory probing reveals that the concept in their head is usually in the order of 'letting them talk about their problems and giving them handy bits of advice'. Such notions reveal a serious ignorance of the subtle skills and targets of counselling, I fear. The counselling conversation is not an ordinary, everyday conversation. It has special features designed to remove certain aspects of everyday conversation and to emphasise others which may not normally be present. This is why some basic training in counselling skills is important since, even with the best will in the world, sitting down to 'do counselling' simply on the basis of trying to be helpful will often lead to a sterile outcome. Thus, we should begin by being clear on what counselling is not about by listing a few common erroneous notions:

Common Misconceptions of Counselling

1. Counselling is *directly* concerned with making people less emotional, or even stemming emotion.

2. Counselling involves giving direct advice to clients or attempting to solve their problems for them.

3. Counselling involves challenging a client's feelings and perceptions in order to impose one's own values and perceptions – these having the feel of being more realistic or accurate.

4. Counselling is an activity which may be instigated in order to satisfy *our* need to make people feel and function better (this is a felt misconception rather than one which is consciously thought).

In fact, if you regard these not just as misconceptions but also hold them as taboos in counselling then you will avoid some of the more serious errors too – which is a rather more significant achievement.

The Targets in Counselling. Taking things a step further, while you are studiously refraining from giving out advice or persuading people to see things your way, you will, of course, be engaged in the positive acts of counselling. Egan (1975) has set out a useful, three-stage scheme to explain what these are. The stages unfold in the following way:

Stage 1 – exploring and clarifying the problem situation
People turn to counsellors when things have gone badly and they are confused and distressed. Quite often, though, they will not be truly clear about what exactly is disturbing them, but are only able to report the consequences, such as agitation and depression. Thus the special working relationship formed in counselling is focused progressively on encouraging in-depth 'self-exploration', so expanding the client's contact with his personal feelings and perceptual habits. This in turn leads to a clarification of the nature of the difficulty.

Stage 2 – setting goals based on dynamic understanding
This is perhaps the phase of counselling which might be described as educational. The client is drawn into piecing together the discoveries from Stage 1 and generating a clearer picture of himself and others in the problem situation. This process includes what is called the 'dynamics' of the situation, that is, the psychological forces (motives, needs, fears, blocks, etc.) which have emerged from the discussion. In other words, a deeper understanding is achieved, including perhaps recognition of issues which previously have been blocked from conscious awareness. Again, it must be stressed that the client is led to

make these insights himself, he is not lectured at or persuaded into acceptance. *Counselling brings out what is already within.* Egan's style is very much action-oriented and so the end point of this stage is the use of acquired personal knowledge to declare targets or goals for change and resolution.

Stage 3 – facilitating action

The targets declared by people will vary enormously. For some they will be highly concrete, such as making headway with the business of social rehabilitation after a long, disabling illness. For others, the targets will be less concrete, say, achieving acceptance after the loss of a body part or the beginning of an illness which narrows life down. Whatever the nature, the counselling relationship is used to help the individual into change. Reappraisal, confronting awkward issues, taking initiatives, seeking ways out of an impasse, and testing out the reality of feared situations become the final focal point of attention.

From this you can gain the general feel of counselling. It is not in-depth therapy. Diagnosis of personality or psychodynamic features plays no real part. It is a limited, supportive activity aimed at developing a person's understanding and placing him or her in a position where it is possible to decide upon and initiate constructive change. The counsellor is active in creating the special relationship and atmosphere of the sessions, but his or her input is subtle, drawing the client towards greater personal insight. The effect is intended to be that of a catalyst.

No doubt, you will be curious about the special style of conversing and the special atmosphere of which I have spoken. These are the product of what normally goes under the heading 'counselling skills'. Once more, I will draw up a list with brief explanations to illustrate these. Some of them will be familiar since they are identical to those needed in emotional care.

Counselling Skills. In any reasonable training course you will be taught and encouraged to rehearse the following skills (these are illustrated in the extended example given later).

Provision of the working inter-personal relationship – as in the other elements of care, the all-important foundation stone to effective counselling is the manner in which the counsellor relates and interacts with the client. The atmosphere needs to be non-anxious, non-threatening, without the sense of being forced. This means, of course, that the counsellor must genuinely be relaxed in the situation and free from personal tension and threat since these will inevitably be transmitted to the client if they are present. The relaxed stance with clients will stem, in part, from the counsellor remaining mindful that her role is not that of providing instant solutions, but is more to do with fostering a relationship which serves as a 'growth medium'. In other words, the style of relating by the counsellor communicates caring support and gives 'permission' for the client (in fact, positively encourages) to search out and express a whole range of inner feelings and experiences. This enables discoveries to be made which lead to personal insight and, later, personal change.

Listening skills — through practice and guidance, a trainee counsellor learns a particular style of listening. It is described as giving full and free attention. It simply involves following very intently what the client is saying while constantly asking oneself, 'What is this person trying to say with his words, his facial expression, his posture, the areas he chooses to talk of freely and the things he is clearly avoiding?' One is *listening to hear, understand and emphasise* and not, initially at least, to make a reply. However, by the use of gaze, posture and occasional remarks, the client remains very aware of the counsellor's attention.

Probing — while listening in this intent manner, the counsellor may notice areas of vagueness or avoidance in the client's communication. Normally it will be appropriate to lead the client to say more on these topics. This is called elaboration and the counsellor will facilitate this by gentle, probing questions.

Reflecting/communicating understanding — the counselling conversation is a joint product put together by the close collaboration of the two (or more) people involved. A constant requirement of the counsellor is to communicate back her understanding and to check the accuracy of this by means of the client's reactions. As opposed to commenting upon or evaluating the client's experience, the counsellor 'reflects' back what has been said, that is, gives a brief repeat version in her own words to show understanding together with other supporting comments which also indicate that attention and understanding are being maintained.

Empathising — as was explained in Chapter 4, to have empathy means to truly comprehend and identify with another person's experiences. If you are in empathy with, say, the feelings of a woman who has to lose a breast, it means that you know her feelings, you can project yourself into her place and, on the basis of what she has said to you, make contact with what it is like to be her. That is, you sense the thoughts and feelings which assail her. Empathy does not come from prior knowledge — that would be false empathy. True empathy comes from exploring with the client the exact nature of her experiences. As you listen intently, it becomes possible to sense her feelings because you have allowed yourself full exposure to her description of the feelings, perceptions and expectations related to the loss of a breast. To some extent, the ability to empathise depends on the level of 'in-touchness' a person has with her own feelings of life. Obviously, if one is 'switched off' to feeling, then the skill of empathy will not be available. Again, though, this is a skill which develops with guidance and practice.

Challenging skills – here I borrow Egan's (1975) term. While the early stages of counselling see little by way of active intervention on the part of the counsellor, as trust develops and the client becomes both accepting and experienced in the counselling 'encounter', so then the counsellor may adopt rather stronger facilitating techniques.

Amongst these are:

1. *Confrontation* – when the counsellor detects evasiveness, inconsistencies, clear-cut blocking or denial, game-playing, the maintenance of a facade, etc. she will confront the client with her observations, suggesting to the client what she believes is happening. Obviously, the skill is to learn how to do this so that it is helpful and leads the client on to productive self-discovery (as opposed to being destructive of rapport, so setting back the working relationship).

2. *Communicating intuitive empathy* – when an experienced counsellor has gained and absorbed a full account of a person's difficulty, she may discover herself echoing the feelings of her client (empathising) to a degree which seems to go beyond what has actually been said. She will sense that the client is feeling something that he is unable to express verbally, perhaps because he is denying the feelings. At appropriate times, the counsellor will suggest to the client that such feelings apply to him. If the client has matured in the work, he will examine the suggestions honestly, seeking to see if they fit, which may then lead to a further advance in insight.

3. *Sharing and self-disclosure* – occasions occur in counselling when the client is assisted if the counsellor discloses her own feelings and experiences to the client. For example, the counsellor may reveal how she felt in a particular situation, describing to a client, perhaps, her feelings after a death has been experienced. The point of such disclosure would be to augment levels of support or further the growth of insight.

4. *Focusing on the here-and-now* – a second form of self-disclosure by the counsellor is the communication of her thoughts and feelings concerning the quality of the relationship that has developed between

the client and herself. She focuses attention on the 'here-and-now' aspects of the work, drawing attention to the significant patterns which may have emerged. This may be relevant as a means of giving feedback to the client on his characteristic styles of relating and interacting, assuming that the pattern of relating in the counselling session reflects behaviour elsewhere which is causing difficulties.

5. *Information sharing* — a client may be entrenched in a way of viewing a situation, a 'perceptual and emotional set', as we say. On occasions, it is helpful to gently feed in factual information which encourages new views and new thinking.

There is something rather lifeless about such lists and brief descriptions as these, so I will try to bring it all to life for you by examples of typical transactions during a counselling session.

Nan Smith (short for Nancy) has been in my office for 30 minutes or so. I have been asked to see her by the ward sister. Her husband, Leslie, aged 62 years, is dying from cancer of the liver. As yet, he has not been informed of this, primarily because Nan has insisted that he must not know. At present, the open talk by staff with Leslie refers only to liver disorders. The request to see her came as a result of events occurring during the evening visit the day before. Nan had travelled in for visiting as usual but Leslie had been withdrawn and incommunicative. He lay turned away from her and apart from a few angry remarks, barely spoke. He had been like this with the nurses as well, a complete change to his stoical, cheery self. To make matters worse, he was virtually refusing to take liquid thus becoming marginally dehydrated. Not surprisingly, Nan was deeply hurt and showed as much to the nurses. They asked if she would like to see the ward counsellor and she felt that she would. Now, here we are halfway into our first meeting.

She is talking easily and openly although in rather short statements and so I have adopted the strategy of keeping the flow going by using facilitating questions. We have covered the background to the incident yesterday which basically involved her describing events during the last few months and expressing her sadness that things should end like this for them. Leslie may have only a few more weeks to live and after a long, happy marriage suddenly, for no accountable reason, he is angry and rejecting towards her:

Nan You see, I don't know what's best. Maybe he'd rather I didn't come. It's as if I've done something wrong but I just can't think what. Like yesterday, I tried to chat to him for a while and cheer him up a little but it's very hard when he just stays silent. He's very poorly, of course, but he's been worse before and never behaved like this. What do you think I should do?

Counsellor I don't know at the moment, Nan. It's really something for you to decide when we've talked it all through. Can I ask you to give me an idea of how this has affected you? (*A question to lead her to an expression of personal feeling while avoiding getting drawn into giving instant advice.*)

Nan I've felt very upset by it. I couldn't sleep last night, I got a bit panicky. All of us have been trying to give him company and take him out of himself a bit. You see, the family isn't used to rows or bad feeling. We're very close and at a time like this — we all know it's cancer but he doesn't — we just don't want him to get upset and start brooding because he'll think of his brother who died five years ago with cancer and then get frightened. We don't want him frightened and upset.

Counsellor You want to protect him up to the end, but this bad atmosphere stops you? (*Reflecting back.*)

Nan Yes, that's it, and I worry that the children will blame me if he gets upset or depressed. What we all want is for him to have an easy time, not get in a state like his brother did — but now something's gone wrong and I feel it's my fault. (*In tears, I help her deal with them and give her time.*)

Counsellor I understand your confusion, Nan, you feel you've done something wrong but don't know what. Let's take it a step further. What are your memories of the visit the day before yesterday? (*A direct question to help develop the description of events.*)

Nan Nothing out of the ordinary, really. He was quiet. I did most of the talking. He seemed a bit depressed at one point — I remember he said he'd never see our daughter again — she's in Australia, you know.

Counsellor How did you reply?

Nan I told him he was being silly again and that he would be better soon and home in a few days. It was then that he first turned away from me. He didn't say anything or do anything, just turned away (*pauses again, near to tears*) and he wouldn't talk any more, except to say it was time for me to go.

Counsellor What were your feelings at that moment?

Nan Well, I felt dreadful. It isn't like him. We've had our differences like anyone else but we've always faced up to one another and said what we think — I couldn't cope with him going silent like that.

Counsellor Try and enlarge on what you mean when you say you felt dreadful. (*Probing.*)

Nan I suppose I felt worried in case it was my fault — guilty, you might say, and to be honest, I felt a bit cross. I didn't deserve to be treated like that. I've been putting so much effort into looking after him and keeping him cheerful. Yes, I felt cross, which is terrible because the poor soul's so ill and I know he doesn't mean any harm. But it wasn't as if I'd been sharp with him or said anything offensive. I was just cheering him up, letting him know that we were all waiting for him to come home. They have to keep up hope, you know, but I couldn't cope with him silent and turned away. That did hurt me. It's been a hard time for me too.

Counsellor You felt he'd turned on you unfairly without good reason, especially after the things you've been through recently. (*Reflecting, showing understanding.*)

Nan Yes, and now I just don't know what to do.

Counsellor Do you have any idea at all what he might have been thinking or feeling? (*Encouraging her to explore.*)

Nan Well, I've been through it over and over again — oh, I don't know, really. He hates being in hospital, away from his home. Both his father and brother died of cancer and in a way, I think he's been expecting it. He's been under a lot of strain worrying.

Counsellor It isn't just him that worries, is it? (*Probing.*)

Nan No, I've probably fretted about it more than him over the last few years — it's something we never talk about but it's always there, if you know what I mean. It's been hanging over my family since his brother died. They were twins, you see. His brother had a rough time of it too. I've worried for us all. I had to see the doctor myself about nerves last month because of this.

Counsellor Nan, I can see that you've carried a great deal of anxiety about Leslie and the risk of him dying of cancer. It feels as if you've been really frightened during the last few years so that it has affected the way you've talked, or rather, not talked, to Leslie about it all, and what you've asked others to say to him. Maybe *your* anxiety has led to a long silence which Leslie now finds difficult. (*Intuitive empathy — a 'challenge' to her to consider a new perspective to do with her own anxiety.*)

Nan (after a long pause) He was badly upset by his father's death and then his brother's a few years later. We just never talked about cancer again. I was thinking that it runs in the family and that he'd be next. It used to make me feel sick. I didn't want him to know I was thinking this way. I mean, he might have been thinking the same but we just sort of never mentioned it. When he got ill a year ago I went to see our doctor on my own to ask him outright — I couldn't bear not knowing one way or the other. The doctor said he wasn't sure but quite likely it could be cancer. I don't know how I got through that week, I felt awful. I had to pretend I had a migraine. But I decided to do my best to get him by as long as possible without knowing it was cancer, that's why I asked the doctors not to tell him.

Counsellor Why was this so important to you? (*Probing.*)

Nan I just thought he would panic, sort of go under, I suppose. I didn't really know if he would, though. It just felt important. The children, well, I call them children but they're all married now, agreed that it was best, too.

Counsellor It's as if by keeping it back from Leslie you could keep your own panic under control, live as if it were not happening. (*A challenge with a gentle, confronting interpretation of events.*)

Nan Well, it was him I was thinking of, not myself. But I suppose you're right, really. I found it easier to cope with, just keeping it to myself. We could go on making plans for the future and keep life going. I didn't know what would happen if he found out — he might have just given up.

Counsellor How sure are you that he doesn't know, or at least strongly suspect? (*A question to encourage exploration.*)

Nan He'd have told me, though, wouldn't he? Perhaps not . . . he might be keeping his thoughts from me in the same way, I suppose. Do you think he knows then?

Counsellor I haven't met your husband, Nan, I truly don't know. But my own feeling about the situation that has arisen leads me to think that he, at least, strongly suspects he has cancer. I want to ask you to do something. Imagine for a moment what Leslie must feel like if he does know. His doctors and nurses are evasive and just talk about waiting for tests. They'll not be straightforward with him since you've asked them not to be. You and the family seem oblivious and are chattering away about getting him home again soon, as if you believe everything is normal. Sometimes he tries to tell you what he thinks, like he'll never see your daughter in Australia again, but everyone rushes to stop him saying things like that and changes the subject. How do you think he feels, put yourself in his place for a moment. (*This is a combination of disclosure, giving my own reactions and a challenging exercise to expand Nan's thinking about the elements of the situation.*)

Nan Oh dear, it's all so confusing. How would I feel? Well, if I really suspected that I had cancer, I'd be very frightened but at the same time I'd resent being treated as if I wasn't an adult and couldn't discuss it. I think I'd get cross and say something.

Counsellor Would it feel lonely? (*A lead to expand the exploration.*)

Nan Well, yes, I suppose so. It would be important to be able to talk about it to at least one or two people, share your fears, as it were . . . what would be more difficult . . . would be not trusting your family and doctors. Suspecting they were keeping something from you but at the same time talking about it behind your back. I can see now what you've been leading up to. You think that Leslie is behaving this way because no-one will actually tell him he's got cancer when he knows he has all the time — and we make it worse by being cheery and pretending nothing's wrong. (*Nan has now achieved the key insight.*)

Counsellor I think you could be right, Nan. You see, people who are seriously ill and dying usually need several things. They need to know what's going to happen and when, so that they can prepare themselves and order their affairs according to their wishes — saying goodbye to people, for example. They also need stable companionship and the opportunity to draw on the support of close relationships. Without these they are very isolated and there can be a terrible feeling of being cut off. Dying is a phase of life we all have to deal with, and it's much more comfortable if it's shared and dealt with in a way which suits the dying person's own wishes. Leslie isn't being allowed these. He's surrounded by family and staff but is really quite alone because no-one will talk to him. He may have a great need to share this phase of his life with you — his close companion. (*Again this is a challenge to consider an alternative perspective. There is some information-giving as part of the challenge.*)

Nan How should I alter things?

Counsellor You know Leslie well, I don't know him at all, so that's for you to decide. But we can talk about some of the different ways of going about it if you wish.

This transcript is a near verbatim record of a counselling session I was engaged in a year ago. Nan talked some more and resolved the problem of how to change the situation herself. I do not know exactly what she said but she did phone to say that she broached the subject in a simple, open way. Leslie didn't speak initially, instead he drank a whole glass of orange juice (if you remember, he was refusing fluids). Later, they talked long and hard, with many tears, but, Nan reported, they became very close and both drew a great deal from the remaining six months which they had together. Leslie died in psychological peace.

Training and Reading in Counselling

As you can probably see, counselling is not a skill picked up through a few quick lectures, nor indeed by simply reading a training text. It is a skill which is fashioned by experience, constant case discussion and a well run training course. Ideally, this would be followed by an extended period of personal supervision. 'Sounds ideal but just where do we get all that?' I hear you say. Believe me, if you pursue the issue, such training is available. Start the search by phoning your local Department of Clinical Psychology and if they cannot provide such things directly (in which case they should be ashamed of themselves), they will at least direct your inquiry towards the right target. Fortunately, many of the training courses for the para-medical professions are now including some basic training in counselling skills and so too are some schools of nursing and medicine. A background in reading will, of course, be a considerable asset and I suggest that you go through at least one of the following: Egan (1975), Brammer (1973), Nurse (1975), Tschudin V. (1983) and Nelson-Jones (1982).

Pitfalls

With the emphasis on training and skills, it must appear all too easy to go wrong in counselling work, to 'put two large feet in it' and end up turning things into a dreadful mess. This is not really very likely. Certainly, caution is important and the development of professionalism is essential, but there is no need for anxiety. I will say with confidence that most of you, as nurses and members of the para-medical professions, will find basic counselling techniques within your scope — provided you can get off to a good start by finding a clear and supportive teacher. You must accept one thing, though. As in any skill, you will probably be clumsy at first and make mistakes. You must budget for making these and not be made tense by an unrealistic need to be powerful and faultless as a counsellor from the outset. Here, for example, are some of the typical bits of 'clumsiness' and errors made by a new or badly trained counsellor:

— directing the conversation in a controlling manner with a nervous stream of questions
— interrupting or finishing off sentences for the client, using restricted choice questions (either X or Y) or restricted response questions (yes or no)
— talking whenever there is a silence because it makes you tense
— giving instant advice or guidance
— being too problem/solution-centred rather than person-centred
— rushing to reassure in order to damp down feelings

— being preoccupied with giving interpretations and forcing insights through

Those of us already involved in counselling have all made such errors and you will too.

In the long term, though, you will acquire a style of your own and, with proper case discussion and feedback, will mature away from such things. Then comes the vulnerable phase, which I fear, lasts for ever. Once we 'go solo' as counsellors and involve ourselves in regular case work there are still pitfalls. These are more to do with the emotional orientation that can develop between counsellors and their clients. We need another whole book to cope with this topic and so, once more, I must console myself by just sketching out the framework of ideas. The basic concept is to do with patterns developing in a counsellor's work which obstruct effective progress and possibly make life uncomfortable for the counsellor. For example:

1. The counsellor becomes identified with her client and his problems to such a degree that she feels a strong personal commitment and urgency to do something to sort things out herself.

2. The counsellor becomes drawn into the client's limited view of a situation and becomes weighed down by the same helpless feelings as the client. There will be a sense of being trapped in an impasse yet with the client leaning heavily and making powerful pleas for help.

3. The counsellor becomes so committed to resolving problems and 'saving' clients that she fails to see that certain clients have a 'vested interest in their problem' and *need* it to deal with other issues in life. A hopeless struggle ensues which will end in the counsellor giving up the case in despair (a case for early referral, probably).

4. The counsellor unwittingly solicits dependency in her clients because it makes her feel powerful. Later, she becomes bogged down by cases that never seem to go away.

5. The counsellor becomes possessive towards a client and clings on to a case. Sometimes this sets up feelings of bitter resentment if other colleagues are involved, or leads to efforts to keep other people out of the case, thereby blocking the natural progression of events such as referring on to a psychological therapist. This may occur if the counsellor becomes bonded to the client in an overly powerful way, emotionally mistaking him or her for another figure in life. Sometimes this possessiveness occurs when the counsellor has a commitment which goes beyond the actual case — demonstrating prowess to colleagues or defending professional territory, perhaps.

It is the likelihood of such patterns developing that makes the importance of regular case discussion, together with genuine receptivity to feedback from colleagues, such an important aspect of professionalism in this work. Without it, you may fail to see gross distortions in the conduct of particular cases.

Knowing Your Limits

In a similar vein, it is essential to have a clear picture of the limits in which you work. The problem of clinging on to a case when what is required is not counselling but active psychological therapy is likely to grow unless the issue has been properly resolved in your own mind and feelings. It is hard to refer on if you have become attached to a person. At the same time, it is unforgivable to hold on to a case to meet *your* needs rather than those of the client. This theme will be expanded in the brief chapter on referral.

When is Counselling Needed?

The three main components of psychological care have now been described. We are left with the issue of how you decide at any one time which of these functions should receive emphasis. When, for example, should you be in the role of counsellor rather than simply giving emotional care? We will discuss this in the final chapter. Meanwhile, the basic idea to carry forward is that people who may benefit from counselling as it has been described here will be better able to make use of the event if any obvious needs in terms of emotional and informational care have been tended to first.

7 ATYPICAL OR SEVERE REACTIONS – MONITORING OR REFERRING ON

Once you have taken an interest in the psychological aspects of illness and have begun to develop your work to include psychological care, then you will inevitably become more psychologically-minded, noticing more of the psychological scenery. In itself, this will be a most valuable asset to the people you care for, but in the context of a fully functioning scheme of psychological care this ability provides the basis for the *fourth component of the approach, namely the task of monitoring the psychological state of your clients and being able to detect levels of distress or actual psychological disturbances which merit referral to a specialist in psychological therapy.*

We are not talking here of you becoming a psycho-diagnostician, attempting to identify the nature of a particular disturbance (phobic, depressive, psychotic, etc.). Rather, the requirement is that you acquire the simple practical ability to recognise that a person's state has changed to a point where basic psychological care will probably prove to be insufficient. This could be on the occasion of your first contact or at some point during your conduct of psychological care with a particular case. Closely related to this is the issue of deciding how to manage referring a case – both from the point of view of your client and how you manage the business yourself. The objective of psychological care is to minimise psychological distress and lead people through the harsh experiences of serious illness. A therapeutic relationship is formed which will, ideally, be a *lasting* resource. At the same time, it is unhelpful to 'cling' to a case when there is really a need for more specialised help. Letting go can be difficult, though. In addition to these issues there comes the not inconsiderable problem of how and where will you find more specialised help.

Who Needs Specialised Help?

Whilst wanting to avoid seeming vague, I have to say that it is very difficult to list hard and fast criteria for dividing your clients into two groups, one of which would be described as 'in psychological difficulties and definitely needing referral to a psychological therapist'. The division is very much confused by various factors, for example, the level of experience of the counsellor involved. A nurse with a good number

156

of years' experience in psychological care will deal quite effectively with a certain case, whereas someone relatively new to the work will feel overwhelmed and need to refer the case on, both for her own comfort and to guarantee its effective management. Similarly, one unit or ward may have time and capacity for plenty of psychological work and will absorb some relatively demanding cases, while another will only be able to cope with basic preventative work and will need to refer cases other than those which can be dealt with by basic procedures. In short, the point at which referral is made is, to a degree, a matter of local adjustment.

A small proportion of general hospital clients will not generate any ambiguity, however. They will be people who have totally lost emotional control or who are clearly disabled psychologically, interpreting events in a bizarre way or clearly experiencing intense disturbances of psychological functions such as delusions, hallucinations, or gross levels of emotional reaction. Such cases would normally lead to an automatic referral to the psychiatric service anyway whether or not there had been developments in psychological care.

Another larger group will prove more difficult to reach a decision about referring on. People in this group will not appear as grossly disturbed, but nevertheless will cause concern and leave you feeling that they are functioning very badly in some aspects of life. There will be a sense that they are afflicted by problems which do not appear to trouble the majority of your clients. Such cases will generate a feeling in you that the client's reaction seems atypically severe; it may be hard to empathise with it. In addition, you might notice that your client's long standing behavioural and emotional patterns (the elements of personality) make him ill-suited to the stressing experience he is going through and that he has entered a period of crisis in which he is becoming increasingly unable to cope – 'going under', in fact. In other words, there will be something of a dilemma centred around sorting out whether this is just a case which needs a little more effort or one for which early referral for therapy would be best.

Probably the best way to convey this to you is with several extremely brief outlines of cases which were referred to me by nurses because they felt the person's problems were at a level where psychological therapy was needed. In all these cases I felt they were correct in so thinking.

1. Most dialysis 'partners' are nervous when they are first trained to place cannulae in the fistula (the vein-artery anastomosis constructed for haemodialysis) of a person preparing for dialysis. Hilary was more

than nervous. As the time approached to put her husband's cannulae in, her hands became very shaky, her face lost colour, there were signs of perspiration and she became physically very tense. She tried her best on three consecutive training sessions but had to give up each time. On the last attempt, she became so agitated that a nurse had to take her to the visitors' room and sit with her for a while because she was so distraught. In the following week she missed two sessions at the Unit, later explaining that she had felt so anxious about coming that she was physically sick as she was getting ready to leave. She had, of course, developed a phobic reaction, for which she needed appropriate psychological therapy.

2. Beth had been seeing a speech therapist following a two-month period of aphonia. The speech therapist was competent in psychological care and blended this with the speech therapy. After two or three sessions, the therapist felt that Beth seemed very withdrawn and depressed, not in a tearful way but in a passive, helpless fashion. Her judgement was that the needs of her client went beyond the care which she could offer in her weekly sessions and so she referred Beth to see me. Her depression turned out to be linked in with the aphonia. Both seemed to originate from the death of Beth's mother two years earlier which had been a tremendous blow, since it left her socially isolated. Her difficulty was best described as an atypical grief reaction and justified some five sessions of psychotherapy which produced definite improvements.

3. Mark courageously decided to continue with his degree in architecture despite needing to dialysis three times a week. He remained remarkably well in physical terms but, as the sister from the Unit who was making home visits reported, he was progressively becoming more irritable, fatigued, unkind to his wife and morosely withdrawn. He confessed to the sister on one visit that he felt near to 'cracking up'. There had been times at college when he had wanted physically to smash his work and, after such occasions, he felt very low and tearful. She discussed with him whether it was best for him to use the unit counsellor or for them to deal with it themselves. The sister privately felt that it might be a bit too much for her since it would probably require several sessions in quick succession, and she did not have the time for that. It turned out that Mark preferred to work on the problem away from home and with a comparative stranger, anyway. Thus the home sister asked me to help him with this particular difficulty. We met for three separate sessions and discovered that Mark had reduced himself to a state of tense, angry fatigue in his endeavours to prove himself equal

to the other students. He was slower in his work now and, because of the prevailing uraemia, compensated by arriving earlier at college, working through lunch and forcing himself to work in the evenings when he should have been resting. He was repeating a pattern of long standing, namely a competitive need to achieve high levels of performance in comparison with his peers. Now, in kidney failure, this level of striving was unrealistic, and he was daily suffering frustrations and defeats as his energy proved insufficient and the distractions of dialysis interfered with his attempts to compete. He was clearly on the edge of exhaustion and near to a depressive reaction. We worked at understanding the origins of these needs and helping him to adjust to more realistic personal targets.

4. Maureen did not complain of psychological tension or discomfort but complained of feeling sick. She was at her worst when the drug trolley came round and her various prescriptions had to be swallowed. At these times, she spoke of severe nausea and several times a week actually was sick whilst attempting to swallow drugs. The sister in charge of her ward felt that the whole situation was rapidly getting out of hand and could clearly lead to serious difficulties. It seemed to her just the kind of thing that psychologists were invented for, and so it was not long before I had put in my first visit to meet Maureen. The difficulty, it transpired, was that she had always avoided medicines and drugs. She had been a health food enthusiast and had not used any drugs at all throughout her adult life. Her reaction to drugs was, 'I know it's irrational, but it's like swallowing poison.' It also emerged that as a child she had been forced to take a daily 'medicine', namely, cod liver oil. She so hated this and became so tense that she was often sick after the daily ritual. She grew into adulthood with an aversion to medicine and turned to health foods as a defence against needing to swallow medicines. What appeared to be happening now was that the 'parental-like' authority of the nurses urging her to swallow drugs (although she recognised that her life might depend on some of them) was producing the same emotional conflict and associated solution as in her childhood, namely, comply by attempting to swallow but defy by then being sick. It was an appropriate referral and therapy took two lines, firstly dealing with the basic conflict and secondly training in the management of tension so that swallowing could be completed without inducing vomiting. Sadly Maureen died from other causes a week or so after we had begun working together.

As you may see, there is no obvious single behavioural or psychological feature which made these four cases 'a suitable case for referral'.

At a general level, we could argue that in all of them there was an obvious risk of further deterioration and to contain this risk an informed psychological investigation together with necessary therapy was needed. It was also clear that the person initially handling each of these cases sensed something rather different about them in comparison to the more usual pattern. The severity of the anxiety reaction, the persistence of the depression, the degree to which efficiency in living was being affected and the power of the psychosomatic feature all suggested that these were clients requiring help with significant psychological difficulties, rather than people for whom good preventative care would suffice. Here, I think, is the key point. The approach to psychological care which I have been teaching is not to be confused with psychological therapy. The whole point is to anticipate difficulties and work in a preventative fashion so minimising the impact that these have. The counselling component of psychological care does extend the work to aiding clients in the resolution of difficulties in life, and there will never be a sharp divide on where counselling stops and therapy begins. It must be a considered judgement in relation to a client's difficulties in which you ask:

1. Does this look and feel like the kind of difficulty which falls within the range of basic counselling and emotional care or does it require help beyond that level?

2. Is it within my personal capabilities and experience to handle it effectively?

3. Can I find sufficient time?

According to your answers, you will work on with a case or commit yourself to making a referral.

To Whom do You Refer?

The provision of support services in the psychological/counselling specialisations vary greatly from one country to another. Similarly, the availability of support personnel varies according to whether a particular hospital is state-financed or run privately, and whether or not it is in a part of the world where people are accustomed to making use of state or privately run psychological services. In some areas of the USA, for example, it is almost second nature to visit a psychologist when problems crop up, which means that there is a good number available. Because of this variability, I will restrict my remarks on this topic to giving a few guiding principles and my thoughts will be directed to the system which I know best, that is, the state-financed British National Health Service. You will have to convert these principles to fit the system in which you work.

The average general hospital will usually have an established procedure for coping with grossly disturbed people. Typically, this involves a nurse drawing the attention of relevant doctors to the plight of her client who will then call in one of the local psychiatrists. To tap into this procedure may not, however, necessarily be a very favourable move as far as the furtherance of good psychological care is concerned with the exception, that is, of instances where a person has deteriorated into psychotic disturbance or gross and unmanageable levels of emotional reaction. The problem is, if I may make a few generalisations, that the conventional 'psychiatric event' will involve a diagnostic assessment and the virtually inevitable prescription of emotion-inhibiting drugs with little else to follow. Not all psychiatrists function in this way, of course, but sadly it is quite prevalent. In terms of the aims of psychological care, the standard psychiatric approach is unacceptable for two reasons.

Firstly, the type of difficulties which we have been discussing basically require treatment by psychological means in order to produce psychological change and activate psychological processes. The pharmacological approach does not have central relevance since, although drugs may bring sedation and temporary relief, ultimately the actual problems have to be dealt with directly as most of them do not conveniently disappear of their own accord. The situation would otherwise be analogous to that of treating toothache by painkillers alone. We know this would not prove effective. The cavity must be discovered, cleaned and filled. With clients who are in difficulties but not grossly disturbed, the same idea applies. Of course, people should be made comfortable if they so wish and hence appropriate drugs made available to them for that purpose *provided* there is full and honest discussion on what these drugs can achieve.

The second reason why the standard psychiatric approach is unacceptable is to do with its obvious implications – the whole message and value of your psychological care work will be undermined by a drug-oriented psychiatric consultation. *The point of drug therapy is to block and suppress emotion, treating it as an illness. This, by now, I trust you will know is not a valued objective in psychological care.* What I am arguing against, therefore, is a referral which leads to nothing else other than drug therapy. At this point I must stress that I am not against the involvement of psychiatrists *per se* – quite the opposite. We need the help and support of psychologically-minded psychiatrists very much. However, there is no point in setting up a scheme of psychological care which is then undermined when referral has to be made to another profession which adopts a contradictory approach. There is, of course, much to be said for a negotiated compromise involving a 'partial referral'. Here, a psychiatrist will assist with drug therapy when it is a clear necessity while you continue with the psychological care work. *What is vitally important, therefore, is that if referral to a psychiatrist is made, he or she must understand and support the objectives of psychological care and complement these in the approach they adopt with your client, i.e. you need to pick your psychiatrist and make sure you get a co-operative, psychologically-minded person who does not experience your work as threatening, nor sees it as irrelevant.* Some effort at inquiry and face-to-face discussion will clarify the position of individual psychiatrists. Do not be intimidated in doing this — remember you are acting as an agent on behalf of your client and if you are initiating moves which lead to a referral, *it is your responsibility to know that the person likely to take over the case will conduct it in a manner which is beneficial to your client.*

This point will be picked up again in the next section because I recognise that it has profound implications for nurses and para-medical professions in terms of 'the right to question the performance of a doctor and other specialists'. To broaden the issue, I will say that this same point applies, of course, to any practitioner in any profession to whom you direct a referral for additional psychological help, whether it be psychologist, social worker or professional counsellor. You are not in a position to evaluate their professional skills. This is not the suggestion. You are, however, in a position to check that they understand the objectives of your work and will complement them in their own approach. In other words, they too must value psychological care and think in psychological terms. There is no point in making a referral if it results in the end of psychological care for your client.

Thus we have established that the psychiatric service exists and should be used as long as there is clear compatibility in approach. Of course, your psychiatrists, like everyone else, will probably be 'very busy'. Here, I think, one argues that sooner is better than later (a case dealt with early on usually requires less work), and if the client is left without help then the psychiatric service would quite probably get the case in the long term anyway.

What are your other options? There will usually be three:

1. Clinical Psychologists. These are in plentiful supply in America (relatively speaking) and in short supply in Britain. Australia seems to be somewhere in between and the situation in Europe is very variable. I would say that if you decide to take psychological care seriously, you should contact the nearest Department of Clinical Psychology (your district administrator will give you the address) and build direct links with the psychologists. They will almost certainly welcome your approach and will be able to handle a limited number of referrals. They will possibly consider working directly with you in the unit or ward (as I do) depending on how extended they are as regards work. They will almost certainly help out with training and advice on individual cases. By the way, it would be false to portray all clinical psychologists as ideal to work with you. Some of the older generation are still locked into the original role with which the profession launched itself into the Health Service, namely, psychological assessment (not therapy). Others have become specialised in areas such as mental handicap, child psychology and so on. Lastly, a proportion are fairly extreme 'behaviourists' and would not agree with my fundamental premise in emotional care, namely that one is dealing with emotional processes and the key role is to facilitate them. To be direct, you have to pick your psychologist, too.

2. Social Workers. So, too, you should approach the social work department. They will be a most valuable source in linking in with and discussing your work, and will probably be able to give direct assistance with a small number of cases. I frankly do not know the proportion of social workers who are competent in psychological therapy. It is not, to be honest, a profession which usually provides two or three years' intensive training in psychological therapy, as happens with clinical psychologists. Nevertheless, many social workers do take a keen interest in case work and have developed themselves to a good level of competence.

3. Professional and Voluntary Counsellors. Once more, depending on the area in which you work, US versus UK, big city versus small country town, etc., there will be a varying provision of counselling services. There are usually various voluntary and sometimes professionally run organisations. It would be inappropriate to equate the services made available by such organisations with that of, say, a department of clinical psychology. They offer intensive and advanced counselling skills, but not formal psychological therapy. However, if you are dealing with a person who needs continuity of care after discharge or who will benefit from intensive counselling which you cannot provide, then it is worth making inquiries as to what is available in your area.

In many places, you will find people functioning as counsellors in the hospital service itself, often on a voluntary basis. Usually they will have had a reasonable training in counselling skills and work with considerable enthusiasm and sympathy for psychological care. They may need orienting to your speciality but will often be pleased to assist with a few clients. For example, from heresay alone, I know of people in my own locality functioning as either voluntary or professional counsellors in an infertility clinic, a contraceptive clinic, a women's clinic, the hospice service, an alcoholism counselling service and so on. Basically, if you want the assistance of counsellors and are prepared to look, there are a good number around. One resource they will have which you probably will not is the time to work in depth with cases. This does not, of course, mean packing your clients off to anyone who claims to be a counsellor. It is necessary to build up a relationship with a few, to acquaint yourself with their ability and learn to trust each other in working together. As always, it remains important to recognise limits and maintain professionalism, even when using voluntary counsellors.

Overall, by far the best bet is to review the options with the rest of the team and then attempt to establish regular links with a few people. Unless, of course, you already have someone on the staff who functions in the capacity of a psychological therapist.

What if you are defeated? What if no-one can be found who will assist with an individual case? Then you are pushed back into relying on your own resources. Offer what you can give and remember that you *can only offer so much*. You will always find someone to discuss the case and advise you — psychologist, psychiatrist or social worker. Telephone them; you will rarely be turned away.

The System for Making a Referral

Who does what when a referral is required? Is it you, the sister-in-charge, the registrar or the consultant that should make the actual referral? As we look at this issue it is useful to discriminate between two types of referral. These are (1) external referrals, where they are made to a specialist outside the membership of the unit or ward team, for example, a psychologist; and (2) internal referrals, where the referral is made to someone who is part of the team, for example, the medical social worker.

If you have slotted into a scheme of psychological care there will be a procedure already. If not, then it is up to you to make a move and negotiate on the business of referral procedure with your colleagues.

Probably the situation concerning external referrals will be the most awkward to resolve. Let's say that you are a nurse. You have been in close contact with a client through your work of psychological care. You will now know him better than your colleagues because you will have spent more time with him than anyone else. Here is a dilemma. Quite often the doctors will be the least well informed on the true psychological status of your client and, because of their own psychological defences, least able to see the associated needs. Left to their own devices, as we have seen, the evidence reveals that the majority of hospital doctors rarely appear to think much on the psychological care of their clients, and even more rarely to notice that a person needs psychological help and so refer to a specialist in psychological care when it is necessary. *Yet*, as we have also seen, the medical profession works hard to retain sole preserve over the decision-making and administrative power required to effect referrals. This is a power which is guarded jealously for a variety of reasons and it creates a difficulty for us. Put succinctly, the people most likely to know when a referral is necessary (those giving psychological care) do not normally have the power of referral, and those who have the power of referral are the least likely to know when a referral to a psychological therapist is necessary. Clearly this is inefficient and against the interests of people using the hospital service. There is thus a diplomatic task to be undertaken since our aim is to create a system which minimises psychological neglect. As initial awareness of the need for referral will probably be yours, you must negotiate out a procedure wherein you at least are free to *initiate* the moves leading to a referral which, if local circumstances require, may then be activated by the collective decision of the team or sole act of the consultant in charge of the case.

A consultant does hold responsibility for what happens to the client – he 'carries the can' if things should go wrong. This burden must be respected and it would be unreasonable of us to expect a consultant to delegate the basic responsibility except in exceptional circumstances. It is also clear that part of a consultant's function involves centralising decision-making and so heading off clinical anarchy. We would, therefore, expect a consultant to be *involved* in a referral. However, it would similarly be unreasonable on the part of a medical consultant if he attempted to dominate the business of referring people who had been receiving psychological care by other staff who were more developed and informed in the work than he. We could not condone the obstruction or neglect of a necessary referral because a consultant had an inability to recognise the need, or was possessed of personal whims antagonistic to psychological care which were based on prejudices rather than scientific analysis.

Overall, the best plan is to work out the issue directly and honestly with your senior nurse and consultant. Ideally, you will negotiate a compromise which recognises your position as the member of staff most likely to be the best informed (assuming you have been working with a client for a while) and accepts the consultant's position of overall responsibility. It should also be recognised that you must liaise with the person receiving the referral in order to brief him or her on the case. A system for joint consultation between yourself and the rest of the team and action based on mutual agreement is obviously the ideal.

This positive action-taking approach may seem foreign to you, particularly negotiating 'terms' with medical colleagues. It is necessary with innovation, though. So let me encourage you to be assertive yet diplomatic and try not to be put off by bluster and bullying. Remember, your *primary* concern is with the needs of your clients. You know and understand the 'set up' in which you work. The objective is to make sure that these needs are met and at the same time maintain harmonious, understanding relationships with colleagues. There is no point in directly attacking medical colleagues over this issue. Negotiate it out and allow time for trust to build up. Ideally, there will be discussion and collective agreement as to what is best. The problem of who to refer to (which we raised above) will feel easier to resolve if it is a shared problem; so too the issue of when to refer. A priority has to be the maintenance of good communication and integration between the professions. Never sacrifice this, nor good will, because your clients will pay the price. At the same time, do not be trodden into the ground. You have principle on your side.

It is relevant to say that my own experience to do with the issue of referral has been quite agreeable. Medical staff in the Kidney Unit like to know if a nurse has asked me to help directly in a case so that they have good information on the 'state of play'. Ideally, they like to discuss it too. But they value a system which functions automatically and so support the nurses in getting on with the job of giving care, including referring a case on to me when it is necessary. Sometimes they refer cases directly themselves. Bear in mind, though, that this is an internal referral system. I work in the Unit and log my activities in the notes. This allows greater flexibility and informality compared with a system wherein external referrals have to be made.

Managing a Referral from the Client's Point of View

Nurse I would like you to see our psychologist.

Client (inner voice) A psychologist, this is terrible. They think I'm going mad. To face this on top of everything else . . . I don't want to see him.

My biggest problem working in a general hospital is that I am called a psychologist. Although I am not there to work with people who are seized by mental illness, madness, gone looney, or whatever term applies, it is frequently assumed that 'seeing the psychologist' implies that one has stopped being normal. I use different devices to get over this, variously titling myself as the Unit Counsellor in the Kidney Unit, the Hospital Counsellor in the wards and Pain Counsellor in the Pain Clinic. It helps. I say this simply to direct your attention to the significance of the act of referral to a psychologist or psychiatrist in your clients' eyes. Does it mean abandonment and that you think they are not worth your time? Does it mean that you think they are going under or already regard them as 'mental'? Does it provoke fear, resentment, unhappiness or quite what?

Referral must be explained well and thoroughly talked through. Ideally, it will be a joint decision reached by yourself and the client. You will explain your position showing why you need someone to take over the case. You will be very clear on who the person actually is that your client is expected to see, what they do and, most importantly, the significance of seeing them. You will make explicit why you feel it would be advantageous to see someone in addition to yourself. The most important requirement is, as always, honesty in the context of a trusting relationship. For example, if you have become worried about some aspect of your client's life but feel it is out of your depth to help them with it, tell them so. At the same time, try to communicate that the event is not horrendous in your eyes, but that the upheaval and stresses of serious illness or major injury provoke personal difficulties (not madness) and these must be dealt with early on — in this case using the help of someone who specialises in giving such assistance. Do not, however, force an agreement to accept referral to us, the therapists, because, in most circumstances, working with people who have 'been sent' is a frustrating and fruitless endeavour. Negotiate the issue to a conclusion and accept a refusal on the idea of referral if that is your client's sincere wish.

Will Many Referrals be Necessary?

There is no reliable way of estimating this. At present, few referrals are made from the general hospitals because much of the psychological distress goes unnoticed and, frankly, because the psychiatric and psychological services tend to be held in low regard by the medical profession. However, the general hospitals are for the physically ill and not the mentally ill. There is, therefore, no reason to expect that an overwhelmingly large concentration of people will need referral, although we know from Chapter 2 that there are a great many in psychological distress. The real lack at present is of *preventative* psychological care to assist people with the known stresses and demands of serious illness and injury. Properly implemented, psychological care will reduce the number of psychological casualties below the present level — the complication being that it will also lead to many of the currently hidden psychological casualties being noticed.

My own experience suggests that the numbers needing referral will not be excessive and that, as the quality of psychological care improves with experience and the number of people offering psychological care rises, the number of cases needing referral will eventually diminish.

8 SYNTHESIS – AND SQUARING WITH REALITY

We have worked through the aspects of psychological care which I judge to be essential for seriously ill and injured people. Of these, informational care and monitoring of psychological state should unquestioningly be provided for all clients. Emotional care and the provision of basic counselling should be readily available and 'on offer' according to people's needs and inclination to accept help. The actual requirements for such care will, of course, vary greatly from person to person. Now, it remains to join the pieces together, stand back and see what we have got, then answer some of the more obvious questions and criticisms.

The approach adopted has been to present the work of psychological care as it will be conducted by the individual nurse or member of the para-medical professions. In making this presentation, the assumption has been held, as I have pointed out with some regularity, that the person involved has the benefit of an environment favourable to such work, with adequate time and facilities together with the genuine understanding and positive support (insistence would be better) of the medical profession, senior nurses, heads of departments, etc. I do realise that this has been an idealisation, and I do know that the majority of readers will not have the benefits of such a favourable setting. I hope, however, that you will appreciate the necessity to teach the work in its 'pure' form, that is, without dilution by shortage of time and staff and without distortion as a result of impoverished understanding and inadequate back up (or even obstruction) from colleagues. The emphasis of the material given is also clearly directed at longer-term clients or at least those who maintain contact through regular out-patient visits, rather than those who have been and gone in the space of 24 hours. Such idealisation on my part must have provoked protest in many readers, especially those who genuinely see the need for psychological care in their own work environment but find the opposite conditions to those which I have apparently assumed. To you I will say stay with me for a few pages more and then we will discuss your position. Keeping the idealisation alive for a last few moments, I want to take a look at the events of psychological care as a whole.

Integrating the Components of Psychological Care

What will be the general approach of people who are thoroughly experienced in psychological care and know how to put it all together? Firstly, may I remind you of the role concept. Experienced 'models' will construe psychological care as a natural and necessary extension of their role. It will be seen by them as important, central in fact, and not as a low priority luxury to be abandoned whenever things are a bit tight. In other words, it will be seen as an essential part of the professional care routinely provided in hospitals. The not uncommon, well intentioned but amateurish 'trying to help' behaviour will be replaced by professionalism. These people will know exactly what they are doing and why, in terms similar to those set out in the main chapters of this book. As each client is taken on, it will be reflexive for them to begin informational care which will be seen as essential as, say, the physical routines of nursing. Similarly, as each client is taken on, it will be reflexive to take up the task of monitoring their psychological state, that is, thinking and inquiring about the client in a psychologically-minded way as well as in a medically-minded way. The basic orientation will be preventative. The stresses and harsh experiences of illness will be countered as these people assist their clients with the tasks of adjustment, acceptance and emotional processing. They will offer a supportive and genuinely caring relationship and be quick to provide emotional care and basic counselling according to the needs of their clients. They will always hold in mind the possibility that referral to a psychological therapist may be advantageous and will, should the occasion arise, make this clear to their clients in a non-threatening, non-possessive way.

'But,' you may want to protest, 'how will I know at what stage to offer the different parts of psychological care — how will I ever really be sure that I am right?'

The answer is a reassuring one. Relax with it all. Be thinking, of course, but do not turn psychological care into a ritual of strict procedures, full of stages and rights and wrongs. Accepting the premise that informational care and psychological monitoring should go on *all* the time, beyond this there are no set sequences and patterns to the work, which will vary from one case to another. It is a matter of blending the various skills which we have studied in relation to the needs of each person. In psychological care, *the master skill is that of identifying the needs of the client and responding appropriately to these*. Regrettably, this ability cannot easily be taught by written word. It is an asset acquired by experience, through spending time working with your clients in an open, receptive way so that they may teach you their needs. You will have to be patient with yourself while you expand your experience. Thus, one client may find your supportive concern and informational care work sufficient for his needs. Another may want to use your ability in counselling to help resolve a particular issue but will have her needs for emotional care met elsewhere. A third person may be in constant need of emotional care throughout the span of your contact, whereas a fourth will require emotional care for brief, intense but infrequent occasions yet draw heavily on you as a counsellor. A fifth person may need all that you can offer but decline to receive any of it. Again, I will stress the value of regular case discussions which will accelerate your learning.

There is, I admit, an obvious flow to the 'typical' case. Initially, relationship building and early informational care work take the time available followed by a move to check whether the client seems to need emotional care and whether he is able to make use of the opportunity for this. Later, when things are stabilised and the relationship formed, the contacts may well naturally turn into the counselling mode of working as the 'problems arising' are grasped. If there are medical incidents, for example, say, a failed transplant attempt or complications following surgery, then additional emotional care work may be necessary. In this way, a man who has just suffered the traumatic loss of an arm in an industrial accident will probably need much emotional care in the early period of recovery. Later, the mode of working will shift increasingly to deal with the wider horizons involved in picking up life and work again and the examination and resolution of personal difficulties through the counselling techniques. Possibly this will be taken on by his occupational therapist as regular contact with the nurse ends. The occupational therapist, however, will have to remind herself to check that any need for emotional and informational care is still being met and not assume that this aspect of the case is history. Thus, you see the answer to the question, 'What do I do at which stage?' is simply *meet the needs of your client.*

Organising a Scheme of Psychological Care

Clearly the long-term objective in the development of this approach to medicine has to be that general hospital staff as a whole become more psychologically-minded and that psychological care becomes an unexceptional facet of standard practice. By implication, there will be co-ordinated schemes of psychological care operated at the ward, unit or departmental level. Consider, as an example, an orthopaedic ward which deals with long-stay injury and surgical cases together with a flow of less serious, shorter-stay surgical clients. How will the psychological care be organised?

It seems to me that the precise way in which such schemes are run is really the business of those in positions of medical and nursing authority. The allocation of psychological care duties and time for psychological work, the maintenance of standards, the provision of training and support, must all be worked out to suit the situation, which will, of course, vary greatly from place to place. *The most fundamental requirement, though, has to be that someone in an executive position (doctor, ward sister, etc.) does regularly ask, concerning each person on the ward, 'Who is handling this person's psychological care and how is it going?' When such a question is heard regularly we will have entered a new era in the development of general hospital care.*

My own thoughts on how to approach some of the organisational problems are on the following lines. Initially, the sister-in-charge must deal with the prevailing problem of training and maintaining professional standards. She needs to use local resources to secure a standard training facility which is suitable for new nurses and other staff who may wish to slot into the scheme. Working with the local psychologist and senior nurses in charge of training, she will negotiate the development of a training package which will automatically be available at various times throughout the year. This will include appropriate reading, video teaching tapes on counselling skills, etc., lectures or tutorials and some experiential training sessions. It may sound a lot, but a course of only several days length along the lines of those already organised with some frequency on, say, care of the dying, ward management, etc., would give a reasonable introductory training. Really, the resources are available already — all that is required is sufficient pressure to set it all in motion. Obviously, if the ward sister in our example combined with several others to say that they all needed a regular training facility of this type for their staff (twice a year, perhaps), then it would make a more powerful demand and be more sensible in terms of cost efficiency. Additionally, the sister-in-charge needs to create a regular case review session, once a month perhaps, where nurses and staff involved in psychological care report back, discuss and offer mutual tuition to one another. This is very important as a device to maintain psychological-mindedness, provide necessary support and keep an ongoing atmosphere of development and training alive.

The organisation of training needs to be made into permanent structure unless the staffing is very stable with few additions throughout the year. Suitable and interested new members of staff, thus, may be given an initial training experience and then provided with regular supervision and teaching. It would seem appropriate that the nurses who have extended their roles in this way would be referred to as *nurse-counsellors*. In a similar manner, the head of a para-medical department, say, speech therapy, would need to make such provision for her staff too. She might well consider joining in with training events for nurses.

A word on 'suitability' at this point. It is a large topic and my plan is to side-step it. We must, however, at least recognise that by no means all nurses or members of the para-medical professions are suitable for psychological care work. You may recall the section in Chapter 4 which gave the profile of a person suited to emotional care work. Similarly, in general terms, one is also looking for a good intelligence, sufficient to allow a genuine grasp of the principles of psychological care and an ability to think through the issues which assail individual clients. Certain other important resources clearly include a good level of sensitivity to feeling (without over-sensitivity and thus a vulnerability to becoming upset oneself), the capacity to function independently and cope with the responsibility of individual case work, general stability and an inter-personal manner which fosters good relationships (in other words, not excessively timid, insecure, trivial, cold, authoritarian, assertive, etc.). How this is assessed in a reliable way is something which I must leave for local discussion and experience. It is, though, important. A sister or head of department must be selective and exercise judgement on suitability.

Incidentally, I cannot help noticing that there is an assumption in the last two or three paragraphs that these basic psychological skills are not, and will not, be taught effectively in the schools of nursing, occupational therapy and physiotherapy, etc. My thoughts are based on the present-day situation, and I have to say that very few people qualifying in these professions whom I have met in recent years identify themselves as adequately trained in psychological *skills*. In fact, none do. As to the future, I sincerely hope that the training schools will teach courses designed around the idea that basic nursing and para-medical roles include psychological care work, and will thus make a component of their courses over to the necessary preparation.

With the preparatory aspects provided for, the sister-in-charge must now organise the provision of psychological care and integrate it with other ward duties. At her disposal will be a 'pool' of nurse-counsellors and hopefully one or two other professional staff (social worker, physios., occupational therapists) who will have declared themselves interested in participating in the scheme – obviously a little recruitment drive with the offer of training where it is necessary will be a help here. Thus, as each new admission joins the ward, one of the 'pool' members will be asked to deal with the psychological care of that person. Many cases will prove to be brief, light duties, involving little more than systematic informational care, attention to psychological state and the provision of a supportive contact which the client realises can be called upon for more extensive help if necessary. Other cases, the type that have served as illustrations throughout this book, where disfigurement, loss and threats to security in life arise, will prove longer, heavier commitments. The sister will, thus, have to co-ordinate the allocation of psychological care duties in the same fashion as she arranges the other routines of nursing. The monthly case discussions meeting will serve as an evaluation and support group and it can also consider issues to do with referral – if to refer and to whom. Thenceforth, a visitor to the ward *will* be able to ask, 'Who is handling the psychological care of the latest admission and how is it going?' The sister or doctor will be able to reply, naming a member of staff with an indication of any ongoing psychological work.

So far, I have omitted a vital aspect. Such a scheme will run at its optimum only if it is understood, valued and supported by the medical team. Whilst not being excluded from offering psychological care themselves, I have argued earlier that they should be exempt from the face-to-face care work if this is their preference, since the necessary, protective psychological defences for those in the role of hospital doctors are incompatible with the type of psychological functioning required for effective work in psychological care. This in no way precludes the medical staff from complementing the scheme of care by assisting in its organisation – ideally *insisting* on its organisation – and guaranteeing that the information-flow to the nurse-counsellors and others is up to date and sufficiently full ('information should be a shared property').

The symptom of non co-operating or incomprehending medics is that the nurse-counsellor is forced to keep asking them for relevant information and is made to feel something of a nuisance for her trouble. The sign of genuine back-up by medical staff is that *they* take the initiative and make sure the nurse-counsellors have appropriate information so that informational care may be conducted properly. A flight of fancy? Well, I was allowed a few last pages of fantasising about the ideal setting. If you are sceptically curious to discover how we will ever move the majority of the medical profession into this position, I have to say it makes my head ache thinking about it too. It is a strange conflict. One wants to be considerate and supportive to medical colleagues. Many have a difficult and stressing job. At the same time, if they are traditionally-minded, they really can 'mess up' attempts to introduce psychological care. This has to be opposed. I am optimistic for the long term, though. With a great deal of patient, hard work there will be slow improvement. Thus, it is important to be assertive and have resolve, remembering that your function is to strive for the clients, not to protect other professions.

Lastly, our sister-in-charge will keep an eye on her 'psychological workers' for signs of things going astray. Over-involvement, possessive clinging to cases, failure to discuss cases regularly, failure to notice psychological needs, fatigue, over-exposure to distress, fading interest with unreliability and poor quality work, will occasion discussion and appropriate assistance.

Developing Psychological Care in Unfavourable Circumstances

The central argument of this book will not find universal sympathy by any means. However, without doubt some readers will want to add their contribution to the development of psychological care in general hospitals and will also want to expand their own knowledge and skills in the area.

Regrettably, not all those with a positive motivation will experience their particular work setting as encouraging. In fact, the less fortunate will discover that the whole atmosphere is one which discourages psychological care, where those in leadership appear neither to understand nor value the approach. How, in the face of such a discouraging environment, might one still make a contribution? A helpful outlook is to view the development of psychological care as at least a two stage event. Stage one is to do with attracting sufficient support and interest such that attempts at stage two, the actual implementation of the roles, will be viable. I do not mean to infer that you should hold back from attending to the psychological needs of your clients as best you can. It is obvious, though, that if you are attempting this in a permanently unfavourable atmosphere without the understanding and positive support of the medical staff and senior colleagues, then your work will be badly undermined and you will become despondent and resentful. Thus, for a while, you must divide your energies. Part of you must become a 'campaigner'. So, in very general terms, your contribution begins by accepting the responsibility to do something about the present situation yourself, no matter what position you have reached in your training and career. Perhaps the most important first action is to think, read and talk about psychological care, then begin a personal campaign to 'sell' the ideas to those of your colleagues who are unaware or unconvinced. To be realistic, you must be braced for brusque rejections from some colleagues. These are usually generated by feelings of threat brought about by a lack of understanding and knowledge and your response, probably over a period of months, should be a patient, reassuring, educating flow of discussion and information. This is the foundation stone which you must work at even if it happens that you are in a junior position. (A *staff* nurse should educate a sister or consultant? Well, who else is there to do it? This is what I mean by accepting the responsibility and taking initiatives.) On the bright side, you will also meet with much agreement and support from other colleagues. Frankly, I find that by no means all nurses or para-medical staff accept the approach or wish to be personally involved. However, it is very definitely the majority who *are* interested. The balance is bound to vary according to the speciality involved.

Let's return for a moment to the suggestion that you may be faced with a setting which is a 'psychological desert'. It will be hard to go it alone, without support, recognition or encouragement. One thing which should prove helpful, therefore, will be to track down like-minded colleagues from other wards and departments and develop an informal special interest group. The advantage of this, apart from the obvious supportive gain, is that it will be easier to obtain some teaching and supervision from the local psychologist or allied professions. Incidentally, never be shy in seeking training and help directly. Lift the telephone and get on with it. Most psychologists will welcome your approach, as will social workers. It is a frequent experience for me to have a direct request from a group of nurses, occupational therapists or speech therapists to give a talk or training session. It is always pleasing to experience their interest.

No doubt, in the type of environment we are considering, there will be a stream of obstructions and devaluations. As a staff nurse related to me only last week, 'I sat down to talk with a lady on my ward because she was in such an upset state. It was obvious that the most important thing was to talk it through with her but after ten minutes my ward sister came up and interrupted us. She said that if I had nothing to do other than sit around chatting then I should go and get the notes ready for the ward round.' With this type of atmosphere, it is easy to become disillusioned and discouraged. However, if you see yourself as working towards the *eventual* provision of proper psychological care in general hospitals, then an important personal contribution will be to strengthen your knowledge and arguments so that you may patiently chip away at the task of interesting and educating your colleagues from a position of strength. The message, therefore, is that as well as trying to implement some of the basic practices in your everyday work, set aside some of your energy for reading, discussions and attending any training experiences which you can discover. You may then make a valid, personal contribution to the first stage of introducing professional psychological care — that is, selling it.

Hopefully, though, you will not have such a struggle on your hands and will find in your senior staff assistance in training and encouragement in developing skills. Should you be highly motivated and impatient to develop your role in the fashion described, then the obvious solution is to find a job where the consultant, sister-in-charge or head of department is already psychologically aware and has taken steps to implement a valid scheme of psychological care. For a while at least, such people will be like gold dust since, although we have reached a point where a good many senior staff now talk of psychologically-oriented types of care (e.g. the nursing process), few have used their senior position to see through their proper implementation. It is a feature which you might check when applying for a job. For example, in my terms a 'good' sister-in-charge will work on the principle that nursing automatically involves 'professionalised' psychological care and will have set up her ward accordingly. Similarly, the head of an occupational, speech or physiotherapy department will see that a proportion of clients passing through the department will be in great need of psychological care and will have organised the means to provide this.

A Critical Perspective

Although much of the material which we have covered is directed to the detail of individual case management, on reflection you will actually see that three parallel concerns are addressed:

1. There is the 'professionalisation' of psychological care as conducted by individual members of staff in general hospitals, with an emphasis on the acquisition of additional skills.

2. There is the organisation of schemes for psychological care at the level of entire wards and medical units in order to ensure that psychological care becomes a widespread, preventative activity in contrast to limited, occasional 'casualty' work.

3. A more personally directed component in the form of a challenge for you to evaluate your current work regime and assess whether or not you are helping to perpetuate a system of impersonal, technical medicine which is primitive and damaging in psychological terms. This being so, to review the role you play in supporting such a regime and to consider what changes you might make as a personal contribution to the development of caring medicine. This challenge is directed to all the major clinical professions which together make the general hospital staff — the doctors, nurses, social workers, physiotherapists, occupational and speech therapists, etc. It is clearly a thoroughly relevant question for allied professions too, such as hospital administrators.

The arguments have now been presented and the techniques illustrated. We have now arrived at the last task — that of stock taking.

I have been uncompromisingly critical of the present levels of psychological care in our hospitals and have implicated both the medical and nursing professions as bearing responsibility for this. Surveying the claims and criticisms thus made, I can find no reason to mellow or withdraw my views in any way. Save on regret — without doubt there exist some physicians, surgeons and anaesthetists who *are* sensitive, psychologically-aware people who are already doing their best to shift medicine from its overly technical basis to a more caring form. They have not had sufficient recognition from me and have, I realise, become caught up in the general condemnation. Perhaps we may recognise them now (I have several in mind personally) and ask of them that they redouble their efforts. Nurses of similar dispositions, of which there are a good number I believe, have been acknowledged several times throughout the text.

Objective Evaluation

It is likely that searching questions will be asked of this approach, as they should be: does it work and is it possible to demonstrate that psychological care achieves that which it is expected to achieve? For example, are the people in a ward which is organised to provide psychological care actually better informed than in a ward run on traditional lines? How have they responded to emotional care? Are they, as a result, more comfortable and emotionally stable? Do they feel better cared for? If objective measures are taken of psychological state, say, the levels of depression and anxiety, will a difference be found between the people on the two wards? (This is a piece of research which needs some sophistication in approach since we must bear in mind that emotional care is not primarily concerned with the instant reduction of emotion, but rather the facilitation of emotional process.) Of great interest, too, will be a comparison of the rates of physical recovery, survival, progress in rehabilitation, etc., between the two groups. Lastly, and of equal significance, how do the staff fare? Does the implementation of psychological care give greater fulfilment in work? Does it reduce efficiency in other aspects of their roles? How has it affected staff relationships?

If you are hoping for immediate answers to these questions then, regrettably, I am about to fail you. The difficulty is that the implementation of psychological care as a standard, stable practice in hospitals such that meaningful research questions of this type may be answered, is yet to come. Research cannot be conducted into something which has not been properly established. Of course, some relevant but indirect studies exist already, for example, those mentioned in Chapter 2 which examined the effects of pre-surgical preparation by means of information and coaching in coping styles. Although positive outcomes were generally produced, these were not a good examination of psychological care. In an effective scheme, the understanding and positive collaboration of the majority of medical and nursing staff will be evident — without this uninamity, psychological care is, to a degree, sabotaged and can only limp along. In these early studies, such factors were not taken into account and thus the true potential of psychological care could not be assessed. To pick up the metaphor from above, worthwhile research may only begin when we have established some 'psychological oases' in the hospitals.

Incidentally, when developments proceed to a point which favours empirical evaluation, the object of the research will be, in my view, to evaluate the potency of various techniques and organisational plans in achieving the aims of psychological care, and examining how best to integrate it with physical care. The question, 'In serious illness and injury, should we attempt to deal with the whole person and in so doing extend our care to cater for psychological needs which are currently neglected?' does not appear to me to be a research issue as such. It is a social and moral consideration and, personally, I have yet to encounter arguments *against* caring medicine which are worth the time of day.

Objections

I have mentioned before that I often find myself teaching psychological care to groups of nurses or trainees from one of the allied professions. Naturally, in such a setting, I come face to face with 'reality' and have to absorb the objections and criticisms of the audience. In similar style, therefore, it seems appropriate that *we* should finish with an airing of some 'popular' objections and examine the responses which can be made to these. Let's imagine we are in a seminar together. It is discussion time. Here are some of the comments and questions which are likely:

'Nurses are too busy, we just do not have the time'
Until a trained team of work-study observers conduct objective studies, we will not have a factually-based answer to this. The next best alternative is to inquire of a large sample of nurses how *they* view the situation. This I do with some frequency. For our purposes it is relevant to relay to you the opinions of several senior nurses whom I have recently engaged in conversation around this point. All have replied strongly in the following manner. 'Too busy doing what, though? A good deal of this busy-ness is centred on tasks of low importance. There is still a strong task-orientation to nursing with unnecessary repetitions and rituals — it's a kind of defence.' This will sound familiar to us from Chapter 2 where there was a description of the defensive strategies which have evolved in nursing as a means of minimising inter-personal contact. The over-involvement with tasks, the task-oriented approach, was noted as a mainstay defence. Thus, a strong possibility arises that some of the duties which appear to weigh nurses down and leave no time for psychological care may, at best, be low priority, labour-intensive rituals which are related more to the preservation of routines than dealing with the actual needs of the clients. At worst, they are essentially devices for avoiding closer inter-personal contact. In this way a series of routine bed baths which are by no means essential to well being will 'tie up' a nurse for hours during a week and eliminate her from other forms of care. Similarly, some nurses' time goes towards doing things for 'patients' which they could well do for themselves, since 'patients' are encouraged to adopt a passive, dependant role. Meal-times are such an example. We, therefore, have to question the validity of this busy-ness.

Please understand that these comments do not come from me but are a composite of comments from various senior nurses, which I simply pass on to you. At this point, though, I will come in with a comment or two of my own. Were psychological care to be allotted its *appropriate* level of priority (which in caring medicine is quite high), then it would take precedence over those elements of nursing which are low priority routines and it would lead to the progressive elimination of the task-oriented defence since closer personal contact would become a valued objective which could be taken on in greater confidence. In other words, more time for psychological work would become available.

I also want to point out that some of the important changes needed in the development of psychological care are not likely to demand much time. I refer to changes in thinking and attitude towards a psychologically-minded style of nursing. Change of attitude itself takes no time out of regular duties at all, yet it can have a positive influence on the care given. Also, note that no matter what turnover and workload exist on a genuinely busy ward, *time will already be given* to some information exchange and supportive contact — it is inevitable. As the minimum development, this time may be used in the rather more systematic and professional activities of informational care and monitoring psychological state together with some input in terms of emotional care. Thus, you see, psychological care may be introduced at various levels of intensity according to the time available. There will *always* be some time available and, therefore, objections to its introduction based on the plea of insufficient time are unsound.

'With the economies and cutbacks, we do not have the staff to cope with psychological care'

The same points apply to this objection as to that concerning the availability of time. However, an important additional issue must be emphasised. The shift to caring medicine and the implementation of psychological care will be a slow process of change, taking place over many years. Even in the 'lean times', the work of laying the foundations can and should proceed, albeit at a slower pace. Since all things have seasons, the current era of cutbacks will inevitably be followed by a stable period and even selective re-expansion. It will be highly advantageous, therefore, to have established psychological-mindedness in the hospitals and to have plans for full implementation of psychological care even though the conditions of the present day may allow only relatively reduced schemes to be introduced initially. The great need is to make the start. Remember, too, the potential for direct assistance by the para-medical professions and make use of these additional sources of 'labour'.

'If the doctors are against it, we can't just go ahead, it would be treading on their toes. If a consultant says he does not want someone informed, you have to abide by what he says'
This is not going to be an easy debate for any of us but the contentious issues must be faced. Issues of both principle and fact are involved. The following are my views on the situation described. Let's deal with the facts first. A medical consultant has indisputable *clinical* responsibility. He is given authority to organise and conduct the medical treatment necessary to restore or maintain physical health and, by implication, must control those aspects of hospital activity which bear a direct relationship to these treatments. *His contract of employment will not, however, instruct him to maintain moral, social, political or psychological authority over his clients.*

Now, as a power-conserving monopoly, the medical profession often gratuitously mandates itself with responsibilities in these areas and assumes decision-making authority. In strict terms, however, if the issues involved are not of a clinical nature, then the 'ice on which the profession stands is too thin'. For example, a man is being treated for cancer of the pancreas. His consultant surgeon will rightly assume responsibility for all aspects of the case management which affect the conduct of treatment and general health of that person. If issues arise which go beyond that brief, then the consultant is exceeding the range of his *exclusive* authority. His view will be important but will have the status of bearing equal weight against that of, say, a senior nurse. Extending the example, what happens if the consultant opposes psychological care and plans to withhold information from the client against the nurse's judgement? *If* he can demonstrate that there are *clinical* reasons for so doing (i.e. it adversely affects the cancer or general physical health), then he is operating within his contract. If, however, the basis on which the decision is generated is anything other than medical, i.e. psychological (for which few surgeons have had any training), social, moral or even personal caprice, then that decision cannot carry real authority. He is operating beyond his contract and has no grounds on which he may *impose* such a decision. He may, however, want to make a case for persuasive purposes. In which case, the only way to resolve the issue would be by consensus method involving the whole team.

Many such decisions seem to me to be areas of great ambiguity and are as much the province of nursing authority as medical authority. My motive for arguing this is not to encourage a fight. The purpose is to find ways of improving psychological care in hospitals, one way or another. If the key concern is to do with the well-being of the client there will, I suspect, be few instances in which psychological care (including the informational care component) will prove injurious to the clinical conduct of a case. Opposition to it could not, therefore, be justified on medical grounds and so the decision to introduce psychological care stops being the exclusive province of the medical profession.

If I am honest I have to admit that this stance might generate a confrontational situation in certain circumstances. For some members of the medical profession it will be threatening and feel like a loss of power. It will tap into the 'my patients, my ward' manner of thought and provoke defensive power-conserving reactions. Attention, though, must be directed resolutely to the unmet psychological needs of the ill and injured – tending to these must take priority.

Having said this, I want to repeat the message given earlier in the chapter. Open fights are usually unhelpful. You need to be firm, thoroughly informed and negotiate from a position of strength. Also, make an effort to be reassuring and work patiently at the task of attitude change. Harmonious professional integration is your target.

(Doctor) 'Yes, probably there is a lot in what you say but I'm not having my nurses' time tied up like this until I'm sure that everything else is done properly'
The composition of nursing duties is the business of the director of nursing and the individual ward sisters. They offer a service to support the medical service and are duty bound to maximise the effectiveness of medical treatment. However, they are not 'your' nurses – they are members of an independent allied profession and the decision concerning what constitutes good nursing care is a nursing matter although, of course, it should be negotiable. It would be inappropriate for a member of another profession to attempt to impose restrictions of such a nature that nurses were forced to conduct what, in their eyes, would amount to bad nursing. Added to which, it is an unrealistic statement, since extending the roles of nurses and para-medical staff in this way will complement and support medical treatments, possibly enhancing their effects at times. It has never been suggested that psychological care displaces any necessary nursing duties.

*'It's not just the doctors. We were trained to look after people's
psychological needs at the School of Nursing. Our tutors really
hammered it in. But here in the hospital, the senior nurses and nursing
management just will not back us up. All they seem to worry about
is basic nursing duties and manpower planning'*

There does not seem much more to add to this than was written a few
pages earlier. If you are keen to develop psychological care but find
yourself in an unfavourable setting then you must contribute initially
by becoming a campaigner. If there is sufficient upward pressure
directed at nursing management by a sufficient number of people,
attitudes will slowly change. Some senior sisters and nursing administrators may find the whole issue threatening since they have no training in psychological care and fear being exposed as inadequate in this
respect. Accordingly, the emphasis should be on a gentle, educational
approach.

*'To be honest, I just feel too emotionally tired. I don't think I could get
involved in people's problems like this. I just want to do my basic
nursing job and go home'*

Honesty of this type is welcome. In the same way that people should
not be forced to receive some of the elements of psychological care,
neither should individual members of staff be forced to provide it. The
result would be poor quality work. A person who feels unable to participate in a scheme of psychological care because they are ill-suited is
being responsible in withdrawing. The only proviso I will make is that
they should still recognise the need for psychological care in hospitals
and support its implementation. Their personal position does not in any
way justify an obstructing stance to the provision of psychological care
by those who wish to provide it.

*'Some people only stay for a night on my ward. You can't do much in
that time, it's not worth it'*

That is so wrong. The general approach and atmosphere of doing things
matters greatly in a hospital, even when intensive psychological work is
not feasible. Psychological care should even pervade an outpatient
clinic. In overall terms, the introduction of formal schemes of psychological care is part of a wider shift from solely technical to more caring
medicine. Never lose sight of this objective. A 24-hour stay on a tradi-
tionally-run ward carries the risk of some disturbing, possibly damaging
psychological experiences, whereas that same event in a ward which at
least thinks in terms of psychological care has a built-in safeguard

insulating people from these risks. Added to this, if the task of monitoring psychological state is conducted properly and there exist facilities for referring on, then arrangements can be made for the occasional client on the ward who needs more extensive and longer-term care.

'We would like to do this kind of work but we have never been trained to do it'
Then take the initiative and arrange some training for yourself. Explore local opportunities for teaching and training — it's easy enough to do. Request your senior nurse in charge of training (or head of department) to make approaches to the people you discover who could help out. Ask her to make inquiries then set something up. Note: *You* take the initiative.

Don't you think that this will make some people worse — it encourages them to become dependent and start thinking about their problems which stirs things up'
Firstly, I am suggesting that what already exists in an 'amateur' way is intensified and made professional. Surely there can be no objections to that.

Secondly, dependency is not a sin, it is an emotional state. If you offer support to people in trouble they will lean on you, particularly if there is trust and you are strong. As you help clients with their reactions and difficulties you can, where necessary, include the issue of dependency as something to be dealt with, aiding them in the development of coping skills. Dependency is a natural *phase* in most instances, not a permanent feature (except in the case of highly dependent personalities who would demand much of you anyway).

As for stirring up problems, the whole spirit of this work is that of an invitation for a client to share reactions and difficulties if he or she so wishes — the issues are at a level of conscious awareness already. Put it like this. If you were to be admitted to hospital after a serious road accident and faced permanent physical handicap as a result, if your mother were to be admitted to hospital for surgery to deal with cancer of the tongue and larynx, or if your husband had to attend a neurological unit with suspected multiple sclerosis, would you worry for yourself and your relatives in these situations *because* there were people on hand to give professional care for the inevitable emotional needs? Would you worry because the staff planned to help with any personal and psychological difficulties arising; planned to maintain a flow of trustworthy information and also expected to give support by representing any psychological needs to the rest of the team? I doubt it. Perhaps, though, you might worry a little if this type of care was known to be missing.

EPILOGUE: 'ALONE WITH ILLNESS'

Lorna A. Sealy

Author's note: in the role of a psychologist in a general hospital, one spends a great deal of time listening to detailed accounts of people's experiences. Sometimes I feel that many of my colleagues in nursing and medicine have never allowed themselves to do that – ever. It is appropriate, therefore, that we should rehearse this skill together. We will give time to receiving the experiences of a woman who nursed her husband for several years and was herself damaged, both by the nature of the event and the absence of psychological care skills on the part of the staff. We will just listen and put the effort into understanding what it was really like rather than making any comment.

I was married to a man who went into chronic renal failure. My perception of events during this time was, of course, subjective and not always easy to formulate concisely and clearly. However, I will attempt to chart out the history of my experiences without too much loss of accuracy. It begins in 1976.

We had both newly qualified as teachers and in the last month at college, Kevin had been offered a teaching job in the south of England. We were engaged at the time and planned to marry the following summer. We moved and I found a job locally as a secretary since there were no other teaching posts available. We had been living in the new location for a couple of months when a routine examination and blood test by the GP we registered with showed Kevin to be anaemic. On investigation, it was revealed that his kidney (he had one removed when he was five due to a urinary infection) was not functioning properly and would deteriorate until finally treatment by dialysis would be needed, probably in about twelve months. Kevin was given an appointment with a consultant nephrologist and a transplant surgeon and I, as his fiancée, was invited to attend.

We met with the two doctors and they gave us their view of the situation and offered treatment by haemodialysis technique with the possibility of a transplant in the future. The other alternative, we were told, was inevitable death. We were young and he had just begun his career as a teacher. To us, the consultant nephrologist appeared to paint

quite a rosy picture of the life to come including adequate work capability, a degree of sport and a 'normal' living pattern being in reach.
We were advised by him not to have a family too early in marriage in
order that we could fully establish our routine of home dialysis first.
If Kevin had a successful transplant he could expect normal health but
would have to take steroids for the rest of his life. These could affect
his fertility and present problems for conception. We left that interview
with a feeling of gratitude towards the doctors and confidence for the
future.

Did we only hear the things we wanted to and disregard the remainder? To a degree we probably did. However, the doctors may have
found it a hard task to put a more realistic picture to two people who
so obviously wanted to be reassured. Kevin's decision to accept treatment would not have been any different had he been given a more
modest picture. I wish at least we had been given fuller information
and that someone had made sure we understood some of the risks and
problems involved. I have no memory at all of being given advance
information on negative aspects of life with dialysis, e.g. the constant
minor physical irritations, continual tiredness and the extent to which
our social life would become totally disrupted.

The six months or so that followed were filled with the mechanics
of training for dialysis and becoming self-sufficient other than dealing
with accident or emergency. We attended the Unit three evenings a
week. Our training was adequate although at times we found ourselves
rebuked by one nurse for adopting procedures taught to us by another
nurse in the preceding session. The business of informing us was haphazard — there was no record of what we had been taught and what
remained for us to learn. Neither was there a system for assessing our
absorption of information and, more importantly, our basic understanding of life on dialysis. We felt drawn to one or two nurses who
obviously sensed our needs as 'people' in the situation. It would have
been ideal if they could have been personal tutors, but as things stood
this was not possible and we never knew from one session to the next
which one of a dozen or so nurses we would be working with on any
particular day.

With the positive remarks of the doctors still fresh in our minds,
we went ahead with our marriage and the purchase of a house. In
retrospect I find it staggering that we received positive encouragement
to marry rather than be advised against it in the strongest terms.
Anyone with a clear understanding of what life is truly like for a
haemodialysis family could never, in honesty, offer encouragement if

they had the welfare of *both* people in mind. I suspect that part of the motive was to secure a stable dialysis partner for Kevin, which I became, although at high personal cost.

Dialysis equipment was installed at home and we were keen to distance ourselves from the Renal Unit in order to gain a degree of independence and flexibility which it was not possible to achieve in the hospital environment. We made the transition accompanied by visits from a home sister for the first two dialysis sessions, after which we were pronounced 'capable'. For a few months all seemed well, then Kevin became ill. It happened suddenly. He developed pulmonary oedema, pericarditis and pericardial effusion. He was in hospital for the next few weeks. We had been aware that there was something wrong and had been to the GP as well as the Unit. It was revealed that Kevin had become fluid overloaded (that is, he had consistently taken in more fluid than was being removed) and from then on our common experience was that we were made to feel at fault by the Unit staff. Yet, we felt we had never been told about the importance of the link between weight control and fluid intake. No doubt we had, but with so much information to absorb during training, much of it had been lost by this time. Thus, as Kevin had slowly put on weight over that first summer, we had been pleased believing it was the muscle weight returning which he had lost as a result of the kidney disease. In our ignorance the link between fluid and weight had not occurred to us and no-one had checked up on what we were doing or thinking once we were at home. Kevin slowly recovered from this but my memory is that at least two years elapsed before his heart, which was badly stretched by the fluid overloading, returned to its pre-stressed size. Our resentment, however, never did recede. We had been striving hard but did not have the knowledge we needed and it felt very unjust to be accused in this way.

The doctors in charge of the Unit always emphasised most strongly their feeling that there was no good reason for a person on dialysis to stop work. Kevin would be seen as having failed not only himself but also the 'team' at the Unit if he did so. Hence he continued to work although it became more and more of a struggle against the exhaustion caused by uraemia and he took increasing time off work sick. The job took every ounce of energy which he had and thus the total responsibility for the 'administration' of our lives passed to me. I can see now the damaging effect that this expectation towards normal working had on us. We were dialysing back at home again and knew few other patients to 'compare notes' with. We were effectively cut off from people who really understood what a life on dialysis meant. All I knew was that I was having to do so much whilst Kevin did proportionately less and had more time off work — a very different experience to that which he had been led to hope for. Kevin felt undermined as a man and saw himself as a tremendous burden to me. He loved teaching but knew he wasn't doing as good a job as he could (his employers, both inside the school and the local education authority were wonderfully patient and supportive — there was never pressure exerted on him by them) and he would have resigned much sooner than he in fact did except the idea of 'letting everyone down' filled him with guilt. I can also admit now to having unspoken feelings of resentment because I wanted to accuse him of not doing the things the doctors said he should be able to do. But I felt guilty at my resentment because I knew my husband was profoundly ill and literally disabled, something our doctors seemed to find difficult to accept.

The next couple of years passed by fairly uneventfully but the routine was unremitting. It felt as though we were becoming more and more deeply entrenched in a day-by-day existence centred on dialysis and that control of our lives was steadily passing from us. In retrospect, this is exactly what was happening, mainly because of our lack of recognition of this change and my lack of determination to alter it. I think it was through a feeling of guilt that I allowed Kevin to adopt more of an invalid's role and myself more of a mother/nurse/housekeeper role — I found it difficult to assert equality in our relationship when there was the unspoken (and occasionally spoken) accusation of 'How can you be so hard — you don't know what it's like feeling ill all the time. You're lucky you're healthy.'

We still hoped for a transplant and during this time there were two 'false alarms', where we were telephoned and told that a kidney was available for transplantation and to ready ourselves for the operation. On the first occasion we were asked to go into the Unit so that Kevin could dialyse before the operation — the kidney was still in Liverpool. By the time we arrived at the Unit they had been notified that the transplant was not proceeding because of damage to the organ. On the second occasion we had come much closer. Kevin had actually finished a five-hour dialysis session when a telephone call from a Birmingham hospital came through with the news that the kidney had again been damaged in transit. That was a terrific disappointment.

Life continued. I found our financial struggling harder to cope with as the months went by. We never had any money to spare and we couldn't see how we would be able to manage if Kevin stopped teaching. We had even contemplated both giving up work just in order to reduce the stresses and permanent rushing about (for me) and throwing ourselves on the State, possibly giving up home ownership for council accommodation. We had seen the then social worker and had talked to her about various options but she never really seemed to pick up the urgency behind our meetings. Maybe we tried to appear too bright about everything and would have been better off if we had just collapsed and relied on outside agencies to sort us out. But we didn't.

I did belong to a sports club and tried to go to it twice a week although this was not always possible. It was the one thing that gave me social contact outside of home other than work and was very important to me. However, some kind of holiday where I actually had a break from the routine for a couple of weeks would have been such a relief. In four years this was never to become available. Firstly, we could not have afforded it and, secondly, Kevin would always bring pressure to bear by becoming very agitated and upset at the thought of dialysing at the Unit for a period of time. He disliked Unit dialysis possibly because he had much more sympathy at home and was made to do a lot less for himself than at the Unit. However, whatever the reason, I was made to feel that I was 'deserting' him and putting him in an intolerable position. No-one at any time elaborated to us the benefits of a partner being able to have a break from the stressful routines and it was only much later that such suggestions were made.

Eventually another opportunity to have a kidney transplant occurred and this time the operation was carried out. Prior to surgery, Kevin dialysed at the Unit. I remember very little about the time spent waiting except that Kevin did sleep for quite a lot of it. I don't recall much communication with doctors and nurses although I do remember them talking to us with general encouragement. As far as transplants were concerned, we did know that 'things could go wrong', rejection could set in (hopefully being suppressed by huge doses of steroids), the kidney might not start functioning, it might work for a while and then suddenly for no apparent reason stop completely, necessitating dialysis again until the next transplant. We also knew that dialysis might be required until the kidney did work at a satisfactory level. I cannot think of any other bits of information we were given, although with all the time spent at the Unit over the years I daresay we had talked about transplant surgery with patients and nurses but on a general level.

Other than telling Kevin that he would be taken to the Intensive Care Unit after the operation, we were unprepared for how he might feel during the next couple of days. In fact, we knew very little indeed about the actual events following a transplant attempt. The anaesthetic used was curare based and shortly after coming round from it, Kevin was aware that he could hardly move at all. He could barely move his fingers and moving an arm or leg was impossible. He had not known this might happen and was not able, so soon after surgery, to understand that this was a temporary thing which would pass within a day or so. It caused him a great deal of distress and fright which I feel could so easily have been avoided. The staff in ITU were very caring but seemed to have little in-depth understanding of the treatment of dialysis patients and transplantees. This in itself was understandable since, if patients in ITU required dialysis, a nurse would come from the Kidney Unit for this purpose. However, there also seemed to be confusion between the treatment of general surgical cases and the treatment of transplantees. When the two were combined, it caused real problems.

One example presented itself somewhat traumatically after the transplant operation. Kevin developed low blood pressure as a result of which his fistula (that is, his access to venepuncture in haemodialysis treatment) collapsed. The new kidney was not working yet and he needed dialysis. A temporary external access (a shunt) had to be inserted into a vein in his leg under a local anaesthetic. Within a day or so of this happening, the staff of ITU were making Kevin get out of bed and move around the room on his leg despite our anxious protests that we didn't think he should put any weight on it. The response was that after an operation (any operation?) the best thing was to use the body rather than lie prone. They did not check this out with anyone experienced in renal medicine and assumed that normal post-surgical procedures would apply. As a result of the transplanted kidney not working, Kevin's legs had become oedemic and on being made to use his leg in this condition, the openings for the shunt were enlarged considerably. Once he was well dialysed (since the kidney never worked well) and the oedema was reduced, he started bleeding profusely from his leg wounds whenever his leg dropped much below the horizontal. I clearly remember being told by the staff at the Kidney Unit that what else could you expect from ITU — they didn't know about it. Why didn't someone take the trouble to tell them?

Another very unpleasant incident in ITU concerned catheters. Kevin had to have a catheter inserted into his bladder during the transplant operation for the purpose of preventing raised urine pressure in the bladder if the new organ started functioning quickly and well. After 48 hours or so (I think this was the appproximate time period) this was removed. Kevin was being given a steady intake of fluid at the time to try, I believe, to stimulate the kidney into action. While the catheter was in place he had not been passing much urine. After its removal, the nurse who was looking after him kept asking him to try to pass urine but he was unable to do so. About four hours later a doctor came in, looked at his records and announced that if Kevin did not pass urine within an hour, she would have the catheter replaced. Kevin was very distressed at this and said how uncomfortable it had been and that when it was removed there had been blood on it and it had not come out easily. I was present the whole time and was upset at the high-handed and dismissive manner of this doctor who virtually ignored his fright other than telling him he would have to have it put back and not to be stupid, things like that didn't hurt. I don't believe that I could be a silent witness to such an incident ever again. What I would say might make no difference but at least I would take the opportunity to express my disgust at such treatment. The deadline arrived and Kevin had still been unable to pass urine. He was in a poor frame of mind when the doctor returned. For some reason I was not asked to leave the room. A local anaesthetic (lignocaine jelly, I believe) was put onto the end of his penis and a few minutes later the doctor starting insert-ing the catheter. I'd seen Kevin crying from emotional distress in the past, for example, when he was told that he would need dialysis and the implications and uncertainties were frightening him, but I'd never seen him cry out of pain. It was, looking back, appalling that so much fright and distress could be added to the problems of anyone in Kevin's position, especially when it was handed out by a person who would undoubtedly profess to be caring. It would have been caring to at least acknowledge the distress and take time to discuss the situation with Kevin. In contrast, the doctor attempted to ignore it, brushing it aside as a nuisance. In the end, she said the gauge of the first catheter inserted under the general anaesthetic (and also this one) must have been too big, hence the pain and bleeding, and she used a smaller one which she fitted relatively easily.

It was a relief to get back to the Kidney Unit and see familiar faces. Kevin was put in a room for barrier nursing. The procedure then for entering the room was initially gowning up, masking and wearing sterile gloves. During this period, some of the staff would come into the room, in particular auxiliaries, 'just for a minute' without follow-ing the procedures. This used to cause Kevin some anxiety, especially since the kidney was not doing well and he did not want to hazard himself by possible exposure to infection. I remember one night nurse in particular who used to come into the room without masking up despite being full of cold and sneezing. When we complained we were told we were making a fuss. However, in the initial couple of weeks back at the Unit, despite dialysis being required, we did feel very supported by the staff. They were all eager for transplants to be successful for the patients they spent so much time with and were always delighted when people could leave dialysis behind, even as a temporary thing.

There was, though, disagreement between the doctors in charge, which came across to the nursing staff and the patients. I couldn't begin to guess at the reasons, but it appeared that personalities clashed and a new appointment had disturbed some of them. Mutual dislike was apparent and this was a very unsettling time for all concerned. We personally found we were being told one thing by one doctor which was then contracted by another. This was confusing and upsetting. It eroded our confidence and affected the nurses who were also receiving conflicting orders, which created tension and difficulties for them.

Kevin's new kidney struggled on for a short while but what little function it had seemed to fade, rejection being the primary problem. Eventually, after about six weeks, a biopsy was arranged and as a result Kevin had a 'blast' of steroids to try and halt rejection. Sadly this did not work and the transplant attempt was recognised as having failed. At this point we felt a subtle shift in the way the nursing staff related to us. The supportive, sympathetic attitudes became much less evident and there seemed, in the background, an air of unspoken accusation. This we found bewildering – surely we weren't to blame for the kidney not working? I imagine few if any of the staff would accept this as having happened, and probably we were in an extremely emotional, sensitive state and were looking for something or someone to take our anger and disappointment out on.

We did, however, feel as if it was 'the two of us versus the rest of the Kidney Unit' at that time. Kevin had a brother living nearby who spent a good deal of time with the two of us. He was the only person who made himself available to us and understood sufficiently our feelings to let us take out behaviour on him which would, outside of these circumstances, have been unacceptable. He was a silent listener, someone who provided us with an outlet, and in that role he was of tremendous value to us. I don't think I ever once acknowledged this to him afterwards, probably because it felt difficult to talk about behaviour that was the result of such emotional distress, but he was very much appreciated. It seems to me, though, that such distress is an obvious and normal feature of such surgery, where the outcome could mean a change of life style from one very impaired and restricted to one of comparable freedom. It might have helped if the staff at the Unit had been more able to understand our needs and help guide us through the period of a failed transplant or refer us to other help. Instead, they appeared to need to work through their own disappointment and could give little help. The decision was made to remove the failed kidney rather than leave it because there was the possibility of some infection. Surgery was carried out eleven weeks after the transplant under local anaesthetic (epidural) and Kevin was allowed home shortly afterwards.

That whole episode seemed to take something vital away from Kevin. I think now that it was hope. His manner became much more introspective and his behaviour changed. The convalescence was slow and he saw himself as an invalid leaning heavily on me and totally unable to do much for himself. I think I was aware of the danger in letting this become too entrenched but again I could not cope with the accusation of being hard, uncaring and unloving. So I capitulated thereby worsening the situation.

It was obvious that Kevin had no wish to get back to work, mainly, I think, because he saw it as unattainable. He would become easily upset if people talked about it even though he was under no pressure. Eventually I suggested he resign and he leapt at the opportunity. It lifted a tremendous worry from him and he became much happier (at least for a while) with the sense of relief. The summer passed slowly with little happening in our lives bar (for me) work and dialysis. With the convalescence after the transplant, my one outlet at the sports club became difficult to sustain. Kevin would complain about being on his own all day and then, on the evenings I went out, being left at night too. I stopped going. He never made much effort to get out and sustain a social life, or just go out with me, and I became more isolated. Yielding to the pressure to leave the club was a bad mistake on my part. Perhaps it would have been different if we had had much family locally but we didn't. Being new to the area we had few friends either and Kevin resisted meeting others. He was becoming more and more difficult socially.

The mechanics of dialysis passed by uneventfully into the autumn and there was not much contact with the Kidney Unit except when Kevin had problems with sleep and 'itching skin and pins and needles', common symptoms with dialysis patients. He would contact the Unit for alternative drugs since those he was given seemed to be of little help to him. His pattern of life seemed to be changing and he would spend an increasing amount of time downstairs at night, distressed because he couldn't sleep. He found that difficult to accept and would fight it, being unable to view the time constructively and do anything positive with it. Instead it was seen as a nightmare. He would take larger and larger doses of drugs to try and induce sleep. When I left the house to go to work he would finally get to sleep and would often still be in bed when I returned home. His difficulties seemed to be compounded as he became more and more lax about his fluid allowance, often drinking way beyond what he should. His resolve to stay in control collapsed. I was quite unaware at first of the way he was treating himself, especially over the quantity of drugs he was taking. It came as quite a shock when I realised this. He was often still asleep when I got home but in a very dopey state when he was wakened. At first, I thought it was because he was still tired but he was probably becoming toxic with the quantity of drugs he was taking. He would think nothing of taking half a dozen sleeping pills, a handful of tranquillisers, anti-hystamines and sometimes quite a lot more in one night. His behaviour was becoming aggressively dependent and harder to live with. I was feeling increasingly that I was fighting an uphill battle for the two of us and instead of a sense of reward, there was only a sense of being trapped and feeling cheated. I felt a growing tension – we seemed so terribly alone with it all. Nobody knew of our daily experiences and the struggle it had become. The people at the Kidney Unit no doubt worked on the belief that we were doing well.

One night during a dialysis session he was very difficult. Suddenly the years of strain and fatigue seemed overwhelming and I broke down. My memory of the events that followed in the ensuing weeks is not necessarily strictly chronicled but is close enough. That night, Kevin realised I was very upset and that perhaps he had gone too far and he rang his brother who came round to see us. I was still out of control and one of the sisters at the Unit was telephoned. She came round to the house, quite startled, I think, because no-one had suspected we had any problems. We always seemed cheerful and able to cope. She was a great help to me at the time, taking the stance of someone outside of our lives who would listen but not judge. However, the next day she reported the incident to the Unit and it was referred to the unit counsellor who contacted us and arranged an interview. I remember this as being a fairly relaxed chat at home. I had not met him before and I suppose he was trying to sound us out and get some idea of how we functioned. I do know, however, that I felt quite at ease and surprised myself at how easily I had given him 'personal' information. In fact, sadly, Kevin had become quite annoyed at my openness and his response seemed to detract from the idea of having a 'combined session' to try and sort things out.

I felt much more in control of my emotions after giving some vent to them with the unit counsellor. However, the following week a minor incident triggered off another similar episode. I then felt I had to have a break and just get away from Kevin, dialysis and everything connected with it, so I packed a bag and went back to my parents. The staff at the Kidney Unit now became extremely sympathetic and quickly slotted Kevin into their dialysis programme while I was away. No magical solutions presented themselves to me, however. I was blocking my feelings and all the trip home did was to buy me three weeks' time. When I came back Kevin avoided talking about the real reason for my absence and the only rationalisation for it was that I had become overtired and needed a rest. Life reverted back to the old routine and, literally, nothing altered to make any improvement. In fact, things actually deteriorated. Kevin had been finding his fluid allowance more and more onerous and was badly overdrinking. As a result, he was overloading with fluid again and felt ill. His solution to the problem was to dialyse more often and he would have liked to dialyse on a daily basis. I capitulated to an extent, otherwise I was faced with someone deteriorating into grave illness. He was at this stage dialysing four, sometimes five, times a week. The strain of this (about seven hours each session) after a full day at work together with keeping the house going was defeating me.

We were going to visit relatives that Christmas and Kevin had promised he would control his fluids closely. His resolve held for a day or so and then crumbled. A situation I dreaded most of all ensued – dealing with someone very ill who felt dreadful and who just wanted to switch off, giving total responsibility for himself to me. Our train journey home stretched me beyond my limits. It was at this point that I accepted that I could not continue living in this fashion, becoming more embittered at what I saw increasingly as the selfishness of my husband. I couldn't make excuses for his behaviour any more. I felt like screaming at him sometimes that he think about other people instead of just himself. But by then, even if he had realised the dangers, it would have been too late to save our marriage.

I talked to the unit counsellor and from that visit it was obvious to him that our marriage was teetering badly. He offered his support to both of us as individuals but did not attempt to prolong the unsatisfactory marital situation. My need to escape became overwhelming and I left Kevin three days later. The week that followed was one of sleepless nights and tortured feelings. We were both devastated by events.

Kevin dialysed at the Kidney Unit where he received a tremendous amount of care and warmth from all the staff. I also received kindness and understanding from them. They finally seemed to recognise the difficulties we were having. Some months passed and Kevin converted to continuous ambulatory peritoneal dialysis (CAPD) treatment which gave him a degree of independence he had not had for years and released him from Unit dialysis. He appeared to be going through a positive phase and was planning on travelling abroad to visit friends for an extended holiday, possibly going back to college to do a further course, and his general health and sense of well-being was better than it had been for a long time. Again, though, outward appearances did not represent the real Kevin and on a grey, autumn day he ended his life. It was a tragic end to a life whose last few years had been full of suffering.

All of us who had cared for him were stunned. It drew us together and, when talking with the nursing staff then, I found for the first time the isolation and distance was broken. The great tragedy is that this genuine contact between the staff and myself came only after Kevin's death — I needed them at the beginning and all the way through.

BIBLIOGRAPHY

Balint, M. *The Doctor, his Patient and the Illness* (Hogarth Press, London, 1964)

Bond, M.R. 'New Approaches to Pain', *Psychological Medicine, 10* (1980), pp. 195-9

Brammer, L. *The Helping Relationship* (Prentice Hall, London, 1973)

Brand, P.C. and van Keep, P.A. *Breast Cancer* (MTP Press, Lancaster, 1978)

Broom, A. and Korshidian, C. 'Are Clinical Psychologists Interested in Chronic Pain', *Bulletin of the British Psychological Society, 35* (1982), pp. 418-20

Byrne, P.S. and Long, B.E.L. *Doctors Talking to Patients* (HMSO, London, 1976)

Egan, G. *The Skilled Helper* (Brooks/Cole Publishing Co., Monterey, California, 1975)

Gardiner, B.M. 'Psychological Aspects of Rheumatoid Arthritis', *Psychological Medicine, 10* (1980), pp. 159-63

Gath, D., Cooper, P. and Day, A. 'Hysterectomy and Psychiatric Disorder', *British Journal of Psychiatry, 140* (1982), pp. 335-50

Gendlin, R. *Focussing* (Everest House, New York, 1978)

Goldberg, D. and Huxley, P. *Mental Illness in the Community* (Tavistock, London, 1980)

Greer, S., Morris, T. and Pettingale, K.W. 'Psychological Response to Breast Cancer: Effect on Outcome', *Lancet I* (1979), pp. 785-7

Hackett, T.P. and Cassem, N.M. 'White Collar and Blue Collar Responses to a Heart Attack', *Journal of Psychosomatic Research, 20* (1976), pp. 85-95

Hacking, M. 'Dying and Bereavement', *Nursing,* First Series, no. 27 (1981), pp. 1168-70

Hauser, S.T. 'Physician-Patient Relationships' in E.G. Mishler, L.R. Amarasingham, S.T. Hauser, R. Liem, S.D. Osherson and N.E. Waxler, *Social Contexts of Health, Illness and Patient Care* (Cambridge University Press, Cambridge, UK, 1981), pp. 104-40

Hawker, R. 'Interaction Between Nurses and Patients' Relatives', unpublished PhD thesis, Exeter University, Devon, UK (1983a)

Hawker, R. Personal Communication (1983b)

Hawton, K. 'The Long Term Outcome of Psychiatric Morbidity Detected in General Medical Patients', *Journal of Psychosomatic Research, 25* (1981), pp. 237-43

Hayward, J. *Information − a Prescription against Pain* (Royal College of Nursing, London, 1975)

Heatherington, R. 'Communication − Some Psychological Aspects of the Nurse-Patient Relationship', *Nursing Times* (18 December 1964)

Illich, I. *Limits to Medicine* (Penguin Books, Harmondsworth, 1976)

Janis, I. and Levanthal, H. 'Psychological Aspects of Physical Illness and Hospital Care' in B. Wolman (ed.), *Handbook of Clinical Psychology* (McGraw Hill, New York, 1965)

Johnston, M. 'Anxiety in Surgical Patients', *Psychological Medicine, 10* (1980), pp. 145-52

Kallio, V., Hamatainen, H., Hakkila, J. and Luurila, O.J. 'Reduction in Sudden Death by a Multifactorial Intervention Programme after Acute Myocardial Infarction', *Lancet I* (1979), pp. 1091-94

Kaplan De Nour, A. 'Prediction of Adjustment to Haemodialysis' in N.B. Levy (ed.), *Psychonephrology I* (Plenum, New York, 1981), pp. 343-75

Kaplan De Nour, A. and Czaczkes, J.W. 'Bias in Assessment of Patients on Chronic Haemodialysis', *Journal of Psychosomatic Research, 18* (1974), pp. 217-21

Lancet, vol. 1, part 1 (1979), pp. 478-9

Levine, J. and Zigler, E. 'Denial and Self Image in Stroke, Lung Cancer and Heart Disease Patients', *Journal of Consulting and Clinical Psychology, 43* (1975), pp. 751-9

Ley, P. 'Giving Information to Patients' in J.R. Eiser (ed.), *Social Psychology and Behavioural Medicine* (Wiley, London, 1982a), pp. 339-73

Ley, P. 'Satisfaction, Compliance and Communication', *British Journal of Clinical Psychology, 21* (1982b), pp. 241-54

Lief, H.I. and Fox, R.C. 'Training for Detached Concern in Medical Students' in H.I. Lief (ed.), *The Psychological Basis of Medical Practice* (Harper and Row, New York, 1963)

Maguire, C.P., Julier, B.L., Hawton, K.E. and Bancroft, J.H.J. 'Psychiatric, Morbidity and Referral on Two General Medical Wards', *British Medical Journal, I* (1974), pp. 268-70

Maguire, P. 'Psychiatric Problems after Mastectomy' in P.C. Brand and P.A. van Keep (eds.), *Breast Cancer* (University Park Press, Baltimore, 1978), pp. 47-53

Maguire, P., Tait, A., Brooke, M., Thomas, C. and Sellwood, R. 'Effect of Counselling on the Psychiatric Morbidity Associated with Mastectomy', *British Medical Journal, 281* (1980), pp. 1454-56

Mawson, D., Marks, I.M., Ramm, L. and Stern, R.S. 'Guided Mourning for Morbid Grief – a Controlled Study', *British Journal of Psychiatry, 138* (1981), pp. 185-93

Mayou, R., Foster, A. and Williamson, B. 'Psycho-social Adjustment in Patients One Year after Myocardial Infarction', *Journal of Psychosomatic Research, 22* (1978), pp. 447-53

Mayou, R., Williamson, B. and Foster, A. 'Outcome Two Months after Myocardial Infarction', *Journal of Psychosomatic Research, 22* (1978), pp. 439-45

Menzies, E.P. *The Functioning of Social Systems as a Defence against Anxiety,* (Tavistock, London, 1970)

Miller, A.E. 'Nurses' Attitudes towards their Patients', *Nursing Times, 75* (1979), pp. 1929-33

Moffic, H.S. and Paykel, E.S. 'Depression in Medical In-Patients', *British Journal of Psychiatry, 126* (1975), pp. 346-53

Morris, T. 'Psychological Adjustment to Mastectomy', *Cancer Treatment Reviews*, vol. 6 (1979), pp. 41-61

Morris, T., Greer, H.S. and White, P. 'Psychological and Social Adjustment to Mastectomy – a 2 Year Follow-up Study', *Cancer, 40* (1977), pp. 2381-7

Murray Parkes, C. 'The Psychological Reactions to the Loss of a Limb' in J.C. Howells (ed.), *Modern Perspectives in the Psychiatric Aspects of Surgery* (Macmillan, London, 1976), pp. 515-32

Nelson-Jones, R. *Theory and Practice of Counselling* (Rinehart, Holt and Winston,

London, 1982)

Nichols, K.A. 'The Nurse and the Psychologist', *Nursing Times* (4 January 1984), pp. 22-4

Nichols, K.A. 'Psychosocial Difficulties Associated with Survival by Dialysis', *Behaviour Research and Therapy* (1984)

Nichols, K.A. and Rafferty, C. 'The Speech Therapist and the Psychologist', *Bulletin*, no. 336 (1980), pp. 4-7

Nurse, G. *Counselling and the Nurse* (Houghton-Miffen, 1975)

Nursing, no. 27 (1981), 'Communication'

Nursing Times, vol. 77, no. 15 (1981), pp. 628-39

Querido, A. 'Forecast and Follow Up – an Investigation into the Clinical, Social and Mental Factors Determining the Results of Hospital Treatment', *British Journal of Preventative Social Medicine, 13* (1959), pp. 33-49

Rachman, S. 'Emotional Processing', *Behaviour Research and Therapy, 8* (1980), pp. 51-60

Rawlings, E.E. 'The Doctors' Potential for Doing Harm', *Psychotherapy and Psychosomatics, 21* (1972), pp. 105-6

Ray, C. and Fitzgibbon, G. 'Stress Arousal and Coping with Surgery', *Psychological Medicine, 11* (1981), pp. 741-46

Richards, C. 'Communication – the Patients' Point of View', *Nursing*, first series, no. 27 (1981), pp. 1189-90

Ridgeway, V. and Mathews, A. 'Psychological Preparation for Surgery: a Comparison of Methods', *British Journal of Clinical Psychology, 21* (1982), pp. 271-80

Stein, L. 'The Doctor-Nurse Game' in R. Dingwall and J. McIntosh (eds.), *Readings in the Sociology of Nursing* (Churchill Livingstone, London, 1978), pp. 107-17

Sternbach, R.A. *Pain Patients – Traits and Treatments* (Academic Press, New York, 1974)

Stockwell, F.C. *The Unpopular Patient* (Royal College of Nursing, London, 1972. Republished by Croom Helm, London, 1984)

Strong, P.M. *The Ceremonial Order of the Clinic* (Routledge and Keegan Paul, London, 1979)

Tessler, R., Mechanic, D. and Diamond, M. 'The Effect of Psychological Distress on Physician Utilization – a Prospective Study', *Journal of Health and Social Behaviour, 17* (1976), pp. 353-64

Towell, D. *Understanding Psychiatric Nursing* (Royal College of Nursing, London, 1975)

Tschudin, V. *Counselling Skills for Nurses* (Balliere Tindall, London, 1983)

Wallace, L.M. 'The Heart of the Matter: a Clinical Psychologist in Coronary Care', *Bulletin of the British Psychological Society*, vol. 35 (1982), pp. 379-82

Waitzin, H. and Stoeckle, J.D. 'The Communication of Information about Illness', *Advances in Psychosomatic Medicine, 8* (1972), pp. 180-215

Wilson-Barnett, J. *Stress in Hospitals* (Churchill Livingstone, London, 1980)

Wirsching, M., Druner, H.U. and Herman, G. 'Results of Psychosocial Adjustment to Long Term Colostomy', *Psychotherapy and Psychosomatics, 26* (1975), pp. 245-56

Woodhams, P. 'Nurses and Psychologists – the First Hand Experience', *Nursing Times* (11 January 1984), pp. 34-5

INDEX